Track of the Mystic

The Spirituality of Jessica Powers

by
Marcianne Kappes, C.S.T.

Sheed & Ward

Sheed & Ward™ is a service of The National Catholic Reporter Publishing Company.

Library of Congress Cataloguing-in-Publication Data

Kappes, Marcianne, 1947-
  Track of the mystic : the spirituality of Jessica Powers / by Marcianne Kappes.
      p.   cm.
  Includes bibliographical references and index.
  ISBN 1-55612-659-X (acid free)
  1. Powers, Jessica—Criticism and interpretation. 2. Christian poetry, American—Catholic authors—History and criticism.
  3. Carmelite Nuns—In literature. 4. Mysticism in literature.
  I. Title.
PS3531.09723Z74   1994
811'.54—dc20   93-46599
                                                            CIP

Published by: Sheed & Ward
              115 E. Armour Blvd.
              P.O. Box 419492
              Kansas City, MO 64141

To order, call: (800) 333-7373

Contents

Credits

Grateful acknowledgment for permission to reprint from previously published materials is made to the following:

Excerpts from "Notes on a Poet's Life," ©1990 by Dolores R. Leckey, in *Spiritual Life* 36 (Fall, 1990), reprinted by permission of the author. See also *Winter Music: A Life of Jessica Powers,* ©1992 by Dolores R. Leckey (Kansas City, MO: Sheed & Ward).

Excerpts from "A Meadow Moreover: Wisconsin Poems of Jessica Powers," ©1989 by Richard Boudreau, from the Jessica Powers Symposium, Marquette Univ., Milwaukee, Wisconsin, reprinted by permission of the author.

Excerpts from "The Silent Poet," ©1960 by Mary Timothy Prokes, SSND, in *Spirit* 27 (May, 1960):52-57, repinted by permission of the author.

Excerpts from *The Carmelite Adventure,* ©1990 by Constance FitzGerald, OCD (Baltimore, MD: Carmelite Sisters), reprinted by permission of the author. The original 1790 diary of Clare Joseph Dickinson is in the Archives of the Carmelite Monastery in Baltimore.

Excerpts from *Carmel of the Mother of God,* ©1942 by Discalced Carmelite Nuns of Milwaukee, and from "Sister Miriam of the Holy Spirit, OCD," ©1989 by Nuns of the Pewaukee Carmel, *Carmelite Digest* 4 (Summer, 1989):8-12, reprinted by permission of the Discalced Carmelite Nuns of Milwaukee.

Excerpts from *Charter of Life,* ©1979 by Carmelite Communities Associated, as a joint contemporary statement of 14 member monasteries expressing the Teresian Charism in poetic style, reprinted by permission of the publisher. All rights reserved.

For the members of my community, the

Carmelite Sisters of St. Therese in Oklahoma,

for the Kappes family in Indiana, and

for Linda Marconi of Saint Louis.

Acknowledgements

Marcel Proust wrote: "The real voyage of discovery consists not in seeking new landscapes, but in having new eyes." I have words of gratitude in my heart for those who have shared their vision with me so that I too might have new eyes.

People who have inspired me to undertake this writing project are: my parents, Marcella and Virgil Kappes; my friends, Rebecca Moeller and Catherine Pangallo; and the women of WITS/Women in Theological Studies at Saint Louis University.

In the midst of their active ministry throughout the state of Oklahoma, the Carmelite Sisters of St. Therese deserve special recognition because they supported this research project. Especially I wish to thank my community members: Joseph Marie Gibbons, CST, and Diann Paulin, CST, who allowed me the opportunity to undertake this study; Immaculata Commet, CST, who helped to gather information; Susan Clark, CST, who was a meticulous and enthusiatic proofreader; and Mary Frances Coker, CST.

Others who have contributed to this research in supportive and encouraging ways are: my brothers, Tim, Steve, Dave, and especially Ted Kappes, who helped me to obtain the necessary technical equipment to finish this project; Ann Riggs, Eileen Cauley, Dr. Margarett Schlientz, Charles Elston, and the Marquette University Archivists, who provided hospitality and assistance during my research period in Wisconsin; staff and residents of the DeMattias Hall, especially Mary Terese Donze, ASC; Ellen Ryan, FSPA, Bede Jagoe, OP, Carmen Womack, OCD, and Bishop Robert Morneau of Green Bay; and the nuns of Pewaukee.

Finally, I would like to recognize members of the Saint Louis University faculty, especially Dr. Helen Mandeville, Elizabeth Kolmer, ASC, Frederick McLeod, SJ, and J. J. Mueller, SJ, as well as Regina Siegfried, ASC, of Aquinas Institute. Without their guidance and dedication, this book would not be a reality.

Foreword

ONE OF THE BASIC PRINCIPLES IN THE FIELD OF BIOLOGY IS THAT OF osmosis. Put simply, this means that what we get near to permeates us, conditions our lives and shapes us into new creatures. From a psychological point of view we talk about *influence*. Certain individuals, theories or actions influence the way we think, the way we feel and the way we act.

Jessica Powers experienced osmosis and, in turn, became an osmotic agent. She voluntarily chose to expose herself to the great writings of St. John of the Cross and St. Theresa of Avila. This was not just a matter of reading and rereading the classics but a decision to ponder prayerfully the writings of these saints and mystics for over fifty years. She told me personally that when she first read St. John of the Cross she thought she had died and gone to heaven.

It should not be surprising, then, that her creative genius, the art of poetry, would be richly influenced by the Carmelite tradition. Through a careful analysis of the poems of Jessica Powers, Sister Marcianne Kappes, C.S.T. has demonstrated, in specific ways, the influence of the Carmelite tradition upon the life and writings of Jessica Powers. Sister Marcianne traces the impact of Powers' Wisconsin years, so deeply influenced by nature, family and early religious training; her friendships in New York and the discovery of John of the Cross marking the years between 1936-1941; then her 47 years as a Carmelite, years filled with praying, nurturing spiritual growth, writing poetry, reading the classics, living in community, and struggling with leadership—all these life experiences finding expression in her poetry. Tracking this mystic is a complex adventure. Sr. Marcianne is a good detective and has given us an excellent report.

Besides being a fine piece of scholarship, this book serves another important purpose. It reminds us of the role of the mystic within our society. A considerable amount of attention has been given to the prophetic call through such writings as Walter Brueggemann's *The Prophetic Imagination*, the writings of Joshua Heschel, and other scholarly writers. But there has not been as much attention given to the call to mysticism, though the writings of Evelyn Underhill made a major contribution here. In his excellent study on inter-religious dialogue, *Dialogue With the Other*, the brilliant scholar David Tracy articulates the need for balance between prophecy and mysticism:

Neither the Christian prophet nor the mystic can live easily with one another. Yet, as the liberation, political, and feminist theologians now insist, only a mystical-prophetic construal of Christian freedom can suffice. Without the prophetic core, the struggle for justice and freedom in the historical-political world can too soon be lost in mere privacy. Without the mystical insistence on love, the spiritual power of the righteous struggle for justice is always in danger of lapsing into mere self-righteousness and spiritual exhaustion.[1]

What is is needed today is a deep appreciation of the role of the mystic. Many people within our society have mystical experiences, direct and immediate experiences of God, but have no way of verifying the reality of these divine encounters. *Track of the Mystic* articulates the life of one individual who was true to her calling. Jessica Powers, often against great odds, continued to listen to the movements of the Spirit in her heart and life, then took that noble leap of describing her most personal and intimate experiences to others. We are the recipients of her insights and her love. Tracking a mystic is a dangerous adventure since we may find ourselves one day caught in the same divine lair that gently holds all mystics.

Just as Jessica Powers was influenced by the Carmelite tradition and her surroundings as by osmosis, so she, in turn, has influenced our culture. Thousands of people have been reading and pondering her poetry for many years. Through the exercise of her gift, Jessica Powers became an evangelist, proclaiming the presence and purposes of God through her poetry. The intrinsic value of the creative process mingles with the baptismal call to evangelize with the result that a new experience of faith is available to all.

One final observation. Lewis Thomas, a doctor and writer (my favorite book of his: *The Lives of the Cell*), died of cancer this past year. Several weeks before his death, he was interviewed by Roger Rosenblatt regarding his experience of dying. Immediately Dr. Thomas turned his attention, not to the art of dying, but to the art of living:

---

1. Grand Rapids, MI: William B. Eerdmans Publishing Company, 1990, p. 123.

There is an art to living. . . . With the same sharp insight that we all have for acknowledging our failures, we ought to recognize how we have been useful, and sometimes uniquely useful. . . . If you can contemplate the times when you've been useful, even indispensable, to other people, the review of our lives would begin to have effects on the younger generation.[2]

Jessica Powers, the mystic, was useful in a unique and indispensable way. She became a clear channel of God's glory and life. It was with prayerful intent that her volume of selected poetry began with "The Mercy of God" and ended with "Doxology." From beginning to end, her sight was on God, the triune God who was the center of her gravity. When she died on August 18, 1988, a homecoming was experienced. If, with the guidance of Sr. Marcianne Kappes, we follow the tracks of Jessica Powers, then we might come to experience a similar welcome home:

The Homecoming

The spirit, newly freed from earth,
is all amazed at the surprise
of her belonging: suddenly
as native to eternity
to see herself, to realize
the heritage that lets her be
at home where all this glory lies.

By naught foretold could she have guessed
such welcome home: the robe, the ring,
music and endless banqueting,
these people hers; this place of rest
known, as of long remembering
herself a child of God and pressed
with warm endearments to His breast.[3]

—Robert F. Morneau
Auxiliary Bishop of Green Bay

---

2. Cf. *New York Times Magazine*, Nov. 21, 1993, p. 53.
3. *Selected Poetry of Jessica Powers*, ed. by Regina Siegfried, ASC and Robert F. Morneau. Sheed & Ward, 1989, p. 53.

Track of the Mystic

There was a man went forth into the night
with a proud step. I saw his garments blowing;
I saw him reach the great cloud of unknowing.
He went in search of love, whose sign is light.
From the dark night of sense I saw him turn
into the deeper dark nights of the soul
where no least star marks a divine patrol.

Great was his torment who could not discern
this night was God's light generously given,
blinding the tainted spirit utterly
till from himself at last he struggled free.
I saw him on the higher road to heaven:
his veins ran gold; light was his food and breath.
Flaming he melted through the wall of death!

—Jessica Powers

Chapter 1

Introduction

AT THE END OF HER LIFE, JESSICA POWERS REFERRED TO HERSELF AS A "gypsy." This word described her wandering over vast inner and outer landscapes of life for 83 years (1905-1988). Jessica used this image of a "gypsy" as a way of linking herself with the roving figure of the Hebrew prophet Elijah, who wandered from mountain top to desert plain faithfully following the call of God. She drew inspiration from the Elijan narrative and similar biblical narratives as she struggled to integrate her spiritual and cultural heritage in an effort to give poetic expression to Carmelite spirituality in an American context. Studies of the literary content of her poetry have been under way for some time, but more recently, there has been an awareness of the need for research to place her in her historical context and extract the theological themes present in her writings. One area of extreme importance and integral to Jessica's identity was the influence of Carmelite spirituality in her life. Besides being a source of creativity for her, Carmelite spirituality functioned as her window into Sacred Scripture. She drew upon her Carmelite spirituality for direction and then wove its guiding lessons into her life's journey at every turn. Jessica Powers cannot be understood apart from her Carmelite viewpoint which links her with the historical development of Carmelite spirituality for nearly eight hundred years. As an American, she creatively integrates her historical perspective with a distinctively American Carmelite spirituality. Thus, this research investigates Jessica Powers as an important and remarkably creative religious poet who embodies Carmelite spirituality within the context of twentieth-century American culture.

Jessica Power's life was a gypsy-like experience of continuous movement and transition: from rural Wisconsin to urban Chicago, from the excitement of New York's Catholic Poetry Society of America to the cloistered life of a Wisconsin Carmelite nun, from the

nature images of a localized poet to universal themes of classical Carmelite spirituality, from Irish immigrant spirituality to post Vatican II
spirituality, from a God who spoke in times past to a living God.
Both inner and outer landscapes are involved in her life's journey.
Jessica Powers' attention to nature links her with other nature-atten-
tive poets, such as John of the Cross and Emily Dickinson, who use
"nature as metaphor to explore human interactions, human/divine relationships, and inner/outer landscapes."[1] Her vision is one of hope
which she captures through a poetic critique of her life experience as
an American influenced by Carmelite spirituality. Regina Siegfried
ASC, who co-edited with Bishop Robert Morneau of Green Bay a
book of Jessica's poems entitled *Selected Poetry of Jessica Powers*
(Sheed & Ward, 1989), has noted: "Her fascination with words and
their power to lead us to the Word is simultaneously purpose and
metaphor for her. She wanted her words, her poetry to draw others
to God."[2] Especially in later life, Jessica expressed the desire that
her writings might influence others to persevere in their search for
God.

After Jessica Powers joined the Carmelites in Wisconsin, the
bishops of her area supported her publications, with Bishop Robert
Morneau of Green Bay often writing and lecturing on the importance
of her work in the study of American spirituality. Jessica's writings
demonstrate a unique blending of American Catholic spirituality and
Carmelite spirituality, resulting in a biblically based yet contemporary
body of writings vibrant enough to enrich Christian theological reflection in the future.

This study traces the chronological development in Jessica's poetry in an effort to demonstrate the process by which she achieves
spiritual integration through her interaction with the changing conditions in American history, the Catholic Church, and the Carmelite Order throughout her lifetime. First, an introductory survey of Carmelite history and spirituality functions as background for her writings in Chapter 2. Next, each major period of her life is considered
through a study of her poetry and writings as they develop over a
period of sixty years within the appropriate time frame and historical
setting of the American society in general and the U.S. Catholic
Church in particular. This chronological study leads a reader through
her early years in a farming community in rural Wisconsin (1905-
1922), her Chicago period (1922-1925), and her return to the family
farm (1925-1936) in Chapter 3, her New York period (1937-1941) in
Chapter 4, her early years in the Carmelite community in Milwaukee,

Wisconsin (1941-1958) in Chapter 5, and her later years in the Carmelite community of Pewaukee, Wisconsin (1958-1988) in Chapter 6. In the person and writing of Jessica Powers, also known as Miriam of the Holy Spirit in her Carmelite community, Carmelite spirituality adapts to American spirituality and releases an outpouring of poetic expression. Without a chronological study of her poetry and without an understanding of the factors linking her to Carmelite spirituality, her writings are denuded of their strength to demonstrate the basic tenets of Christian spirituality, to explain what it means to be a mystic in modern day America, and to outline the process for others who are called by God to follow a similar path.

In the main body of this research, special note is given to the images and themes which arise in each period of Jessica's life and the way in which these themes develop in continuous patterns in order to draw out the spiritual and theological significance of her writings. Images and themes of spiritual yearning are treated in Chapter 3, images and themes of discontent and dislocation in Chapter 4, poetic reflections influenced by her lived experience in a cloistered Carmelite community in Chapter 5, and poetic reflections on meaning and passages in life in Chapter 6. Lastly, a critique of Jessica's ability to synthesize within her poems and writings the many and various strains of American landscape and Catholic tradition with biblical perspective and Carmelite spirituality is undertaken in an effort to evaluate her unique contribution to historical theology in the American context and Carmelite tradition.

Chapter 2

The Historical Setting

JESSICA POWERS WAS INTRODUCED TO CARMELITE SPIRITUALITY through the works of Carmelite writers and poets, like Teresa of Avila, John of the Cross, and Therese of Lisieux, many years before she joined the Discalced Carmelite Order. Upon joining a Carmelite community herself, Jessica was immersed in the dynamics of the life-style which these Carmelites and countless others had experienced before her. At its core, this lifestyle balances a daily rhythm of manual labor with communal Eucharist and solitary contemplative prayer based on scripture. The insights which Jessica gained from her experience as a member of a Carmelite community influenced her writings as much as the classic works of Carmelite literature. Therefore, a brief study of basic Carmelite writings and the history and spirituality of Carmelite communities, especially those which influenced the first Carmelite houses in the United States is necessary in order to place the life and writings of Jessica Powers in their proper historical and theological context.

The Influence of Classic Carmelite Writings

The spiritual sources which influenced Jessica Powers most heavily throughout her life were those which function as base documents in the development of Carmelite Spirituality in the Teresian or Discalced tradition: the Bible, the *Rule of Saint Albert*, the writings of Saint Teresa of Avila, the writings of Saint John of the Cross, and the writings of Saint Therese of Lisieux. The way in which scripture influenced the *Rule of Albert* and the spirituality of the three greatest classic writers in the Discalced Carmelite tradition, Teresa of Avila, John of the Cross, and Therese of Lisieux, is important to note in a study of Jessica Powers, because she also uses the same scriptural themes which these pieces of Carmelite literature employ. For example, the prophet Elijah (ninth century B.C.), the events surrounding his ministry in Israel, and his spiritual legacy function as the symbolic founding figure, event, and charism in Carmelite tradition.[1] Therefore, it is not surprising to find Elijan themes or images gleaned from these scriptural passages woven into the fabric of her poetry at frequent intervals.

An additional characteristic of the classic Carmelite writers which Jessica Powers embodies is displayed in the way in which they identified with the quest of the lover for the beloved as poetically expressed in biblical passages such as those found in *The Song of Songs*. Carmelite mystics have employed these passages to describe in bridal imagery their unitive encounters through prayer with God.[2] Like other Carmelite writers before her, Jessica Powers exhibits a multi-faceted experience of God as Trinity, tender life-giving parent, incarnate Christ, passionate lover, holy and living Spirit. Daily encounters with God through the experience of Jesus Christ as realized in the gospel narratives and in Eucharistic celebration open up a Christocentric world of nature to the gaze and pen of these Carmelites of kindred spirit.

The most pivotal figure in the Discalced Carmelite tradition is Teresa of Avila (1515-1582). The life work of this Spanish mystic centered upon the return of Carmelite communities to the inspiration of a document which she supposed to be the primitive rule of Saint Albert. Actually the rule in her possession was a reworking of the primitive rule which took place during the papacy of Innocent IV in 1247.[3] The original or primitive rule, known as *The Rule of Saint Albert*, was written between 1206 and 1214 by Albert, the Latin Patriarch of Jerusalem (d. 1214). It consisted of twenty points, the majority of which were scripturally based.

After careful reflection on the reworked version of the primitive or the Innocentian-modified rule and related scriptural passages, Teresa formulated a plan for reforming religious life in the Carmelite tradition. She reaped tremendous success in her initial efforts to implement her ideas within the Carmelite Order. However, opposition to her movement eventually resulted in a split within the Order so that today there are two groups of Carmelites: the Calced Carmelites who resisted Teresa's influence in the sixteenth century; and the Teresian or Discalced Carmelites who followed Teresa's inspiration.[4] The two groups exist today as two separate orders with each under its own Superior General.

Teresa was a Christian humanist who experienced a profound mystical life remarkable for its clear Christocentric element in which the humanity of Christ functions as the doorway to union with God. Her ideal of Christian community life was based on small groups of Christians living simply, reflecting on the Sacred Scriptures, returning to the inspiration of the more primitive Carmelite rule, using common sense in all aspects of daily life, and immersing themselves in a balanced prayer life with both solitary and Eucharistic dimensions. For Teresa, the discernment process that guided her life was based on this balancing of two poles, one individual and one communal. Monika Hellwig has described this Teresian discernment process in these words:

> She had a subtle, carefully nuanced way of submitting herself to the judgment of the Church while never abandoning her conviction that God speaks in our experience and can be trusted to speak to us so that we understand and are not deceived.[5]

According to Hellwig, Teresa realized that "maturity lies in the balancing of one's own experience and understanding with guidance from community and tradition and balancing one's own needs and quest with self-gift to others."[6] The means by which Teresa acquainted herself with scripture to accomplish this balance were very limited because it was highly suspect for a woman in sixteenth- century Spain to read the Bible. Therefore, Teresa had to glean biblical passages from secondary sources and sermons in an effort to reconstruct portions of scripture to use as the basis of her reflection and meditation.[7] In spite of all this, Teresa's writings contain over six hundred references to scriptural passages, and she wrote a commentary on *The Song of Songs*.[8] Best known for her prose writings which earned her the honor of being one of the first women in Roman Catholic Church history to be given the title "Doctor of the Church," Teresa wrote numerous poems as well.[9] From her time in sixteenth-century Spain to present day twentieth-century America, the writing of poetry has functioned as one of the important avenues for exploring mystical theology as well as a prime communication tool for sharing the fruits of such explorations in Carmelite literature.

Another important figure in the sixteenth-century reform movement within the Carmelite order was John of the Cross (1542-1591), who has been recognized by the Church as a doctor of mystical theology and by literary circles in Spain as one of the greatest of Spain's classic poets. He is best known for his descriptions of "the dark nights" of the spiritual life wherein God's absence is felt as an acute suffering which purges the human being for, and during, mystical encounters with God.[10] Like Teresa, John based his theological investigations of the mystical life on scripture and recognized the place of bridal mysticism in Christian spirituality.[11] An analysis of his poems and the commentaries which he wrote on them reveals over a thousand references to biblical passages contained in his works.[12]

The best known and most important single figure in the history of Carmelite spirituality after the initial period of the Teresian Reform is Therese of the Child Jesus and the Hidden Face (Therese Martin, 1873-1897), a French Carmelite nun who is often referred to as Therese of Lisieux or "the Little Flower." She became a pivotal figure in early twentieth-century American Catholic spirituality through her writings which include an autobiography, poetry, numerous letters, dramas, and notes of her last conversations.[13] Especially her autobiography contains a simple biblical and Christocentric message. It is here, in some two hundred pages of her autobiography entitled *Story of a Soul*, that Therese refers to scripture passages from both Old and New Testament over 180 times.

Like her namesake, Teresa of Avila, Therese's spirituality was biblical and Christocentric with the person of Jesus Christ functioning as the doorway to her understanding of God.[14] Therese emphasized a simple following of the gospel message in daily life and ordinary ways. In her spirituality, holiness can be claimed by all, for God is seen as a loving parent. Because her writings were read worldwide by millions of people,[15] the spiritual shifts present in her autobiography helped to break the hold of medieval piety's emphasis on extraordinary religious experiences as indicators of God's favor. These shifts gave proper place to the basic Christian insight that the most direct way to God is in the embrace of daily human life lived with great love in the uncertainty of faith as Jesus did.

The Teresian Expansion

In Discalced Carmelite literature, a monastery of nuns is often called a Carmel. The most important Carmels or Carmelite houses of women with direct links to later United States Catholic history are those in the Lowlands. Several of the first English speaking American women to become nuns were members of these Carmels which were directly linked with Teresa of Jesus through their first leaders, Anne of Jesus (Anne Lobera, 1543-1621) and Anne of Saint Bartholomew (Anne Garcia, 1549-1626).[16]

Anne of Jesus was one of the closest friends and most faithful of the followers of Teresa of Jesus; Anne of Saint Bartholomew had been Teresa's secretary and nurse throughout the last part of her life. Both women were part of the group of six Carmelites who were victims of ecclesiastical blackmail on the part of the French Cardinal, Pierre de Berulle (1575-1629). In 1604 they were forced to leave Spain and travel to France because Berulle had obtained a decree from the papal nuncio threatening excommunication to the Spanish Carmelite general unless Berulle was allowed to handpick and export the nuns from Teresa's monasteries that he wanted for his new foundations in France. Berulle made his selection of these women based on their reputation as the closest and most faithful followers of Teresa.

Once Berulle had transported the Spanish nuns to France, he tried to impose upon them his own ideas of spirituality. First, he wanted the nuns to take a special Marian vow which was not part of Teresian spirituality. Secondly, Berulle tried to institute the practice of perpetual adoration in Carmelite communities. These additions of his French devotional practices were disturbing enough to the Spanish Carmelite nuns without the fact that they were forced to exist in France under Berulle and his colleagues' direction and authority rather than under the jurisdiction and direction of the Discalced Carmelite Order.[17] Berulle wanted to do away with the basic governing structure of Teresian Carmelite communities, the election of community leaders by the local membership of each house, and replace these locally elected leaders with appointed superiors. Also, Berulle tried to force the Carmelites to accept several young women of questionable mental stability, whom he personally recommended on the basis of their extraordinary mystical experiences. By the end of their first year in France, Anne of Jesus was so disillusioned with Berulle's ideas of spirituality that she and several of the Spanish Carmelites retreated to the Lowlands which were under Spanish rule at that time. There she founded Carmelite houses with the Teresian spirit: Brussels (1607), followed by Louvain (1607), Mons (1608), Tournai, Malines (Mechlin, 1616), Valenciennes, Gand (Ghent), Douai, Bruges, and Lille.[18] Anne of Saint Bartholomew, aided by a French noblewoman and cousin of Berulle, Mary of the Incarnation (Barbe Acarie, 1566-1618), worked for nearly an additional five years to bestow the character of the Teresian reform upon the Carmelite communities in France. This was only partially carried out due to much interference on the part of Berulle who continued to have his own ideas of what Carmelite spirituality should be. Eventually, Anne of Saint Bartholomew left France in 1611 to joined Anne of Jesus in the Lowlands.

In 1612 Anne of Saint Bartholomew founded the Carmelite monastery at Antwerp and remained as its guiding spirit.[19] Led by Anne of the Ascension (Anne Worsley, 1599-1644), English-speaking women from the Antwerp Carmel and other Lowland Carmels began a foundation in Antwerp, on the rue Houblonniere in Hopland (1619) for English women. This community with its two daughter houses at Hoogstraten (Hoogstraet, 1678) and Lierre (Liege, 1648), became the only Carmelite monasteries for English-speaking women for nearly two centuries. The Lowland Carmels developed as important centers of spirituality for English women who wished to embrace convent life after Henry VIII disbanded monasteries in England.[20]

These houses founded by Anne of Jesus and Anne of Saint Bartholomew in the Lowlands are also important in the history of Christian spirituality because they resisted the seventeenth-century French spirituality of Berulle and later French Jansenistic influences in their efforts to preserve the basic insights of Carmelite spirituality influenced by Teresian thought. Recent scholars of Carmelite spirituality and church history laud the Lowland Carmelite communities founded by Anne of Jesus and Anne of Bartholomew because "they stand within the moderate humanistic French school as it was mediated to them through the English Jesuit inheritance and through central elements of Teresian/Carmelite spirituality."[21]

Maryland Carmelites in the Lowlands

Some of the daughters of Catholic planters in Maryland migrated to English-speaking Carmelite communities in the Lowlands during the eighteenth century. James Hennesey lists nine women as part of this migration in his article, "Several Youth Sent From Here: Native-Born Priests and Religious of English America, 1634-1776."[22] Because penal laws forbidding the establishment of convents were enforced in the English colonies of America before the American Revolution, English-Speaking American women ended up on continental European soil in their quest for convent life. At the time of the American Revolution that gave birth to the United States, two Maryland-born women[23] were in positions of leadership in the Carmelite communities in the Lowlands and today are recognized as guiding spirits and founders of Carmelite spirituality in the United States: Bernardina of Saint Joseph (Anne Matthews, 1732-1800) was the prioress at Hoogstraten and Margaret of the Angels (Mary Margaret Brent, 1731-1784) was the prioress at Antwerp. It was Margaret of the Angels who gave embodiment to the dream of an American Carmelite foundation in the United States; it was she who organized the initial plans for the foundation and carried out the necessary correspondence to put the plans into motion; but she was dead six years before the time the American foundation was able to be put into effect.[24]

Margaret's spirituality molded the founding group. As a Maryland Catholic, she was open to the English Jesuit tradition and as a Carmelite in the Lowland tradition of the gentle Spanish mothers, she was open to Teresian understandings of contemplative prayer. There exists samples of her poetry based on paraphrases found in *The Rule of Saint Albert*; the Carmelite focus on the centrality of solitary prayer is developed in some of her other writings which seem to rely on a knowledge of *The Institutions of the First Monks*, another Carmelite text. Margaret saw affections of the heart, including human friendship, as conducive to spiritual growth; she also believed that contemplation was basically a profound love experience pervading human life. She was influenced by Teresa of Avila's classical descriptions of contemplative prayer as she tried to record her own religious experiences.[25] The most common Christological development in the Lowland Carmelite communities was their humanistic devotion to the Sacred Heart of Jesus. In *The Carmelite Adventure*, Constance FitzGerald explains:

> First of all, it [devotion to the Sacred Heart] had been taught by the Jesuits and practiced in the Maryland mission. Mary Brent and Anne Matthews probably grew into it as children and through it established the kind of identification with Jesus that made them desire and pursue Carmelite life. Secondly, in its emphasis on the humanity of Christ, on love and interiority, it provided a fertile soil for the teachings of Teresa (and also of Ignatius) for whom Jesus Christ is central. Thirdly, in its deepest meanings and development, devotion to the Sacred Heart as it became infused with Carmelite tradition opened into the experience of contemplative love.[26]

Furthermore, Constance FitzGerald remarks that "this emphasis on love and experience is seen in so many of the founders' poems, not only Bernardina's and Mary Margaret Brent's, but Clare Joseph's from early days in Antwerp."[27]

Carmelites in the United States

In 1790, English-speaking American women from the monasteries of Antwerp and Hoogstraten in the Lowlands began the first convent of any kind in the original thirteen colonies. Bernardina of Saint Joseph, their leader and the first prioress of a Carmelite monastery of nuns on United States soil, was a close collaborator of Margaret of the Angels in this project. It was Bernardina who passed on the best of colonial Maryland Catholicism and Carmelite spirituality to her spiritual descendants in the United States. Bernardina sailed to America from Europe with her Maryland-born nieces, Aloysia of the Blessed Trinity (Ann Teresa Matthews) and Eleanor of Saint Francis Xavier (Susana Matthews) in May 1790. The fourth member of their group was an English Carmelite, Clare Joseph of the Sacred Heart (Frances Dickinson, 1755-1830), who was named subprioress of the new community.[28] Clare Joseph is remembered today for her journal about their ocean voyage and for her poetry which chronicles the details of the life of their community in Port Tobacco, Maryland from July of 1790 onward.[29]

These four Carmelites were accompanied on their pilgrimage from Europe to America by a faithful Jesuit-trained chaplain, Father Charles Neale (1750-1823). Neale was a relative of the three Maryland-born Carmelites. As a young boy, Charles Neale had been educated in the Lowlands by the English Jesuits and entered their society in 1771. After the society was suppressed in 1773, he remained in Lierre as the confessor of the Antwerp community and went regularly to Hoogstraten as a confessor.[30] From this time until his death, Charles Neale remained the chaplain of the Carmelites, loyal to them and supportive of them as they made their passage from Old World to New World. He was instrumental in purchasing the site of their original foundation at Port Tobacco in Maryland with his own patrimony; he assisted them in establishing their community there, managed their farm and business details for them, entertained them with poems at their community celebrations, and ministered to them continuously as their resident chaplain.[31]

After Bernardina's death in 1800, Clare Joseph became prioress of Port Tobacco. She and Charles Neale had enormous influence on the development of the Carmelite foundation at Port Tobacco in Maryland, because for thirty-three years they worked as friends to insure its success. When offered leadership positions in the restored Jesuit Society in 1805, Neale declined rather than abandon his pastoral role with the Carmelite community. Constance FitzGerald writes: "Their friendship and collaboration were the bedrock on which the new Carmel grew."[32]

Although influenced by Maryland Catholicism and English Jesuit training, Neale was more rigoristic in his approach to the spiritual life than the Teresian Carmelites under his pastoral care.[33] Likewise, Clare Joseph seemed to lean toward the more rigorous spirituality of the seventeenth-century French school than had her predecessors, Margaret of the Angels and Bernardina. Born in England, Clare Joseph had been sent to an Ursuline boarding school in Paris and exposed to rigorous French spirituality as a young student. This seventeenth-century French school of spirituality differed from the Teresian school of spirituality in several ways. First, the French school lay heavy stress on the role of the superior and obedience to the rule as the norms for discovering the will of God in one's life, while the Teresian rule saw God's will as mediated through inner dispositions discerned in accordance with scripture and in dialogue with authority within the Christian community. Second, in the French school, interior movements of the passions, emotions and will were suspect, while rational control exercised by the intellect was encouraged. In the Teresian school, the role of human emotions and the mystical movements of the interior life were not to be suppressed by rational control of the intellect; instead, recognition was given to the place of human emotions, especially love and desire for the Beloved, as the doorway to contemplative prayer. Third, the French school insisted that religious experience should be mediated by ecclesiastical structures under the firm control of clerics and religious superiors, while the Teresian school also acknowledged the possibility of God speaking directly to human beings without intermediary ecclesiastical structures, although once again, Teresa always insisted that everything must be in accord with scripture, the traditions and teachings of the Church, and in consultation with competent spiritual directors.[34] Based on shared research with Joseph Chinnici, Constance FitzGerald states:

Although the American Carmelites stressed the experience of God, theirs was a very practical, dignified, restrained piety with definite ecumenical overtones. While placing little emphasis on miracles and visions, it stressed interior dispositions and the acceptance of daily life and tasks in a spirit of love and availability to God's will. Grounded in a deep respect for the movement of the Holy Spirit in each person, which is basic to an understanding and experience of contemplative prayer, their spirituality correlated well with their inherited position of political liberty and the rights of conscience.[35]

In spite of their leanings toward the more rigoristic tendencies of the French school, both Charles Neale and Clare Joseph were persons noted for their honesty, good sense of humor, and steadfast compassionate devotion in the service of others. They were aided in keeping from developing too narrow a spirituality by a high level of culture and lively intellectual life which was characteristic of Maryland gentry and the Lowland Teresians. The founders of the Carmelite community in Maryland bought with them from Antwerp over one thousand books in an effort to build a broad theological library at Port Tobacco. Many works on spirituality, prayer, and Carmelite life were among the volumes that lined their reading room shelves.[36]

Teresa of the Heart of Mary (Elizabeth Carberry, 1746-1812) became the first citizen to make religious profession of vows on United States soil in 1792. Born in southern Maryland of Irish and English parents, she brought all her practical skills and American know-how with her upon her entry into Carmelite life in the United States. Small, wiry, and active as a child, she was a tomboy "who could climb like a squirrel."[37] She learned all the tasks of wool-winding, quilting, and food preserving necessary for survival in rural eighteenth-century colonial life; however, she loved to escape the household tasks and roam the forests and streams, picking berries and gathering nuts along the way. Much of this period of her life can be seen mirrored in the early years of Jessica Powers a century and a half later.

The home of Elizabeth's father was a message center for the outlawed circuit-riding Jesuits who ministered to the outlands of southern Maryland under the constraints of English penal law in colonial times. Silent and discrete, Elizabeth learned how to serve God and her neighbor under their influence and example of courage.

While her sisters and friends talked of marriage, she thought of becoming a nun and serving God quietly in a secluded spot. Guided by Father Ignatius Matthews (1730-1790), the brother of Bernardina, who ministered to Catholics in Southern Maryland from 1765 onward,[38] Elizabeth Carberry patiently waited half her life for her chance to become a Carmelite nun.

After her father's death, Elizabeth had saved a small cash legacy to cover her travel expenses to Belgium and dowry for entrance to the Carmelite monastery there, but history intervened. The outbreak of the Revolutionary War in 1776 made travel impossible, and Elizabeth was needed to manage the family farm while her brothers went to war. After the war there was not enough financial backing for her to leave with Ann Teresa and Susana Matthews and join the Carmelite community in the Lowlands; but most of all, she began to realize that she did not really want to leave America.[39] She began to pray that she would be able to fulfill her dream in her own country where she had worked and prayed and her brothers had fought for freedom. In this delay in undertaking her life's vocation, especially the period when she helped to manage the family farm for her brothers and the economic hard times which followed, Elizabeth's life parallels portions of the life of Jessica Powers.

When the Carmelite nuns finally arrived from Europe in the summer of 1790, Elizabeth presented herself as a novice for the community. She was received on November 1, 1790 and proved to be an invaluable member of the community, for she was the only one who had practical skills of running a farm. She knew all about sheep-raising and shearing, as well as planting and harvesting crops, spinning and weaving, and score of other pioneer household skills.[40] In a letter to the Carmelite community of Antwerp residing at Lanherne, England during Napoleon's invasion of the Lowlands, Elizabeth gave the following description of life among the Carmelites at Port Tobacco, Maryland:

> Without rent or revenue we depend on Providence and
> the works of our hands, productive of plentiful crops of
> wheat, corn, tobacco, a good will supplying our large
> and healthy community with every necessary of life. We
> raise a large stock of sheep, yielding a considerable
> quantity of wool, black and white, which we spin and
> weave to clothe ourselves and negroes. The situation of
> our monastery is pleasant, rural and healthy, being on
> top of a large hill. We have excellent water and exten-

sive enclosure containing nearly three acres of land. The place is solitary, suitable to our eremitical order.[41]

After the death of the founding members, lawsuits over the Port Tobacco land and other monetary troubles forced the Carmelite community to relocate in Baltimore in 1831 under the leadership of Mother Angela Teresa (Mudd).[42] Here from 1831 to 1851, they ran a school for girls to meet the needs of the local Catholic population and provide for their own maintenance. Two of the members of the Baltimore community were educated by Mother Seton at Saint Joseph's Academy in Emmitsburg, Maryland, and the Sisters of Charity actively assisted the Carmelites in learning how to operate their school. In 1851, Francis Patrick Kenrick (1797-1863) was made bishop of Baltimore. Under his guidance, the Carmelites closed their school and returned to their original observance of the Carmelite rule. However, no provision was made for the monetary support of the community, and it is not known today how they supported themselves after the school closed.[43]

For the next ten years, the Baltimore community grew steadily. Finally the community was able to make its first foundation of a daughter house in St. Louis (1863). This foundation was followed by: New Orleans (1877), Boston (1890), Philadelphia (1902), Brooklyn (1907), Seattle (1908), Santa Clara (1908), Bettendorf, Iowa (1911), and many others in the United States.[44]

In tracing the Carmelite roots that shaped the life of Jessica Powers, Bettendorf, Iowa, is important to note because the Milwaukee Carmel was a daughter house of this group. Jessica was six years old when the Bettendorf Carmel was founded as a daughter house of the Baltimore Carmel; she was thirty-five years old when the Milwaukee Carmel was founded by members of the Bettendorf community; she was fifty-four years old when she acted as director of the Milwaukee community during its move to Pewaukee, Wisconsin; and she was sixty-four years old when the Albuquerque Carmel (f.1955), originally a daughter house descending from the Carmel of Tulancingo, Mexico, by way of Dallas (f.1928) and Santa Fe (f.1945), left New Mexico to join her Pewaukee community.

The following chapters contain accounts of the history and spirituality of Carmelite communities in the United States intersecting and interweaving with the life of Jessica Powers, which is set within the American historical context and significant developments in the Roman Catholic Church occurring within that context.

Chapter 3

Jessica Powers: A Wisconsin Poet
(1905-1936)

JESSICA POWERS' LIFE ILLUSTRATES THAT HUMAN EXISTENCE IS FILLED
with paradoxical elements, but it becomes an adventure when lived in
relationship to a loving God. Her biographer, Dolores Leckey, explains: "Her life spanned almost this whole century from 1905
through 1988, [and] . . . she carries with her the story of women and
women's choice through several periods of American history and
church culture."[1] This chapter highlights the personal relationships,
outlines the major events, and explores the cultural and religious context which shaped Jessica Powers' thoughts.

The early period of Jessica Powers' life was spent in rural Wisconsin on the family farm (1905-1936) before and after a brief expo-
sure to city life in Milwaukee and Chicago (1922-24). The way in
which Jessica Powers synthesized her insights and experiences in
these formative years is illustrated by her writings. Special note is
given to the images, symbols, and themes which arise in her poetry
during this period. With each shift in her historical circumstances,
Jessica Powers participated in a process of active engagement with
life and developed a poetic ability to grapple with the underlying
questions of significance in human existence. Eventually, her search
for the answers to these questions led her on a physical journey
across half of the North American continent and a spiritual pilgrimage through the "immigrant spirituality" of rural America, through the
paths of Franciscan spirituality, and into the hidden ways of Carmelite contemplation. The restlessness of deep and unsatisfied spiritual yearnings mark each turning point in these years of Jessica Powers' life.

The Family Background

Born on a farm in central Wisconsin, Jessica Powers grew up with simple but ready grist for the mill of her poetic mind. Juneau County contains fields and forests, rivers and lakes, the Powers' farmland and family home, the town of Mauston and Saint Patrick's parish; but, most of all, it harbors the singing birds of the bluffs and the sweeps of cattails in Cattail Valley which point to a benevolent God of beauty. Richard Boudreau's description of Jessica's birthplace is brief but rich in its details:

> The lowlands on which the farm lies border, on the south and west, the coulee or driftless, that is, unglaciated region of western Wisconsin. Covered by a mix of hard- and soft-woods, particularly oak and cedar, the bluffs form a dominant uplift, running from the southeast to the northwest . . . the land on which the farms round-about are located . . . is the bed of old glacial Lake Wisconsin, marked frequently by small pot-holes of swale here and there, and . . . larger swamps sometimes containing the delicate-looking but hardy tamarack trees, and at larger intervals by rather fantastic, free-standing limestone rock formations.[2]

Nature was Jessica's teacher, and the lessons which she learned in this school molded her vision for life. Dolores Leckey explains that Jessica "had a gift of seeing beauty even when others could not. She knew how to make beautiful music with her poems, an important attribute, for beauty is a catalyst for change."[3]

Life in rural Wisconsin was filled with ordinary people and ordinary events surrounded by glorious countryside. Jessica wrote once that Mauston was a place "where human contacts were not measured by profit."[4] Some of the first settlers on the farmlands of Cattail Valley were Irish settlers, like Jessica's great-grandparents, the Keenas. They came in the summer of 1849, following an Indian trail to a point in section eight of the present town of Kildare, named in honor of the first settlers of this section who came from County Kildare, Ireland.

In 1850, James Trainer (1826-1888)[5] and his brother, Daniel Trainer,[6] came to America from Scotland and settled in Kildare, Wisconsin. Before long they were known as the two best woodsmen of the area and experts in the construction of corduroy and plank roads.

In the late 1850s James Trainer "built a road to the Keena cabin and was married to Catherine Keena about a year later."[7] It was on this same land that James Trainer and Catherine Keena (1835-1910) raised eight children, including Jessica's mother, Delia Veronica Trainer (1867-1925).

The Powers family was from County Waterford, Ireland and had its family stories also. Jessica's Gaelic grandmother on this side of the family was Catherine. Hyde Powers. With her first-born baby in her pocket, she walked a plank from one ship to another on the high seas, when the ship she and her husband had taken from Ireland to America began to sink. The high sea rescue was the most vivid remembrance of the voyage, of course, and made a great story retold for many years. Jessica's father, John Powers (1865-1918), was born in America, next to the last of Catherine Hyde Powers' ten children. Catherine settled with her lumberman husband in central Wisconsin, and she charmed her grandchildren at family gatherings with her Irish wit and lively stories.[9]

Jessica's parents, John Powers and Delia Trainer, met in the little town of Lyndon, Wisconsin, married, and settled on the family farmlands.[10] John and Delia welcomed their third child into the world on February 7, 1905, and named her Agnes Jessika Powers.[11] John Walsh and Nellie Keegan acted as Jessica's godparents when she was baptized at St. Patrick's Church in Mauston by Father Peter Becker on February 26, 1905. Jessica's older sister, Catherine Dorothy Powers (1899-1916) and older brother, John Trainer Powers (1901-1977) were present. The scene would be repeated the following year when Jessica's younger brother, James Daniel Powers (1906-1956) was born.[12] In later life, Jessica reflected on her family roots and wrote:

"Prayer For My Family"

Out of the meadow we come
running like children
all holding hands—
none of us clean
and none of us deserving
of your vast love,
but holding on
to one another.
Take us, O God,
into your great arms,
and take us all.[13]

The Historical Context

The period of Wisconsin and U.S. history, in which Jessica Powers was born, is often referred to as "The Progressive Era." No state was considered more progressive than Wisconsin between 1900 and 1924. Most of the Wisconsin farmers owned their own land and received good prices for their crops and dairy products in the beginning of this era; however, as migrations began to the cities and industrialism became more widespread, power was concentrated in the hands of a few wealthy capitalists who gained control of Wisconsin political institutions. In his work, *A Short History of Wisconsin,* Larry Gara describes the situation in these terms:

> Political bosses representing the lumber barons or railroad magnates controlled the state legislators as well as congressmen and senators in Washington. The system worked for the benefit of many but in its smoothly running operations, democracy itself appeared to be threatened. Railroads and other big business enjoyed immunity from heavy taxation, and graft and corruption permeated political life on every level. Wisconsin's response, in the form of the Progressive movement, focused worldwide attention on the Badger State and on its leader, Robert M. La Follette.[14]

Elected governor of Wisconsin in 1901 and U.S. senator in 1905, Robert La Follette (1855-1925) became a symbol of the Progressive movement when he made an attempt to challenge special interest groups and reform state government and institutions according to the agrarian era's concepts of morality and political democracy. Influenced by the idealism of educators, such as President Bascom of the University of Wisconsin, La Follette tried to involve the state education system at the university level in efforts to solve the problems facing Wisconsin society. In addition to this, co-operatives and federations were formed to help farmers and small producers while state laws were revised to curb the unlimited power of rich industrialists. Soon the state exemplified an experiment in progressive government that the entire nation discussed with interest. Gara relates that "the Wisconsin Idea, as it came to be called, involved efficient government controlled by the voters and the use of specialized experts in the interest of the state."[15]

Reminiscing about her father in this period of history, Jessica explained that her father had a bright mind and used to hold public offices. She relates: "I used to have more fun, more pleasure, just sitting in the room and listening to my father talking politics and things like that."[16]

The Religious Context

To understand the religious sentiments and practices which influenced Jessica in her formative years, it is necessary to look at the history and spirituality of U.S. Catholics in the first quarter of the twentieth century. In *Immigrants and Their Church,* Dolores Liptak devotes an entire chapter to the religious history of Irish immigrants in the United States. Liptak quotes a New England bishop who describes Irish immigrants in the 1860s as "generally attached to their faith . . . attentive . . . although often rude and ignorant . . . poor and generally laborers. They suffer much from the prejudice of Protestants."[17]

This negative image of Irish immigrants began to change slowly after the Civil War. Upward mobility came to the Irish as new waves of immigrants from Germany, followed by those from southern and eastern Europe, flowed into the United States. Helped by their command of the English language, the Irish gained a new sense of self-importance and affirmed their religious roots as Catholic numbers grew to challenge Protestant control of business and politics. The Irish supported their clergy, contributed money to the building of parish churches and schools, and controlled the principal ecclesiastical offices in the U.S. Roman Catholic Church during the early part of the twentieth century.[18]

A more detailed view of the spiritual life of these Irish ancestors of Jessica Powers and of the communities which they formed can be gleaned from Joseph Chinnici's book, *Living Stones: The History and Structure of Catholic Spiritual Life in the United States.* Chinnici discusses the components of nineteenth-century U.S. spirituality in Roman Catholic circles which influenced Catholic spirituality from 1900 to 1930.[19] According to Chinnici, several aspects of a nineteenth-century "immigrant Catholic church" mentality still dictated the views of the majority of U.S. Catholics in the early part of the twentieth century. The social experience of Irish Catholics was just beginning to emerge from a period of religious persecution by Protestants and victimization by a free-market capitalistic system, which was being challenged during the Progressive Era in the U.S. Many Irish Catholics still clung to ideals and longings for former times in European history when Ireland and all of western Europe was in a romantic golden age of Catholicism. Ideas of social reform were centered on maintaining institutions for the poor, building parochial schools, and defending the rights of individual ethnic groups.

In this "immigrant" mentality, the Church was seen as a divine and corporate institution and as the ultimate moral teacher preaching a Jesus who redeemed humankind through his crucifixion. As a result of concepts derived from the Puritan core of American culture and from Irish Jansenism, the human person was seen as full of passions, rebelling against God, and saved by industrious and honest labor. Such practices as sacrifice for others, mortifications of the flesh, and obedience to authority were extolled as basic components of Catholic spirituality. Prayer was taught as methodical meditations and devotions centered on adoration of the Blessed Sacrament, veneration of the saints and the cult of Mary, especially under the title of the Immaculate Conception.[20]

All of this began to change, ushering in a new kind of Catholic spirituality especially after the 1880s, as "Americanist" groups of Catholics began to develop new understandings of associationism and to see history as a series of providential developments. In the Americanist religious literature, the human person was described as made in the image of God, imbued with natural virtues, and full of spiritual yearnings, and the Church was identified as an extension of the Incarnation of Christ, an organic communion, and an agent of personal sanctification through the reconciling action of Jesus Christ.[21]

With self-denial remaining as a basic spiritual axiom, asceticism took a new turn toward self-reliance and free, intelligent piety.[22] Instead of "saying prayers" or "getting prayer in," Catholics were encouraged to "pray," the contemplative element of prayer being rediscovered. Devotion to the Holy Spirit became more prominent in religious literature as a result of Isaac Hecker's influence,[23] and the effects of the European Catholic liturgical revival began to be felt in the United States, especially through the pioneer efforts of the European Benedictines and others which later influenced Benedictines at Saint John's Abbey in Collegeville, Minnesota.[24] With such shifts in religious mentality, new ways of looking at social reform emerged: labor organizations became accepted, the value of common education for all was supported, and visionaries and idealists began to talk of programs for the reconstruction of society.[25]

The interaction of these two streams of spirituality, "immigrant" and "Americanist," upon twentieth-century Catholic spirituality in the United States gave rise to a generation of spiritual pilgrims who exhibited signs of being the recipients of "a fractured inheritance" in terms of their spirituality.[26] The "immigrant" spirituality of the majority of U.S. Catholics, supported by conservative Vatican positions and statements, attempted to moderate the Americanist vision as it tried to shape the religious views of men and women born on American soil after 1900. However, these American Catholics were destined to have experiences which would aid them in modifying the "immigrant" spirituality which nurtured them without rejecting the essential elements which constituted the church itself. To this generation of spiritual pilgrims belongs Jessica Powers.

The Early Years

Educated in a rural school (1911-1916) and in a parochial school (1916-1918), Jessica was first encouraged to write poetry by Sister Lucille Massart, a Dominican who was her eighth grade teacher at the parish school in Mauston.[27] About this time, new experiences began to shape Jessica's understanding of life: her sister Dorothy died at age seventeen of tuberculosis in 1916; her father, who had been crippled earlier by a falling tree, died at age fifty-three of a heart attack while helping to load coal for the church in 1918; and her mother found it necessary to mortgage the farm to cover mounting financial losses. While attending high school in Mauston (1918-1922), Jessica began to realize that life asked many questions of her which she could not seem to answer in Juneau County.[28]

Upon graduating from high school in 1922, Jessica went to Milwaukee hoping to get answers to these questions. From 1922 to 1923, she attended Marquette University, taking classes in the school of journalism since, at this time in the history of U.S. Catholic education, Marquette did not accept women into the school of liberal arts.[29] While at Marquette, Jessica was influenced by two people in particular, Ruth Mary Fox and Reverend John Danihy, SJ. Ruth Mary Fox, who taught a course "Dante Lights the Way," introduced Jessica to the writings of the Carmelite poet and mystic, John of the Cross;[30] Father Danihy, who was the dean of the College of Journalism, taught a poetry class at Marquette in which he encouraged students like Jessica to write.[31] Of her days at Marquette, a 1942 newspaper clipping from *The Catholic Herald Citizen* records that:

Old classmates remember that she [Jessica Powers] had a
witty way of saying things, and she seemed always to be
laughing, a full-throated Irish laugh. She spent much of
her spare time pecking away at her poetry in Johnston
Hall.[32]

Out of money and in poor health as a result of a bout of tuberculosis, Jessica ended up living with an aunt in Chicago, doing secre-
tarial work, and reading poetry in the city's public libraries (1923-
1924).[33] Her circle of friends widened when she joined a group
made up of Dominican seminarians and acquaintances who met regularly at the River Forest priory in suburban Chicago to share poetry
in a literary salon. Christopher Powell was a member of this group
who kept in contact with Jessica through a lively correspondence for
years.[34] Loneliness, romantic longings, and dreams of being a poet
filled Jessica's thoughts. Her first published poem reflects these rev-
eries and appeared in *American Poetry Magazine* in 1924:

Dreams of You

My dreams of you are like the fallen leaves,
colored with brilliance, nomad rustling things,
tossed by the winds of olden memories—
they prate of golden summertimes and springs.

When skies were gray, you flung them all away—
but I, who loved them, hoard such gifts as these.
By day I revel in their gilded lights;
at night they whisper tender sympathies.[35]

Life changed radically for Jessica in September of 1925 when
her mother died. Because her two young brothers were left to manage the family farm alone, Jessica decided to stay in Mauston and
help them with the household tasks and farm chores. From 1925 to
1936, Jessica Powers followed the conventional path open to women
in her day. She cooked, cleaned, sewed, did farm chores, and tried to
make sense of her life. Her time for writing was limited, and what
poems she did manage to write ended up in local newspapers, or oc-
casionally in a column entitled "The Percolator" in *The Milwaukee
Sentinel*.[36] Through her writings in "The Percolator," Jessica made
friends with Jessie Corrigan Pegis, the wife of a professor at Marquette University. Their correspondence would develop over the

years and eventually they would meet face to face in New York City in 1938.[37]

Although she tried, Jessica could not settle down in Mauston to marriage, motherhood, farmwork, and housework. The most she could manage was a few dances and those things necessary to help her brothers keep up the mortgage payments on the family farm. Dolores Leckey gives this description of Jessica Powers in this period of her life:

> Her Mauston friends remember her walking the Cattail Valley country lanes, on her way to a ballgame, carrying a book of poetry, talking about living another kind of life than the expected one. She didn't specify what that life would be, but I suspect she may have envisioned it as marked by the continued discovering and uncovering of beauty, some risk taking, a space to work, some sense of adventure, a straining toward extremes. And where is the Holy Spirit in all of this?[38]

Once her brothers were married, Jessica was no longer needed to manage the household tasks on the family farm, but these were the years of "The Great Depression" in the United States. Because she had no financial backing, Jessica's family tried to discourage her from carrying out her dream of living in a distant city. She found an outlet for her interior struggles in her poetry, and soon Jessica established a considerable reputation for herself as a Wisconsin poet. Her best poems from this period reflect local nature themes and lessons learned from the birds and are intertwined with themes of religious questioning and spiritual yearnings played out in a variety of place settings.

The Images and Themes of Spiritual Yearning: Reflections Found in the Early Poems

A study of Jessica Powers' early poems reveals her kinship with the great American religious and nature poets who preceded her, especially Emily Dickinson. Thomas P. McDonnell, Richard Boudreau, and Regina Siegfried remark on the similarity between Jessica Powers' early poetic style and that of Emily Dickinson.[39] Bernard McGarty makes the observation that both poets, Dickinson and Powers, share profound observations with their readers through their use of simple verse.[40]

Although Jessica used the quatrain as the base form of her earliest poems, she also wrote some triplets and sonnets. The majority of her quatrains contain the abab rhyme scheme, but there are some examples of the ballad stanza as well. Like Emily Dickinson, Jessica often used a poetic device known as the enjambment, the carry-over of the poetic line into the following stanza.[41]

Regina Siegfried compares Dickinson and Powers in these words:

> I see similarities in their love of solitude, their uncanny ability to cover thoroughly and well the tracks of their inner life and, at the same time, write on a universal level. Their ability to use household and housekeeping images and their love for birds and flowers indicate kindred spirits.[42]

Siegfried sees Jessica Powers as an American nature poet, as well as a religious poet, who "used nature as metaphor to explore human interactions, human/divine relationships, and inner/outer landscapes."[43] In this way, Jessica was able to express her understanding of God and her "deep sense of the divine, an area where [she] may ultimately prove to be more at home, more profound, and more sure of herself than Emily Dickinson."[44]

Night is a metaphor used by poets, like John of the Cross and Emily Dickinson, for walking into the inner darkness of faith. As early as 1926, Jessica Powers was making use of this metaphor in her poetry to describe the paradox of suffering and death in relationship to life and God.

Petenwell Rock, one of the local scenic wonders of central Wisconsin, was the site of a dance which Jessica attended one night in the "Roaring 20s." In a poem published in 1926, Jessica describes this night of dancing:

Petenwell Rock

I never shall forget the first gay night
I came for dancing here;
Out of a long black road there bloomed this bright portion of revel, near
a tall pine-wreathed rock, as certain as a wall.

Out of the night suddenly lights had mellowed
to warm young gold glistening against a hall
where dancers swayed like songs, and music
                bellowed
its anger against grief; and laughter flying
fell on my ears like sounded waterfall.

But overhead the whip-poor-wills were crying,
crowding all loneliness into one cry,
and a great rock maintained a wise old silence,
lifting its strength into a starlit sky.

O silver loneliness!
    O golden laughter!
O grief that only loneliness should last!
Madness will die, and youth will hurry after.
Into some shadowed past
dancers will bow like dust; laughter will crumble,
while still beneath the silver of the moon
for loveliness and joy that died too soon
these plaintive birds will cry,
and this tall rock will watch with calm indifference,
holding itself aloof against the sky.[45]

Conflicting messages are recorded in this poem: "music bel-
lowed its anger against grief;" "dancers will bow like dust;" and
"laughter will crumble." The human dancer is haunted by anger,
loneliness, grief, madness, and death in the midst of "warm young
gold" and "golden laughter," gaiety and brightness, "beneath the silver of the moon." Some elements of nature are sympathetic to the
human plight and some are not: the whip-poor-wills echo the human
cry of loneliness by "crowding all loneliness into one cry," but the
rock watches "with calm indifference, holding itself aloof against the
sky." The speaker of this poem declares that "I never shall forget the
first gay night I came for dancing here" and ponders this experience
of life's paradoxes.

Certain words and images will reappear in Jessica's poems repeatedly, plunging the original written words to ever deeper levels of
meaning. In comparing the poem "Cabaret" to "Petenwell Rock,"
one notices a repetition of setting: the dance floor; repetition of time:
night; repetition of sound: the music, the laughter; repetition of sight:
light, dazzling, bright; and repetition of feeling: loneliness, grief,
darkness. Both poems were published in the same year (1926), and
both raise the same questions about the meaning of existence, but
"Cabaret" seems to go a level deeper.

Cabaret

I shall spend a penny of love,
and a penny of grief,
And a penny for song,
wine that is red, wines that are purple and white;
I shall find a place in the dazzling room of life,
and sit on a chair and sip my wine all night.

Dancers will come like red and gold leaves blown
over a crystal floor, and I shall see many a reveller wander out alone
through a black door beyond all revelry.

There will be music come on little feet
into my soul, and laughter to be spread
over young wounds, and kisses honey-sweet,
and shining words to keep me comforted.

And I shall wait till the Keeper comes to say
that my hour is done, and he drowns each glaring
light
in endless black . . . and the dancers go away . . .
and I stumble out alone into the night.[46]

In going deeper into life's paradoxes presented in the "cabaret,"
Jessica found it necessary to weave several images together. John of
the Cross' classic description of the journey into the dark night of the
soul, "One dark night, fired with love's urgent longings . . . I went
out unseen,"[47] is juxtaposed with a contemporary cabaret's restaurant
bar and dance floor. The night is dark and "many a reveller wander[s] out alone / through a black door beyond all revelry" and are
lost in meaninglessness. Yet this speaker who "waits till the Keeper
comes to say / that my hour is done," is conscious of being called to
undertake an inward journey, to "stumble out alone into the night."

In reality, a cabaret is a restaurant where short programs of live
entertainment accompany a meal; in this poem, the cabaret takes on a
symbolic meaning and Jessica's use of the image raises many questions. Does one go to this cabaret to be in touch with life or to be
distracted from the questions posed by life? Is the cabaret described
in this poem "the dazzling room of life?" Or does one, although
bodily still in the cabaret, have to withdraw interiorly through the sip
of wine and by sitting quietly on a chair balanced on the edge of the

cabaret, in order to enter and "find a place in the dazzling room of life?" What is the real meaning of her use of the word "cabaret?" Does Powers make mockery of earthly cabarets or does she envision a connection between the earthly and the heavenly in the cabaret of life?

The speaker in this poem is poised on a chair that is tipped: to spend a penny cautiously and see what happens or to spend all one owns to participate fully in the dance of life. The first action will keep one on the edge of life while the second action will bring one to participate in the dance on the "crystal floor."

Is it a penny of grief, small strings of attachment to past sorrow, that keeps this speaker from dancing on the "crystal floor," or is it a fear that "the Keeper [will come] to say that my hour is done, and he [will drown] each glaring light in endless black" that makes this speaker sit upon a chair, drowning all in wine? Is this fear and grief capable of winning out in the end of the poem over the promises of the third stanza:

> There will be music come on little feet
> into my soul, and laughter to be spread
> over young wounds, and kisses honey-sweet
> and shining words to keep me comforted?

What has this speaker experienced that the promises of the third stanza cannot dispel?

The poem speaks of the wine of life. Is this wine of life "gift" to bring happiness and meaningfulness, or is it a narcotic to deaden the haunting thought that "dancers will come like red and gold leaves blown / over a crystal floor" only to be lost forever beyond "a black door beyond all revelry?" Jessica records in her early poems the questions which compelled her to undertake the inward journey that enabled her to make the transition from a poet who treats of localized nature scenes to that of a poet who treats of universal themes.

In addition to this, Jessica's earliest writings demonstrate the power of nature and the lessons of its birds to open up a symbolic language which she uses to chronicle the movement of the Holy Spirit in her own life. Her first attempts at this are modest ones like this poem published in 1927:

Robins at Dusk

I can go starved the whole day long,
draining a stone, eating a husk,
and never hunger till a song
breaks from a robin's throat at dusk.

I am reminded only then
how far from day and human speech,
how far from the loud world of men
lies the bright dream I strain to reach.

Oh, that a song of mine could burn
the air with beauty so intense,
sung with a robin's unconcern
for any mortal audience!

Perhaps I shall learn presently
his secret when the shadows stir,
and I shall make one song and be
aware of but one Listener.[48]

The spiritual yearning is released in words like "starved" and "hunger" while phrases like "how far from day . . . lies the bright dream I strain to reach" give direction to the heart's quest: "I shall make one song and be / aware of but one Listener." By the next year (1928), Jessica is able to publish a poem which has phrases similar to Francis Thompson's "Hound of Heaven,"[49] as she writes: "I can release the hound / of love upon whose bruising leash I strain." Also word patterns such as "where You skim the sod," echo Gerard Manley Hopkins' classic poem, "God's Grandeur."[50] These images are carefully woven with a developing sense of the place of the Holy Spirit in her thought, her prayer, and her poetry to produce this piece:

Celestial Bird

O sweet and luminous Bird,
Having once heard Your call, lovely and shy,
I shall be hungry for the finished word.
Across the windy sky

of all voiced longing and all music heard,
I spread my net for Your bewildering wings,
but wings are wiser than the swiftest hands.
Where a bird sings

I held my heart, in fear that it would break.
I called You through the grief of whip-poor-wills,
I watched You on the avenues that make
a radiant city on the western hills.

Yet since I knew You not, I sought in vain.
I called You Beauty for its fleet white sound.
But now in my illumined heart
I can release the hound

of love upon whose bruising leash I strain.
Oh, he will grasp You where You skim the sod,
nor wound Your breast, for love is soft as death,
swifter than beauty is, and strong as God.[51]

The image of the "Bird" takes on a deeper meaning as the human subject "having once heard the call" now hungers "for the finished word." This bird's singing is not set in tree or wood; rather, "I watched You on the avenues that make a radiant city on the western hills." Jessica Powers was acutely aware of her love for the Wisconsin countryside, but she also was passionately enamored by the throbbing streets of Chicago, and later, New York. Repeatedly her poetry is filled with concrete images which link these two landscapes.

"Lo Spirito Santo" was first published in 1929. Like "Celestial Bird," it explores the theme of the Holy Spirit but this time in explicit terms:

Lo Spirito Santo

The Spirit of God
is wind and water,
fire and a bird.
Substance and sod,
earth and matter
have formed one word.

For who has looked
on a fire blowing
and has not seen
banners erect
and waves going
and a bird lean
on a shoulder of wind?

And who has stood
near a sea burning
under the blind
sun's eye and could
by no thought's turning
look on fire,
or a wind racing,
or a bird thrown
higher and higher
toward towers facing
the sea, toward stone?

So beauty's bird
wind-wisdom seeking,
and sorrow's flood,
and love's flame stirred,
are one voice speaking
a word called God.

For Fire a word
with light its daughter
(and their golden Breath),
name for a Bird
and wind and water
that have no death.[52]

With these lines, Jessica conjures up concrete images in an effort to express the all-pervading power of the Holy Spirit permeating her world. The symbols, images, and themes mirror biblical ones used to describe the encounter of Elijah with the Spirit of the Lord in the first and second book of Kings: wind, water, fire, earth, bird, sea, voice, and word. She links these images with her own key word of beauty, "so beauty's bird"; with her own key image of "bird thrown higher and higher"; with her own theme of a feminine dimension in divine or Trinitarian contemplation, "for Fire a word with light its daughter (and their golden Breath), name for a Bird . . . that have no death"; and with John of the Cross' theme of "love's flame stirred."[53] The result is a glimpse of her vision of the incarnate God: "Substance and sod, earth and matter have formed one word," and "one voice speaking a word called God."

These years found Jessica writing on other themes besides that of the Holy Spirit. Groomed and nurtured by a decade of studying the works of other poets, like John of the Cross, Henry David Thoreau, Elinor Wylie, Robert Frost, Francis Thompson, and Gerard Manley Hopkins, Jessica tried to integrate ideas and feelings in an experiential symbolic language. Upon reflecting on Elinor Wylie's poem, "The Velvet Shoes,"[54] and on the experience of being a woman, she wrote this poem which was published in 1929:

The Granite Woman

The hour she enters hush your lovely song.
She has no road for velvet-slippered feet;
her mind that bore earth's agony so long
would crumble underneath a load so sweet.

Her heart that shut its doors on love's wide
              calling
that was as granite where the storms begin,
would break beneath the weight of petals falling
out of the music of this violin.[55]

Simultaneously strong yet vulnerable, Jessica's "granite woman" leaves the world of "lovely song" and "velvet-slippered feet," travels the road of "earth's agony," and arrives at a pivotal point in life. All the deadening and hardening effects of life's journey are capable of being negated by a new force; all would break beneath "the weight of petals falling out of the music of this violin." For Thoreau, it was the beat of a distant and different drummer that gave direction to life; for Powers, it was the music of this violin that reopened the heart's doors to "love's wide calling."

Longings and spiritual yearnings filled Jessica's mind as she undertook the daily chores of a farm woman in the winter of 1932. Her spirit often found itself on city streets of Chicago searching for God, even while her physical being was firmly stationed in rural Wisconsin. Christmas of the year 1932 was a dismal one, laden down with the burdensome effects of the Great Depression in the United States. Jessica captured the mood in a poem entitled "Michigan Boulevard, Chicago."[57] Set on her favorite street in Chicago, her speaker bears "hunger, loneliness, and poverty" instead of "myrrh, frankincense and gold" as gifts for the Christ Child. The wandering speaker is guided by a star above this street, much as the Magi of old were guided by the Christmas star.[58] Jessica's ability to identify with the marginalized in society in an ennobling and not a condescending way developed in her poetry throughout the thirties. Later these poems were valued and printed in such publications as Dorothy Day's *Catholic Worker*.[59]

An early example of Jessica's poetic prowess in dealing with themes concerning the marginalized in the American society can be found in her poem entitled "The Uninvited." Here Jessica juxtaposed the plight of the urban poor in the 1930s in the United States with biblical images and published this poem in 1935:

The Uninvited

There is a city that through time shall lie
in a fixed darkness of the earth and sky;
and many dwell therein this very hour.
It is a city without seed or flower,
estranged from every bird and butterfly.

Who walked these streets of night? I know them
well.
Those who come out of life's sequestered places:
the lonely, the unloved, the weak and shy,
the broken-winged who piteously would fly,
the poor who still have starlight in their faces.

They are the outcast ones, the last, the least,
whom earth has not invited to her feast,
and who, were they invited in the end,
finding their wedding clothes too frayed to mend,
would not attend.[60]

Jessica writes of the urban poor, proud and with starlight in their faces, as those uninvited guests to the wedding feast in the New Testament parable of Jesus.[61] She knows them well and knows the power of their presence. They are the ones "who, were they invited in the end, finding their wedding clothes too frayed to mend, would not attend." Without their presence, the party is not full, is not complete, is not a real one; rather, it is only a partial, incomplete imitation of life and not what God has willed for those who wait for the coming of the kingdom.

Interaction with the marginalized in her society led Jessica to embrace a mystical vision of the human person in relationship with God and others that was balanced with the real world about her. By means of her poetry, Jessica could capture the paradox of the human being pitted against odds of sure defeat yet being aided by divine grace and redeemed in the end.

Although it would be almost ten years before Jessica Powers would enter the Carmelite community in Milwaukee, the poem, "The Track of the Mystic," reveals the seeds of her Christian spirituality latent with both mystic and Carmelite overtones. Her handling of the classic themes of John of the Cross, which she had been familiar with since the early twenties, and the medieval classic, "The Cloud of the Unknowing," are now explicit as her pen travels this road. The speaker in her poem, "The Track of the Mystic," starts out with proud step in search of love, encounters torment in the struggle, and in the night of God's light experiences the paradox of death in triumph not in defeat. Ultimately, her message is one of hope written in concrete terms and images. First published in 1932, Jessica's poem, "The Track of the Mystic," invokes a powerful vision of the human person transformed by grace:

The Track of the Mystic

There was a man went forth into the night
with a proud step. I saw his garments blowing;
I saw him reach the great cloud of unknowing.
He went in search of love, whose sign is light.
From the dark night of sense I saw him turn
into the deeper dark nights of the soul
where no least star marks a divine patrol.

Great was his torment who could not discern
this night was God's light generously given,
blinding the tainted spirit utterly
till from himself at last he struggled free.
I saw him on the higher road to heaven:
his veins ran gold; light was his food and breath.
Flaming he melted through the wall of death![62]

As she herself became more aware and sure of her poetic call, Jessica became more determined to seek out the means to realize this call. By 1934, she saw the link in her own life between the movement of the Holy Spirit, her poetry, and her need to journey in search of a place to realize her call, as she wrote:

Shining Quarry

Since the luminous great wings of wonder stirred
over me in the twilight I have known
the Holy Spirit is the Poet's Bird.

Since in a wilderness I wandered near
a shining stag, this wisdom is my own:
the Holy Spirit is the Hunter's Deer.

And in the dark in all enchanted lands
I know the Spirit is that Burning Bush
toward which the artist gropes with outstretched
    hands.

Upon the waters once and then again
I saw the Spirit in a silver rush
rise like the Quarry of the Fishermen.

Yet this I know: no arrows of desire
can wound Him, nor a bright intrepid spear;
He is not seen by any torch of fire,

nor can they find Him who go wandering far;
His habitat is wonderfully near
in each soul's thicket 'neath its deepest star.

Let those who seek come home through the vain
    years
to where the Spirit waits a shining captive.
This is the hunt most worthy of all tears.

Bearing their nets celestial, let them come
and take their Quarry on the fields of rapture
that lie beyond the last gold pendulum.[63]

The catalyst for change in Jessica's life was twofold, wonder and beauty, and both were always calling her forward. In this poem, her speaker becomes a hunter, like those who sought deer in the Wisconsin woods, but this hunter is trying to track and make captive the Spirit who calls out in wonder and beauty. Like an artist who "gropes with outstretched hands," the speaker is trying to reach out and touch the "Burning Bush,"[64] again a thing of wonder and beauty existing always beyond the human grasp. As a fisherman trying to net the "silver rush" of the quarry,[65] the human subject is trying to net the Spirit only to discover that the Quarry cannot be taken except "on the fields of rapture" that lie beyond time, "beyond the last gold pendulum." The paradox of the speaker driven to undertake a life-long pilgrimage in search of God is voiced in lines like: "He is not seen by any torch of fire / Nor can they find Him who go wandering far;" or "His habitat is wonderfully near / in each soul's thicket 'neath its deepest star;" or "Let those who seek come home through the vain years / to where the Spirit waits a shining captive."

Finally, spiritual yearnings, such as those expressed in her poetry, forced Jessica Powers to bid good-bye to her family and travel eastward in search of a place in which she could appease these yearnings. Her first stop was a brief one in Chicago in 1936. After a few months spent visiting family and old friends there, Jessica was off to New York in 1937.[66] Meanwhile, her contributions to the development of poetic literature in Wisconsin were recognized by August Derleth and his friend Raymond E. F. Larsson, both co-editors of an anthology of Wisconsin poetry published in 1937 under the title of *Poetry Out of Wisconsin*.[67] They included in their book several of her poems and a brief biographical note of her life.

In summary, poems like "Petenwell Rock" and "Cabaret" mark the beginning of a serious shift from the general themes and romantic musings in Jessica's earliest poetry to the type of theologically reflective stance that stamps the vast majority of her subsequent poems. The paradoxes of life, suffering, death, and resurrection raise questions which capture her attention from the mid-1920s onward.

Jessica's earliest writings also demonstrate the power of nature and the lessons of its birds to open up a symbolic language which she uses to chronicle the movement of the Holy Spirit in her own life. Thus, her poetry begins to resemble that of Emily Dickinson. Now spiritual yearnings exist side by side with the earlier romantic longings of her girlhood. The language of these longings and spiritual yearnings reflects her study of poets, like Francis Thompson and Gerard Manley Hopkins, as well. Having been introduced to the writings of John of the Cross and Therese of Lisieux in the early twenties, Jessica begins to experiment with juxtaposing her own life experiences with biblical narratives and classic Carmelite themes. The poem which best demonstrates Jessica's early experiments along these lines is "The Track of the Mystic."

A dual awareness, her innate love for the Wisconsin countryside and her passion for the throbbing streets of Chicago, constitutes another aspect of Jessica's poetry which evidences itself clearly at this time. Repeatedly her poetry is filled with concrete images which link these two landscapes. Jessica's ability to identify with the marginalized in both settings in an ennobling and not a condescending way develops in her poetry throughout the early thirties.

Finally, the catalyst for change in Jessica's life is twofold, wonder and beauty, and both are always calling her forward. Like classical figures in Carmelite spirituality before her, Jessica struggles to abandon the fear of a wrathful God as her guiding principle in life and strains to follow the promptings of the Holy Spirit by risking all to undertake the search for a loving God.

Chapter 4

Jessica Powers: The Poet on a
Journey (1936-1941)

THE YEARS 1936-1941 WERE A TRANSITION PERIOD FOR JESSICA POWERS.
In 1936 she was in Chicago for a brief visit with old friends and
relatives. Due to the Great Depression that gripped the entire U.S. in
these years, things had changed since she had lived and worked there
in 1923-1924. Slowly she began to realize that Chicago was not the
place where she could realize her dreams. Therefore, aided by her innate courage and spirit of adventure, Jessica traveled, alone and without financial backing, to New York in 1937.[1] Jessica had great
hopes. She sought to develop her poetic abilities, to sharpen her
Christian insights, and to answer the questions life had asked of her
in the preceding years. Her words, transcribed from a taped interview with Robert Morneau and Regina Siegfried when she was in her
eighties, set the scene for this chapter in her life:

> I wanted to go to New York so bad. Everybody told me
> not to go. . . . I think I had a good reason to go, I wanted
> to lead a more spiritual life. I wanted to get closer to
> literary sources. I started out and I didn't have much
> money [and] not hardly any clothes. I just thought very
> confidently, I know God will take care of me. . . God did
> take care of me. When I got off the bus a man came up
> to me and said, "Are you looking for work in New
> York? I can find work for you." I knew he was flatter-
> ing me. I said, "No, I know where I'm going." I went
> into the booth to call and I didn't know how to dial the
> phone. . . . [I did not know] a soul, but the only thing I
> had was a little clipping . . . It said, "If you are in New
> York go to the Leo House." I stayed in there [the phone
> booth] for a while. He was still there. I said I know
> what I am going to do, so I walked out the door and the

cab driver was there. I said, "Do you know where 8th
Avenue is?" and he said, "We are on 8th Avenue right
now." And I said, "Do you know where the Leo House
is?" He said, "A couple of blocks." So I went there.[2]

Jessica made her cross-country trek during one of the bleakest
times in United States history, "The Great Depression," and ended up
in one of the most crowded and impersonal places in United States
geography, New York City. Dolores Leckey writes that "Poetry was
her reason for being in that city, a place she 'could revel in, but not
love,' to use her own words."[3]

The Historical Context

When this period in Jessica Powers' life began, eight years had
elapsed since October 29, 1929, when the New York Stock Exchange
had collapsed. The resulting financial ruin, which devastated the entire nation throughout the 1930s, can be summed up briefly in the
following passage:

> Within a few hours, more than $10 billion of America's
> "fruits of accomplishment" were gone. Within the next
> three years, with declining consumer purchasing, manu-
> facturers closed plants or reduced the work force. Some
> 100,000 workers, on the average, were fired each week.
> The number of unemployed stood at 2 million in 1929, at
> 4 million in 1930, at 8 million in 1931, at 12 million in
> 1932. . . . Over 5000 banks and 9 million savings ac-
> counts were wiped out; tens of thousands of mortgages
> were foreclosed. Families found themselves evicted
> from their homes and barely able to exist.[4]

New York City in the 1930s, of which Jessica Powers had so
long dreamed about as a poet's haven and in which now she found
herself, was a teeming city containing millions of people, most of
whom were unemployed or in her same, if not much worse, financial
straits. The Great Depression was hard on the artists and writers of
New York City. Musicians and poets of the black district known as
Harlem were especially devastated by the economic reverses that sti-
fled their first long-deserved experiences of success in the 1920s.
Their movement, known as "The Harlem Renaissance," had been a
glorious celebration of a true self-consciousness of black culture.[5]

In her later years, Jessica remembered the Harlem writer, Jean Toomer (1884-1967), as one of the best poets of her times.[6] Among other works, Toomer had written the novel *Cane*, his series of black portraits that ranged over unexplored parts of black life and was perhaps "the most brilliant single achievement" of the Harlem Renaissance in the 1920s.[7] However, Toomer became disillusioned, for "the Harlem artists who thought the Renaissance would bring acceptance and success had only deceived themselves."[8] When the Great Depression hit, the black artists found themselves out of vogue and abandoned by their white patrons and publishers. Toomer's light-complexion allowed him to cross the color line altogether. Giving up his dream of acceptance for black Americans and racial equality, he abandoned the black renaissance movement and pursued a form of consciousness expansion and meditation espoused by the Greek-Armenian spiritual teacher, Georgii Ivanovich Gurdzhiev.[9]

When Jessica arrived in New York City, the iron hand of the Great Depression still maintained its grip. The year was 1937: the year of Steinbeck's *Of Mice and Men*, Japan's stepping up its expansion through invasion program, United Auto Workers' sit-down strikes, and the Second American Writers' Congress. By the next year (1938), Wilder had written *Our Town*, Brooks and Warren had published *Understanding Poetry*, the AFL expelled the CIO unions, 10.4 million Americans were still unemployed, Welles's "War of the Worlds" radio broadcast paralyzed U.S. listeners with its tale of a Martian invasion, and Hitler stepped up the persecution of the Jewish people in Europe. Jessica and the rest of U.S. citizenry found themselves in a world with a mainspring wound like a corkscrew.

In 1939 Jessica published her first book of poetry, *The Lantern Burns*, while the literary world around her produced such masterpieces as Steinbeck's *Grapes of Wrath*, Hellman's *The Little Foxes*, C. Brooks' *Modern Poetry and the Tradition*, and Hollywood produced Ford's *Stagecoach*, Selznick's *Gone With the Wind*, and Fleming's *Wizard of Oz*. At the same time, the wider world saw the beginning of World War II with the Nazi-Soviet Pact and the Soviet invasion of Poland and Finland as the year 1940 dawned. By the close of 1940, a new wave of literary events had unfolded with the publication of Hemingway's *For Whom the Bells Toll*, McCullers' *The Heart is a Lonely Hunter*, DuBois' *Dusk of Dawn*, and Cummings' *Fifty Poems*. Meanwhile Germany conquered Norway, Denmark, Belgium, France, Holland, and Luxembourg, and the AXIS alliance formed.

In regard to the social philosophy that influenced the political scene, Hofstadter characterizes this period in U.S. history in his book, *The Age of Reform* in the following lines:

> The Great Depression, which broke the mood of the twenties almost as suddenly as the postwar reaction had killed the Progressive fervor, rendered obsolete most of the antagonisms that had flavored the politics of the postwar era. Once again the demand for reform became irresistible, and out of the chaotic and often mutually contradictory schemes for salvation that arose from all corners of the country the New Deal took form. In the years 1933-8 the New Deal sponsored a series of legislative changes that made the enactments of the Progressive era seem timid by comparison.[10]

By the end of the thirties, it became clear that something new had been added to the social base of the movement known as reformism. Under the influence of a large and powerful labor movement linked with the demands of the unemployed, the New Deal took on a social-democratic dimension that included responsibility for social security, unemployment insurance, wages and hours regulations, and housing. Large-scale spending and unbalanced budgets became standard operating procedures of the federal government in response to the immediate and desperate needs of the majority of both rural and urban U.S. citizens.[11]

A prophetic note was struck by Lord Keynes when he wrote an article in 1940 for U.S. publication in which he pointed out how politically impossible it would be "for a capitalistic democracy to organize expenditure on the scale necessary to make the grand experiment . . . except in war conditions."[12] In addition to this, Keynes argued that an economy based on the production of armaments might be the "stimulus to greater individual consumption and a higher standard of life" for Americans.[13] Depression, war, and prosperity were being linked together in this order as a cure-all for the nation's ills as the United States tottered on the brink of entering World War II in 1941. In the work, *The United States,* the chapter on "The Great Depression and the New Deal" closes with the comment that "the eagerness with which all Americans accepted national planning for the purpose of waging war raised some troublesome questions that would persist long after the war had ended."[14]

The Religious Context

In reflecting upon Jessica Powers' sojourn in New York City during the height of the Great Depression, Dolores Leckey writes:

> Not only did there seem to be a story of an adventuresome spirit, but the Jessica Powers story was also a window onto a fertile, vibrant period of Catholic intellectual and artistic life. The Catholic Poetry Society was born in the 1930s. The English Catholic publishers Sheed and Ward opened their New York office during that period. Radio gave us "The Catholic Hour," which included priest-speakers, choral music . . . what came to be known as the Catholic Revival was in full swing.[15]

The U.S. Catholic world and its citizens were experiencing radical changes in the 1930s. Due to stricter immigration laws and quotas for the first time in over a hundred years, the Roman Catholic Church in the United States was not being flooded with tides of poor immigrants from Catholic regions of Europe.[16] As a result, the Church's energies could be redirected into new channels: ministry to the marginalized in the American society and the development of a vibrant intellectual and artistic life in stabilized Catholic circles.

To illustrate the first point, ministry to the marginalized, Leo House had been established by German Catholic clergy and laity in New York City as a home for poor trans-Atlantic immigrants; now, during the Great Depression, it provided shelter for homeless travelers, like Jessica Powers.[17]

In addition to transformed structures, like Leo House, new movements appeared. For example, the Catholic Worker, a radical group of social activists founded by Dorothy Day, a leftist journalist and recent Catholic convert, and Peter Maurin, a French Catholic peasant philosopher, made its appearance in New York City on May Day 1933. To make the Catholic church "the dominant social dynamic force" was the goal of the movement.[18] The ideals of the Catholic Worker movement took concrete root in their houses of hospitality where the homeless and unemployed could find hot food, a clean bed, and a table around which to carry on a respectful dialogue about anything from politics to theology. The movement's newspaper, called the *Catholic Worker*, periodically carried Jessica Powers' poetry as well as regular features like Maurin's essays and Day's reflections on the American scene. Later Dorothy Day's radical commitment to pacifism prompted many to leave the movement during World War II.[19] In 1942 Marilynn Miller wrote that "Jessica Powers is a kindred spirit of Dorothy Day" and that "Powers' poetry is expressive of the philosophy that Dorothy Day is so earnestly living."[20]

Along the same lines, Catherine de Hueck, an impoverished Russian aristocrat, opened the first Friendship House in Harlem to promote interracial justice in 1938. Out of her efforts grew a movement which spread across the U.S. much in the same manner as the Catholic Worker movement. Friendship houses provided direct help to the needy in forms of food, clothing, and housing; they sponsored educational lectures, workshops, and publications; and they promoted social action by conducting surveys and nonviolent demonstrations against discrimination in their efforts to effect change at all levels of society.[21]

To illustrate the second point, the development of a vibrant intellectual and artistic life in Catholic circles, it is necessary to recognize some of the components of this Catholic Revival of the 1930s: the Catholic Poetry Society of America founded in 1931 in New York City to encourage the writing of poetry; the National Catholic Theater Conference founded in 1937 in Washington, D.C. to encourage drama consistent with Christian principles; the Thomas More Association founded in 1939 in Chicago to disseminate the best in Catholic reading to the American population; and the Catholic Renascence Society founded in 1940 in Milwaukee to stimulate interest in Christian thought and culture. The single most important component of this Catholic Revival relevant to this study, is the Catholic Poetry Society of America.

This society was the brain-child of John Gillard Brunini (b. 1899) and several other Catholic poets, among whom were Clifford Laube and Francis Xavier Connolly (1909-1965). Besides encouraging the writing of poetry, the society sponsored lectures and conferences and, with Brunini as editor, it published a magazine of poetry known as *Spirit*, which prided itself on introducing new poetry and creating a network for Catholic poets, their critics, and lovers of poetry.[22] The poetic renaissance in American Catholic circles in the 1930s owes much to this society. According to some commentators, perhaps more than any other single U.S. organization, it fostered the maturing of Catholic poetry while raising the quality of much religious verse through the standards it set for the appreciation and understanding of poetry."[23]

More recent scholars, such as Margaret Mary Reher, take another view of the literary climate fostered by the Catholic Poetry Society of America and its companion organizations and pronounce a negative judgment on its efforts to "control" Catholic literary tastes in the United States. Following the lead of George Shuster and reflecting upon his critique of the inferior state of Catholic literary endeavors during this period, Reher denounces the Catholic Poetry Society of America for trying to create a separate and elitist literature for its members so that they would have a safe harbor and not be contaminated by association with other U.S. writers. Reher speculates in the same vein as Paul Messbarger that "part of the failure of American Catholic literature has been traced to the literary critics of *The Commonweal* and *America* as well as to the formation of the Catholic Poetry Society."[24]

Whatever may be the ultimate verdict in regard to the contribution of the Catholic Poetry Society of America to Catholic literary development in the United States, it was within this circle that Jessica Powers found the network which she needed in order to publish her poetry in the late 1930s. However, later her name is not linked with this circle but with names like Thomas Merton and Robert Lowell. Already by 1949, commentators like Mary Luke Baldwin see Jessica Powers to be more of a kindred spirit with a new generation of Catholic thinkers:

> Her friend Clifford J. Laube . . . unhesitatingly included her . . . [with] such women poets as Christina Rossetti, Alice Meynell, Katharine Tynan, Eileen Duggan, and Sister Madeleva. Most frequently, however, her name is literarily linked with Thomas Merton and Robert Lowell. She has been called an authentic religious poet.[25]

A New Circle of Friends

Leo House was Jessica's first stop in New York City. Next, in response to an advertisement in the newspaper, she found a position doing domestic work.[26] Jessica continued in this residence and employment until she came in contact with Jessie Corrigan Pegis, a friend whom she had made through "The Percolator" column of the *Milwaukee Sentinel*. Jessie Pegis was a published author who had admired Jessica's poems and had written to her for years.[27] Between 1931 and 1936 her husband, Anton Pegis (1905-1978), taught philosophy at Marquette University in Milwaukee; in 1937 he was teaching Thomist philosophy at Fordham University while Jessie split her time between raising their brood of young children and writing.[28] Upon learning that Jessica was in New York City, Jessie Pegis invited Jessica to come and live with them. Jessica accepted the invitation and moved to Tuckahoe in 1938 and to Scarsdale in 1940 to help Jessie with caring for her children and her housework. As a result, the women were able to develop a fast friendship and support each other while they devoted time to their literary pursuits.[29]

Those were fruitful years at the Pegis' home, marked by evening dinners filled with stimulating conversations and followed by word games. Jessie Pegis described Jessica's life with them in these words:

> We used to do the housework in the mornings, and write and play with the children and talk about life in the afternoons and evenings. The world never quite satisfied her. Not that she did not enjoy life in the world. She did. No one could have been more fun to be with than Jessica. No one could have seemed to get more fun out of living. . . . The children were crazy about her. They adored her from the day we first saw her shortly after we came to New York. They used to beg her to "play sheepdog." The idea of sheepdog was that she was to pull her hair down over her face, with a little not-too-gentle help from their young hands.[30]

Tony, as Anton was called, helped Jessica as she learned to write book reviews, and Jessie taught her a great deal about writing as well.[31] During this time, Jessica wrote a great deal of poetry and numerous book reviews, in addition to short stories under various pen names.[32]

As mentioned earlier, New York City was the home of the Catholic Poetry Society of America, which met at the Waldorf-Astoria Hotel in Manhattan.[33] Here Jessica found a group of gifted people who appreciated her poetic talents.[34] One of the group, Alfred M. Barret, SJ, encouraged her greatly in her writing.[35] Another member of this group, Clifford James Laube (1891-1974), who became one of her most steadfast supporters, was the suburban editor of *The New York Times* and the associate editor and a co-founder of *Spirit*, the magazine published by the Catholic Poetry Society.[36]

Laube had set up a printing press, called the Monastine Press, in his own home and published a volume of his poetry entitled *Crags* in early 1939.[37] Later the same year, he published a volume of Jessica's poetry entitled *The Lantern Burns.* August Derleth, who co-edited with Raymond Larsson the anthology *Poetry Out of Wisconsin* in 1937, gave Jessica the idea for the title of her book,[38] which was a great success and established Jessica's reputation as a first-rate Catholic poet. During a New York interview in 1939, Laube insisted:

> She [Jessica Powers] is the most important woman poet who has appeared in the resurgence of Catholic poetry that has developed since the inception of the Catholic Poetry Society. I think she's a greater poet than Edna St. Vincent Millay, because she has a profound religious significance and deep human pity and a strong spiritual impact.[39]

Besides the Pegis family and the members of the Catholic Poetry Society of America, Jessica had several other good friends in New York City. Two people, who migrated from Wisconsin to New York in the 1930s and kept in contact with Jessica after she entered the Carmelite community in Wisconsin, were Eileen Surles and Raymond Larsson.

Eileen Surles was from a family on the east side of Milwaukee and had known Jessica since the twenties. In New York City, she worked in a book department and did some writing herself. Some of Jessica's fondest memories of New York City were: "I like poking around Manhattan—its libraries, churches, and its teashops—with Eileen Surles [now of the Cenacle]."[40] For decades after Jessica entered the Wisconsin Carmel, Eileen, who became a member of the Cenacle, visited Jessica to make retreats and to nurture their friendship.[41]

Raymond Ellsworth F. Larsson was a second friend from Wisconsin who moved to New York at the same time Jessica lived there. As mentioned previously, Raymond was familiar with Jessica's life and writings because he had helped his friend, August Derleth, co-edit an anthology entitled *Poetry Out of Wisconsin*, which was published in 1937,[42] and for which he had compiled biographies of Wisconsin poets and made selections from their works for the anthology. The most detailed critiques of Jessica's poetry written in this period flow from his pen under the initials R.E.F.L. Raymond also wrote poetry especially for her, as demonstrated in the following example

presented to her under the title "A Little New Year's Poem for Jessica
Powers: Staten Island: 1940-41," and subtitled "Last Days: December
Rain:"

> A mist: each twig
> budded with crystal.
> Silence, even from wind.
>
> Silence: what birds
> are waited?
> What wonder more than nightingale's
> waits for the days,
> for season inexplicably to burst
> from a leaflessness of winter
> with water's bud?
>
> Silence: what birds
> are waited, what season comes?
>
> (Or are these buds
> upon these very trees
> the buds
> forming of love?)[43]

Whatever the relationship Raymond had with Jessica at this
time, it was soon cut short. One of his last published pieces, "Letter
from the House of the Exile,"[44] strikes a reader as being written by
someone who was suffering from severe depression, and this piece remained for over forty years in Jessica's scrapbook. A scrap paper entry in Jessica's diary, written thirty years later in 1971, reads:

> Two poets who dropped out of sight were R.E.F.L., the
> best Catholic poet of his time and the best of the early
> followers of T. S. Eliot, and Jean Toomer. Larsson be-
> came ill and spent over thirty years in the hospital.[45]

Jessica never saw Raymond again after his hospitalization in
Poughkeepsie, New York, but they kept up a correspondence for
many years, especially noteworthy being his letters dated from 1956
until 1964.[46] It was Raymond who wrote an introduction for Jessica's book *Mountain Sparrow* in 1963 after suggesting the title
"Mystical Sparrow" for this work in 1962.[47] Neither was used by
Jessica when she published her book, but the letters were carefully
preserved.

As a daily communicant over a period of many years, Jessica had established the practice of setting aside a portion of her day for prayer. In October of 1938, she deepened this commitment to developing the spiritual core of her life by becoming a secular Tertiary of the Capuchin branch of the Franciscan Order.[48] Catherine O'Hearn wrote an article about Jessica for the February 1940 issue of *Torch* in which she stated:

> She [Jessica Powers] was professed on November 26, 1939, shortly after her little volume of verse had come off the press, and has given her reason for becoming a Tertiary in these brief words: "To grow towards perfection."[49]

Meanwhile, Ruth Mary Fox, who had influenced Jessica in her early days as a student at Marquette University, had a sister known as Mother Fox at the Cenacle in New York City to whom she recommended Jessica.[50] At one time Jessica had thought of entering a mission order or joining the Cenacle Sisters: "I talked to the Cenacle Sister at one time and she came to me with her face glowing saying she had an OK from the mother general in Rome for me to join the order, but I wasn't ready."[51]

In the 1930s, Jessica was neither ready for nor acquainted with the religious group which would eventually claim her, namely, the Carmelites of Milwaukee. Yet she was familiar with Carmelite literature, having been introduced to John of the Cross while she was at Marquette University in the twenties by Ruth Mary Fox. In addition to this, Jessica had read the autobiography of the French Carmelite nun, Saint Therese of Lisieux. Of this experience, she said:

> The Little Flower, I read her life and I just cried when I read it. And I still am moved by her. . . . the tremendous greatness of her soul. I was just reading the other day how the last months of her life her prayers weren't answered, she couldn't go to communion, it was like she was abandoned.[52]

Under the influence of Therese's writings and those of the Carmelite poet, Saint John of the Cross, Jessica felt God was calling her to enter a Carmelite community. A retreat led by a Jesuit priest at the Manhattan Cenacle around 1940 strengthened her resolution.[53] Because Jessica did not discuss her intention of entering a religious community with her New York circle of friends, her decision to apply for entrance into the Carmelite community in Milwaukee came as a surprise. Jessie Pegis, for one, cried over her impending departure.[54]

Images and Themes in Poems Written in the New York Years

During these New York years which were a transition period in Jessica Powers' life, her poetry demonstrates a greater variety of poetic forms as she moves away from the quatrain. Still, she makes use of rhyming elements. Robert Boudreau explains the significance of this shift in these words:

> This is reflected as well in a shift from the simple use of simile and metaphor within the early poems to the extended metaphor, that is, to poems framed by one image, one vehicle . . . It is only a step from that metaphoric framework to the use of symbol and ultimately of allegory, both of which inform her later, more spiritual poetry.[55]

Jessica wrote a great deal of poetry in this period of her life. Important transitions in style accompanied her transitions in thought. The urban landscape of New York City and the grip of the Great Depression upon this city's poor inspired Jessica to write "The Master Beggar,"[56] which employed her customary poetic style and was published in 1937:

> Worse than the poorest mendicant alive,
> the pencil man, the blind man with his breath
> of music shaming all who do not give,
> are You to me, Jesus of Nazareth.
>
> Must You take up Your post on every block
> of every street? Do I have no release?
> Is there no room of earth that I can lock
> to Your sad face, Your pitiful whisper "Please"?[57]

This poem is addressed to the person of Jesus of Nazareth who is identified with the blind beggar on a New York street corner. There is no escape from this gospel encounter for the subject, because Jesus of Nazareth is the one addressed as, "You take up Your post on every block / of every street," and "there [is] no room of earth that I can lock / to Your sad face." The poem continues:

> I seek the counters of time's gleaming store
> but make no purchases, for You are there.
> How can I waste one coin while you implore
> with tear-soiled cheeks and dark blood-matted
> hair?
>
> And when I offer You in charity
> pennies minted by love, still, still You stand
> fixing Your sorrowful wide eyes on me.
> Must all my purse be emptied in Your hand?
>
> Jesus, my beggar, what would You have of me?
> Father and mother? the lover I longed to know?
> The child I would have cherished tenderly?
> Even the blood that through my heart's valves
> flow?[58]

Time becomes "a gleaming store" at whose counters the subject can make no purchases for fear of wasting a coin. Yet, pennies are not enough for this beggar God. Jesus, the master beggar of this poem, asks for all to be given—father, mother, lover, child, even "the blood that through my heart's valves flow." The call to follow Him is a radical, scriptural one.[59] The poem concludes:

> I too would be a beggar. Long tormented,
> I dream to grant You all and stand apart
> with You on some bleak corner, tear-frequented,
> and trouble mankind for its human heart.[60]

This poem is an example of one which makes simple use of simile and metaphor. It transcends the limits of its landscape, yet is concretized by that very same landscape as the victims of the Great Depression are granted dignity through their association with a divinely noble companion who has chosen to share their human plight.

Constantly, the theme of the indwelling of the Holy Spirit in the human heart surfaces in Jessica's lines. For example, "The First Pentecost,"[61] another of her poems published in 1937, focused on the action of the Holy Spirit in the Pentecost event joined with the figures of the Apostles and Mary, "the Galilean mother."[62] Here the scriptural event is linked to the present moment by the use of images not bound by time or place, a poetic technique illustrated by words like:

Blood melted in the frozen veins, and even
the least bird sang in the mind's inmost grove.
The seed sprang into flower, and over all
still do the multitudinous blossoms fall.[63]

Although physically planted in New York City, Jessica's mind traveled often to her Wisconsin home.

"The House of the Silver Spirit"[64] captures a mood riveted by memories of times much harder than any she experienced in New York. Thus Jessica grew stronger in her resolve to survive the reverses of life in New York City as reflected in the words of her speaker: "I am a February child. I love these things—/ This broken shell of a house and the terrible song it sings. / And winter shrieking wildly at this door." Continuing, the speaker in her poem declares:

I came to birth here in a month of snows,
and it is only winter my mind knows—
the incantation of wailing pines,
the hills in moonlight etched in frostly lines,
the cold lamenting of the whip-poor-wills.[65]

It is a poem filled with "frozen hope" and dreadful remembrances of childhood fear when the wolves howled all night in the tamarack swamps and "my mind's house, a whole age younger, / cried with the wolves the same wild ache of hunger, / a sound more deep and terrible than fear." Winter brought sickness and "the white fields of death" with "echoing loneliness" in times past; hence, a command is given:

My music, you must never be
fragile and sweet and a profanity;
Let all my tones be clear and sharp and wild.
This old house bore me in her frosty womb
and cradled me in sound and gloom;
I am their desolate and frightened child.[66]

Painful past remembrances and present difficulties do not make sense and can rob life of its meaning unless the human spirit can find nourishment in the realization of the immediate presence of God or in a vision of future hope. Jessica Powers was a poet of her times who documented and articulated the disquieting and disturbing experiences of her generation; nevertheless, she refused to lose heart and hope so that, in the end, her poetry gives testimony to the presence of God in

her world. In her work, *Catholic Intellectual Life in America*, Reher
states:

> It has been argued that the Catholics of the 1920s needed
> and cultivated the myth of American innocence as a
> mark of their distinctiveness. It gave them a sense of
> unity and security against the larger culture by which
> they had been rejected.[67]

When Jessica Powers was writing in the 1930s, she used the
word "innocence" in her poetry. In doing this, her speaker questions
"innocence" and is answered with a vision of Christ such as the one
recorded in the poem, "The Mountains of the Lord," which was published in 1939:[68]

> Innocence never lost and innocence restored—
> these two went up the mountains of the Lord.
> And I addressed them, glowing and intense:
> under the auspices of innocence
> what amid holy places did you see?
> And the untarnished spirit answered me:

The answer given to the speaker in this poem contains multiple
scriptural references. The first reference calls to mind Matthew's
Gospel: "You are the light of the world. A city set on a mountain
cannot be hidden."[69] The second one refers to lines from the Gospel
of John, "you would have asked him and he would have given you
living water,"[70] and Psalm 23, "Besides restful waters he leads me; he
refreshes my soul."[71] Likewise, the reference to living water appears
in the poem of Saint John of the Cross entitled, "Song of the Soul
That Rejoices in Knowing God Through Faith."[72] In a like manner,
the third allusion to scripture relates to Psalm 23, "You spread a table
before me."[73] These scriptural themes are woven together with sen-
sory images: of sight, fire burning branches; of hearing, the music of
the harp serenade; of feeling, the cool wind; of smell, the scent of
petals; of taste, cool water and heavenly bread; and of the spiritual
sense, mystical union with God in the innermost depth of the human
being. The poem reads:

> I saw a City gleaming on a hill,
> and one triumphant road divined its site.
> I saw a Fire no storm could ever still,
> feeding upon the branches of delight.

I heard a Harp pluck its own serenade;
I drank the Living water from cool streams.
I breathed the Wind that blows far down
      earth's shade
The scent of petals from eternal dreams.

Tables were spread on greensward and in grove
with Bread the angels coveted afar.
I walked beneath the shadow of a Dove
who made a marriage with a Morningstar.[74]

Laden with these scriptural allusions which are set in a land-scape that speaks simultaneously of both the urban and the rural, Jessica's lines climax with echoes of classical themes taken from the master Carmelite poet, John of the Cross: "the way that leads to the summit of the mount;"[75] "fired with love's urgent longings"[76] or "living flame of love;"[77] and "on a dark night" and "in darkness."[78] The paradox of the ascent to light through the depth of darkness impelled by burning love, is described in terms of bridal mysticism: "I walked beneath the shadow of a Dove / who made a marriage with a Morningstar" and "it was the Bridegroom's voice and called my name."

Jessica recognizes an "innocence never lost," perhaps the myth of American innocence referred to by Reher, but she speaks of a second innocence, an "innocence restored" or an "innocence renewed by grace." Her speaker struggles to be free of the "world" on one hand while re-entering it with a longing embrace on the other. The redemptive process culminates in a vision of "the radiant face of Christ the Lover" wet with tears and perceived everywhere. Her lines conclude:

Then I went upward where the summits
    glistened,
lighted by love, the unconsuming flame.
I heard a Voice, and when I stopped and
    listened
it was the Bridegroom's voice and called my name.

I questioned innocence renewed by grace:
what did you see on hills beatified?
What voices heard you in the holy place?
With words of light the penitent replied:

Under the night's impenetrable cover
wherein I walked beset by many fears,
I saw the radiant face of Christ the Lover,
and it was wet with tears.[79]

Jessica Powers may have associated with self-complacent poets in the Catholic Poetry Society of the 1930s dismissed by critics like Reher as bourgeois; however, she was honest and penetrating in her efforts to describe the inner journey which she found herself compelled to undertake.

In contrast, Jessica had a lighter side. Known from childhood and throughout her school years for her Gaelic wit, Jessica charmed New York circle of friends with humorous poetic lines such as these published in 1938:

Manuscript of Heaven

I know the manuscript the Uncreated
writes in the garden of His good estate.
His creatures are the words incorporated
into love's speech. O Great

immortal Poet, in Your volume bright
if one may choose a portion, write me down
as a small adjective attending light,
the archangelic noun.[80]

Jessica's shift from the simple use of simile and metaphor in her earlier poems is now seen developing in this example of her use of an extended metaphor. The result is a delightful view of a poetic God not only speaking THE WORD but also uttering "the words."

Her lifelong love of bird-watching and the lessons the birds taught her about life enabled Jessica to strike an optimistic tone in the poem "Bird at Daybreak" published in 1938[81] and a sobering one in "Bird at Evening" published in 1939.[82] In "Bird at Daybreak," the speaker enters into a lighthearted dialogue each morning with a singing bird, "a small bird cast as John the Baptist," announcing the new day by saying, "I come from heaven to prepare the way. / Now in the east approach the feet of day." This extended metaphor captures the joyful mood in the speaker who, with relish at the prospect of embracing life once again, says: "my little bird, / who makes his coming such enchanting news, / who with the sweetest music I have heard / unloose the golden lachet of his shoes."[83]

In "Bird at Evening," Jessica captures the opposite mood in another carefully woven extended metaphor: "Here is a very Magdalen of bird / weeping her music at the feet of day, / who in a moment more will be interred / and in his shroud of silver laid away."[84] The figure of the Magdalen will enter Jessica's lines periodically throughout her many years of writing ahead. This extended metaphor with its scripturally inspired imagery is superbly fashioned as the poem unfolds: "This is the bird that lately had anointed / the radiant flesh with the cool oil of song. / These feet are still; the night is three-days long."[85] Jessica had the ability to encapsulate a scriptural passage and give it concrete expression in a simple scene that could be enacted in any American backyard. She drew her readers from all walks of life, from the simplest to the most elevated, and invited them to take a reflective stance as they experienced the daily events of their ordinary lives. For her, scripture was alive; through her poems, it came alive once again for her readers.

Reflections on themes of nature and grace lie as foundational material underneath many of Jessica's poems. In the 1939 publication, "Valley of the Cat-Tails,"[86] Jessica takes her reader on a journey through the geography of her early life experiences: "My valley is a woman unconsoled. . . . There is no dark tale that she was not told; / there is no sorrow that she has not had." In this poem, she recognizes the mistake of praising "her dolors in the words of the dark pines, her trees, and of the whip-poor-wills, her sacred birds," because "her tragedy is more intense than these." Life was not meant to be a tragedy, a mere meaningless existence: "The reeds that life from every marsh and pond / more plainly speak her spirit's poverty." Rather life is meant to be recast by grace: "Here should the waters dance, or flowers be," for "the caroling earth" possesses other "primers" besides the dark fears taught by "reeds" which are spoken of as proper symbols of a mother full of dark fears teaching her young through "the alphabet of tears."

Jessica makes use of another image from her Wisconsin childhood, an old bridge, to discuss the components of the journey that climax in the crossing over from fear to freedom:

Old Bridge

Here is the bridge my childhood marked with fear.
I thought an ogre waited under it,
quick to devour if I should venture near.

I ran at sight of it; my sandals hit
the brown dust of the roadway going by.
Oh, it was like a day of lifted dread
when I grew bold enough to peer and pry,
seeking the monster, finding peace instead.

Fled is that childish fear; my thoughts are
                              couched
in grown-up wisdom now, and yet I find
that worse than ogres are the dark shapes crouched
lurking beneath the bridges of my mind.[87]

To cross life's bridges requires courage, and no peace will come to dispel fears unless the speaker in the poem is willing to risk looking underneath the bridges for life's ogres, the worse ones being beneath the bridges of the human mind. Another poem, "The Place of Ruin,"[88] which was published the same year (1939), invites the reader to undertake a similar journey in search of a place where life has meaning. This time, its opening lines are set in a New York City, "this gray shack above a cluttered walk," with the journey's end being "some house from which even a poet / would hide her frightened face, / where God, grown weary of the brush of beauty, / had used the burning pencil of His grace." The speaker in the poem extends the call: "O come and take my hand, you whom I love, / and let us find that place." The journey needs a guide and companions along the way.

Slowly New York City was becoming as thoroughly an unsatisfactory a place as the Wisconsin farm had been for Jessica. Try as she would, popular as they were, her poems kept returning to themes of dislocation and loneliness as Jessica began to realize that her journey was not over; rather, it had just begun. In 1939 she wrote "Morning of Fog,"[89] which begins: "Between this city of death with its gray face / and the city of life where my thoughts stir wild and free / a day stands. It is a road I trace / too eagerly." Whatever life had in store, wherever it would lead, the speaker of this poem could not say. However, the speaker was sure of one thing: "This is a city of phantoms. I am lost / in a place where nothing that beats with life should / roam." Indecision gives way to a resolve to make a break, "I shall go exiled to the fall of night."

The Atlantic Ocean fascinated Jessica with its moods. Loneliness is a mood she chronicles in a poem by the name, "Belmont Harbor."[90] Here the speaker says: "Dusk after dusk here at the harbor found me, / and here I made my choice," and "Here I was wed to loneliness." Putting "the silence that earth spread around me / above the sound of any human voice," the speaker reflects on how "slowly the heart learns, and with what error / and what regret!"

The mood becomes intense and the feeling of dislocation completely overwhelming in the following poem, "Human Winter," which was written before Jessica entered Carmel in 1939 or 1940, but not published until 1942:

Human Winter

No fire could warm this place
though the air hang in sultry shred and the roof
perspire;
nothing here is amenable to fire.

Words fall in slow icy rain and freeze
upon the heart's sudden dismantled trees,
and branches break and fall.
From the wind of inclement glances I cannot shield
myself
who find their frost too subtle to forestall.
I am waiting for the snow of my own obscurity to
settle
and cover me, frozen ground,
to blunt all sharp insufferable sound,
to meet the angles of cold and obliterate them all.
I long to rise in this room and say, "You are not
my people,
I come from a warm country; my country is love.
Nor did I wish to come here; I was misdirected."
But their frost is not defied and their cold is
not rejected.
So chilled am I by this presence of human winter
I cannot speak or move.[91]

The description of the external landscape lays bare the internal landscape, a sacred landscape which has been violated by "the wind of inclement glances" and the destructiveness of "sharp insufferable sound." In the poem, "No One Can Stay,"[92] the situation is described in even fewer words, "Your invitation is with fraud extended," as the speaker formulates the resolve, "no more / will I let any trick of light betray / me to a house that is nothing but a door."

Jessica had supposed that a change of external geography was the solution to her quest for life's answers. To live in New York City had been her destination, her goal, for many years. Now standing on Fifth Avenue, she began to reflect again more seriously on her internal geography and the questions it asked concerning destination, concerning goal. The result was a poem published in 1939:

The Terminal

It was Fifth Avenue, and it was April.
Who could have dreamed such wind and flying snow?
The terminal gleamed gold far in the distance.
And then I thought: where truly do we go?

Is it not thus we wander out of time
down the bright canyons of white whirling air,
too cold and tired for beauty, and too sad
to utter secrets that are warm to share?

Some nights were meant for tears, and some for
                                        laughter;
and some to hold in trust, and some to spend.
But portents were astir that night we sighted
the terminal that stands at the world's end.[93]

Faith grounded Jessica and guided her onward during the period of dislocation which she experienced in New York. In "Night of Storm,"[94] she wrote: "The times are winter. Thus a poet signed / our frosty fate. Life is a night of snow. / We see no path before us, nor behind." In this night, the speaker begins the journey as an exile faced with "terror in a trackless place." The first stanza of the poem ends on a note of gloom. "Or what is else?" and it's newfound answer: "There is your world within." For the speaker in this poem, it is time to stop wandering and time to return home: "O most wretched and blind, come home!" The theme of the Holy Spirit resurfaces and illumines past experiences in a new light:

Where love has been
burns the great lantern of the Holy Ghost.
Here in His light; review your world of frost:
a drifting miracle! What had been night
reels with unending eucharists of light.[95]

All of the experiences set in this place of dislocation are redeemed and, illumined by the light of the Holy Spirit, they become as drifting miracles, charged with new meaning.

Likewise, "The Kingdom of God"[96] encourages the speaker to contemplating the mystery unfolding within, in words which are charged with the challenge to take up an inward journey: "Not towards the stars, O beautiful naked runner, / not on the hills of the moon after a wild white deer, / seek not to discover afar the unspeakable wisdom,—/ the quarry is here." The images and themes of the earlier poems of the twenties, Wisconsin woodlands with forest creatures and "the quarry," reappear in a new landscape as the outer becomes internalized. The image of "the house at rest," first coined by John of the Cross,[97] comes through loudly and clearly in the lines: "There is a Tenant here. / Come home, roamer of earth, to this room and find / a timeless Heart under your own heart beating, / a Bird of beauty singing under your mind." Here the concrete image of a room is utilized in an effort to mirror the inner sanctum of the human person.

The idea of undertaking another journey, this time in terms of beginning again, began to take root in Jessica's mind. Her poem, "Let There Be Light," reflects the decision of the speaker to trust in the Holy Spirit's power to create light out of darkness:

> Over the water of the world again
> the Spirit broods:
> Over the chaos the minds of all
> and down the dream-deserted solitudes.[98]

Recognizing the helpless and brokenness resulting from the chaos reigning in the human mind, this poem speaks of the renewal of the human person through the action of the Spirit brooding over the water of the world. The speaker will cease to be victimized by loneliness and shattered dreams and this promise of hope emerges:

> I know His ominous presence, and I hear
> His prophecy of flight
> over a world of thought at the first clear
> and thunderous dismissal of the night.[99]

The speaker longs for the fulfillment of the prophecies of scripture. Salvation hinges on this divine presence dismissing the darkness of night.

How shall that burst of radiance be greeted
as, from the black abyss,
the first day wakens when it hears repeated
that cry to light, torn out of Genesis?[100]

The response of the speaker is teased out, invited forth by a voice
raising a jubilant question, "How shall that burst of radiance be
greeted?" Without the human response, can there be a "Genesis?"
The speaker in the poem recognizes that God does not play a game
of life-giving within God alone. Humanity is called out of nothingness to participate in the life-giving process.

Published in 1939, the poem entitled "The Books of Saint John
of the Cross"[101] capitalized on the joyous mood inspired by the prospects of a new beginning: "Out of what door that came ajar in
heaven / drifted this starry manna down to me . . . Who bore at midnight to my very dwelling / the gift of this imperishable food? The
speaker can ask the question of "who?" but ultimately the design of
God is a mystery. Neither can an answer be given to the question of
"why?" posed by the divine encounter that leaves its recipient filled
with "gift of this imperishable food" and its accompanying "certi-
tude." God's mercy dictates all in hearts open to divine encounter.
In the conclusion of this poem, the word "mercy" comes into focus
as an important keyword which will be developed in later poems:
"Mercy grows tall with the least heart enlightened, / and I, so long a
fosterling of night, / here feast upon immeasurable sweetened / wa-
fers of light." Likewise, the term, "fosterling of night," will reappear
in later writings.

Although no fitting answer can be found to the question posed
to the speaker in the above poem, a human stance can be taken. In
1940, Jessica's poem, "If You Have Nothing," was published. Here
the speaker makes a response to God in gratitude for the gift of life:

If You Have Nothing

The gesture of a gift is adequate.
If you have nothing: laurel leaf or bay,
no flower, no seed, no apple gathered late,
do not in desperation lay
the beauty of your tears upon the clay.

No gift is proper to a Deity;
no fruit is worthy for such power to bless.
If you have nothing, gather back your sigh,
and with your hands held high, your heart held high,
lift up your emptiness!102

When the poem, "The Heart Can Set Its Boundaries,"103 was published in 1941, Jessica had a sense that she was on the brink of a momentous turning point in her own history, much like the world around her was on the brink of writing a new chapter in its history. In "Boundaries," the speaker declares: "Only when God is passing by, / and is invited in to stay / is there a split of earth and sky." The realization is documented: God takes the initiative but the human response is part of the divine design that reorders earth and sky.

In 1941 Dorothy Day set herself up in an unpopular role as a prophetic witness by denouncing U.S. mobilization plans for war and by endorsing pacifism. Likewise, Jessica Powers took up the weapon of her pen in a poetic protest to write:

The Little Nation

Having no gift of strategy or arms,
no secret weapon and no walled defense,
I shall become a citizen of love,
that little nation with the blood-stained sod
where even the slain have power, the only country
that sends forth an ambassador to God.

Renouncing self and crying out to evil
to end its wars, I seek a land that lies
all unprotected like a sleeping child;
nor is my journey reckless and unwise.
Who doubts that love has an effective weapon
may meet with a surprise.104

Here the speaker cries out to the powers of evil to end all wars, refutes the charge that a pacifist journey is reckless and unwise, and speaks of the surprising effectiveness of the weapon of love.

Her response went deeper than this poetic protest. She wrote a "Letter of Departure," and departed from New York to enter the newly formed Carmelite cloistered community in Milwaukee, Wisconsin in 1941. Published in 1941 and republished in 1946, 1969, and

1984, "Letter of Departure" acts as a fitting summary for this chapter of Jessica Powers' life:

> "There is nothing in the valley, or home, or
> street
> worth turning back for—
> nothing!" you write. O bitter words and true
> to seed the heart and grow to this green answer:
> let it be nothing to us that we knew
> streets where the leaves gave sparsely of the sun
> or white small rested houses and the air
> strung with the sounds of living everywhere.
> The mystery of God lies before and beyond us,
> so bright the sight is dark, and if we halt
> to look back once upon the burning city,
> we shall be paralyzed by rage or pity,
> either of which can turn the blood to salt.[105]

In this poem, the biblical image of Lot and his family leaving Sodom and Gomorrah provides a backdrop for the speaker's reflection.[106] Recognition is given to the belief that "the mystery of God lies before and beyond us" and the paradox is named in the words, "so bright the sight is dark." The city left behind, reminiscent of New York with its towering skyscrapers, has "streets where the leaves gave sparsely of the sun" and the speaker has nothing of worth within its confines to birth a temptation to look backward. Yet, out of love for its people, both rage and pity at the conditions of the city are recognized as emotions powerful enough to paralyze the subject and abort the departure if a backward glance should be chanced. The poem continues:

> We knew too much of the knowable dark world,
> its secret and its sin,
> too little of God. And now we rise to see
> that even our pledges to humanity
> were false, since love must out of Love begin.
> Here where we walk the fire-strafed road and
> thirst
> for the great face of love, the blinding vision,
> our wills grow steadfast in the heart's decision
> to keep the first commandment always first.

We vow that nothing now shall give us cause
to stop and flounder in our tears again,
that nothing—fire or dark or persecution—
or the last human knowledge of all pain—
shall turn us from our goal.[107]

This speaker does not part from the city in innocence. There has been an experience of sin and of betrayal on the human subject's part, "that even our pledges to humanity were false." The pilgrimage in down a "fire-strafed road," not a lily-lined one, with a distant goal only kept in sight by the human will's determination to keep the first commandment in the foreground: "Love the Lord, your God, with your whole heart, with all your soul, and with all your mind."[108] The poem concludes with the lines:

With but the bare necessities of soul—
no cloak or purse or script—let us go forth
and up the rocky passes of the earth,
crying, "Lord, Lord," and certain presently
(when in the last recesses of the will
and in the meshes of the intellect
the quivering last sounds of earth are still)
to hear an answer that becomes a call.
Love, the divine, Love, the antiphonal,
speaks only to love,
for only love could learn that liturgy,
since only love is erudite to master
the molten language of eternity.[109]

Again the scriptural command issued to the first disciples of Jesus, "Do not take gold or silver or copper for your belts; no sack for the journey, or a second tunic, or sandals, or walking stick,"[110] is reiterated in the lines, "With but the bare necessities of soul—no cloak or purse or script—let us go forth." The journey will lead "up the rocky passes of the earth," once more, the image of the ascent of Mount Carmel.[111] Finally, the speaker is able "to hear an answer that becomes a call," as "Love, the divine, Love, the antiphonal, speaks only to love."

In summary, Jessica was a poet of her times who documented and articulated the disquieting and disturbing experiences of her generation without sacrificing her testimony to the presence of God in her world. She drew her readers from all walks of life across the United States and invited them to take a reflective stance as they experienced the daily events of their ordinary lives. For her, scripture was alive; through her poems, it came alive once again for her readers.

Jessica wrote a great deal of poetry in this period of her life in which important transitions in style accompanied her transitions in thought. Now with consistency, her poetry transcends the limits of its landscape, only to be concretized by that very same landscape. She describes the call to follow Christ in a radical, scriptural way as mediated to her through the external landscape of New York City in the grips of the Great Depression.

Reflections on themes of nature and grace lie as foundational material underneath many of Jessica's poems. In her theological perspective, life is meant to be recast by grace and given lasting meaning. She invites her readers to undertake an inner journey in search of a place where life has this ultimate meaning. Now in New York City, Jessica reflects again on her internal geography and the questions it asked concerning destination. Faith grounds and guides Jessica onward as she experiences a prolonged period of dislocation. Through this experience, Jessica gains first-hand knowledge of helplessness and brokenness resulting from the chaos reigning in the human mind. Simultaneously, she testifies to the renewal of the human person through the action of the Holy Spirit. The theme of the indwelling of the Holy Spirit in the human heart surfaces constantly in Jessica's lines during these years as she longs for the fulfillment of the prophecies of scripture. Salvation hinges on divine presence dismissing the darkness of night. As a result, her poetry begins to demonstrate ever-increasing depths with the images and themes of her earlier poems of the twenties and Wisconsin woodlands reappearing in a new inner landscape as she strives to internalize the outer.

At this same time, Jessica considers another question in her poetry: "Without human response, can there be a Genesis?" In pondering this question, Jessica comes to the realization that God does not play a game of life-giving within God alone. Humanity is called out of nothingness by God to participate in the live-giving process. Eventually such thoughts spur Jessica to entertain prospects of a new beginning for herself.

Reviewing insights gleaned from her study of Carmelite spirituality, Jessica writes the poem, "The Books of Saint John of the Cross," in which she admits that ultimately the design of God is a mystery and that God's mercy dictates all in hearts open to divine encounter with God. At length, mercy comes into focus as an important keyword which will be developed in later poems. Reflecting on

God's mercy, she makes a response to God in gratitude for the gift of life. God takes the initiative but the human response is part of the divine design that reorders creation. At last, Jessica hears an answer that becomes a call. The remainder of her life unfolds quietly as she makes a radical response to the call of God by becoming a Discalced Carmelite nun and as she reorientates her poetic endeavors in an attempt to faithfully chronicle the inward journey this call entailed for her.

Chapter V

Jessica Powers: The Carmelite Poet (1941-1958)

WHEN THE DISCALCED CARMELITE NUNS OPENED A HOUSE IN Wisconsin in 1940, Jessica Powers was one of the first candidates to enter their newly formed community. The local newspapers carried full coverage of the event, since Jessica was a well-known and widely read Wisconsin poet.[1] In addition, following the successful publication of her volume of poetry, *The Lantern Burns*, in New York City in 1939, she was considered to be a national literary celebrity with *America* placing her "in the front rank of living Catholic poets," in a 1940 review of her writings.[2]

During an interview in her later years, Jessica recalled that "I had a lot of problems when I first entered: I didn't think I really belonged. Even now in my old age, did I do the right thing, was it God's will at all, but we probably all have that worry."[3] When questioned about the significance of this move in regard to her future development as a poet, she offered this simple evaluation:

> It deprived me of some things . . . someone said to me
> "you would have been a lot better poet if you never
> came to Carmel." I think maybe my poems, the tech-
> nique . . . might have been a lot better. . . . [but] I
> wouldn't have had these thoughts. I could see, that was
> one of the reasons I wanted to go to Carmel. I could see
> that I was tending toward sophistication in writing. I'd
> copy these poets that were worldly and it has no food for
> the soul.[4]

It is possible that Jessica was right in her self-analysis. Had she stayed within the circle of the Catholic Poetry Society and the New York social world instead of heeding her contemplative calling, perhaps she wouldn't have developed the poetic depths which would ultimately link her name with such writers as Thomas Merton, Robert Lowell, and Flannery O'Connor, kindred spirits in later periods of history.[5]

The Religious Context: The Background of the Wisconsin Carmelites

In tracing the Carmelite roots that shaped Jessica's life from 1941 onward, Bettendorf, Iowa, plays a role. While on a visitation of American Carmels in 1935, the Discalced Carmelite Father General William of Saint Albert met Joan of the Cross (Clara Meyer) in Bettendorf, Iowa. Upon hearing that she was originally from Wisconsin, he inspired her and the other nuns with the idea of founding a Carmelite monastery in Milwaukee.[6] When Paula of the Mother of God (Adela Doersching, d. 1941) wrote to Archbishop Samuel A. Stritch to ask his permission to make the foundation in Milwaukee in 1935, he disapproved of the idea, although later in 1939, he received the petition more favorably and allowed everything to be arranged. However, Stritch was transferred to Chicago and it was left to his successor, Moses E. Kiley, to give official approval to the plan and welcome the nuns to Milwaukee in 1940. The Bettendorf community began the necessary plans for the daughter house, with financial help provided by several of the sisters' families. Florence Doersching, a sister of Paula of the Mother of God, purchased the site of the first convent, 4802 W. Wells Street, while the Meyers, Joan of the Cross' family, gave financial backing and practical aid in the details of the foundation. Albert E. Meyer, later Cardinal Meyer, was the first religious superior of the community.[7]

Regular community life in Milwaukee began in November of 1940 under the leadership of Paula of the Mother of God. The founding nuns were all from the Bettendorf Carmel: Mother Paula of the Mother of God (Adela Doersching), Sister Grace of the Eucharist (Helene Mead), Sister Joan of the Cross (Clara Meyer), Sister Elizabeth of the Trinity (Charlotte Kinsella), and Sister Ann of Jesus (Susan Misera). With the exception of the changes of Canon Law of 1928, the Constitutions of Alcala were observed in the new foundation. Archbishop Kiley decided that simple perpetual vows would be taken instead of solemn vows until the Carmel was well established.[8]

The members of the Carmelite community in Milwaukee described the basic elements of their spiritual life in the 1940s in a booklet entitled *Carmel of the Mother of God* that was edited by the nuns and privately printed in 1942. In this booklet, women seeking entrance into Carmelite community life are evaluated in these words:

> Candidates should be persons of prayer, sincerely aspiring to perfection, and detached from the world. They should be at least seventeen years of age, of sound health, intelligent and able to recite the Divine Office and to assist in Choir.[9]

The mission of Carmelite life in the Church, which the nuns of 1940 Milwaukee understood themselves to embrace, was explained by Archbishop Cross in one of his sermons given in their chapel:

> There are Orders that, like the tongue, speak to the world; other that, like the head, minister to all its wants; others, like the feet, traverse the world to make known Our Lord Jesus: In the sacred Body of Jesus there was that Blessed Heart, unseen, unheard by men, but which glowed with love for God and men, and was the very shrine of infinite holiness. May I be permitted to say that in Christ's mystic body—the Church—the Order of Carmel reminds me of the sacred Heart of Jesus; for, like It, unseen, unheard by men, hidden away, it glows with love for God and man, and is the sanctuary where blooms so many a flower known to God only.[10]

The "Little Way of the Little Flower," a particular popularized version of the spirituality of Therese of Lisieux, was very influential in the Milwaukee Carmel in the 1940s, and Therese's words, "My vocation is love," appeared in much of Carmelite literature in the United States at this time, with the Milwaukee Carmel being no exception. In describing their prayer life, the Carmelites of Milwaukee wrote:

> The great means which Carmel presents to those who aim at this sublime charity is contemplation. It is in prayer and by prayer that the Carmelite will attain Divine Union. The Rule, Constitutions, and customs of Carmel, and above all the spirit in which they should be followed, tend to one end—to dispose souls for prayer, to make them contemplative souls. St. Thomas Aquinas defines contemplation as a "simple view of the truth terminating in love." For the Carmelite this "simple view" is seeing God in all persons and things until she comes

to realize that life in Carmel is not something but Someone.[11]

The Milwaukee community also endorsed a spirituality which
taught that sacrifice and suffering were an integral part of Carmelite
life and that manual labor and resignation to the will of God prepared
the soul for sanctification. The kind of sacrifice which they envi-
sioned can be found in these word: "Holy Mother Church bids her
[the Carmelite] sacrifice to God the sacrifice of praise and she places
on her lips the inspired word of God in the psalms and canticles of
the Divine Office." Prayer based on scripture has a central place in
this sacrifice of praise. The praise of God flowing continuously from
human lips in union with Jesus Christ is seen as redeeming time:

> In His Presence, using His words, and praying in His
> Name, the religious is the mouthpiece of Jesus Christ
> and of His Church. Every moment of the day and night
> the Divine Office is being chanted somewhere. This uni-
> versal choir of voices and of heart united in one same
> language, in one same thought, in one same love, and
> re-united in the Heart of Jesus, ascends directly to the
> throne of God and does Him a holy violence.[13]

The Milwaukee nuns took Jesus of Nazareth as their model and
used the practices of the early Fathers of the Desert for guidance
when they wrote:

> The Holy Rule wisely ordains that the time not conse-
> crated to spiritual exercises should be employed in man-
> ual labor . . . in union with Our Lord Jesus Christ to
> render homage to the life of poverty He led upon earth.
> The Fathers of the Desert always regarded manual labor
> as a most powerful means of perfection.[14]

Although the terms they employed were often that of a nineteenth-century religious terminology described by Joseph Chinnici as
"immigrant spirituality" in his work, *Living Stones: The History and
Structure of Spirituality in the United States,* a basic core of Teresian
thought was preserved in the documents written in the initial days
when the nuns were trying to establish a Carmelite community in
Milwaukee on a solid spiritual basis. However, a brief look at the
way the Milwaukee nuns describe their devotional practices in the
1940s reveals much more of an influence of seventeenth-century
French spirituality than the founding mothers of Maryland ever evi-

denced in their writings. Writing of the "Devotions of Carmel" in the 1942, the Milwaukee nuns emphasized that they had two great devotions which they called the "Mother devotions of the Order" and listed these pillar practices as devotions to the Most Adorable Sacrament of the Altar and to the Blessed Virgin Mary whom they referred to as the foundress of Carmel.

In addition to these two "pillar devotions" believed by the Milwaukee nuns to be the essence of Carmelite spirituality, other devotional practices were listed as important in their writings. These practices included: 1) devotion to the Infant Jesus of Prague; 2) devotion to Saint Joseph as protector of the Order; 3) devotion to Elijah, prophet of Carmel; 4) devotion to a medieval Carmelite, Albert of Sicily, and use of holy water blessed with his relic to bring about miraculous cures; and 5) the "Gospel of the Holy Name" devotion, based on a reported vision to a French nun in 1845, who said if believers were willing to wear a little sachet containing a leaflet with the words "When JESUS was named/Satan was disarmed" around their neck, they would be saved from lightning, the snares of the devil, sudden death, facilitation in virtue, and would receive the assurance of final perseverance.[15] A careful study of the literature of the Milwaukee nuns produced in the 1940s reveals that this particular Carmelite community was a product of its culture, reflecting a popular trend toward devotional practices widespread in the type of Catholic spirituality prevalent in the United States in the 1940s.

Jessica's Early Life in the Wisconsin Carmelite Community

Jessica Powers entered the Milwaukee community of Carmelites as a postulant on June 24, 1941. She was followed within a few months by more candidates, including Mary Bernadette of the Immaculate Conception.[16] Soon afterwards, Paula of the Mother of God died of cancer and Grace of the Eucharist, who encouraged Jessica to keep up her writing, became prioress in 1942. Jessica, battling a renewed case of tuberculosis which was the ghost of a previous bout with this disease in the early 1920s, had been forced to take a sick leave. Her condition necessitated a complete rest in a sanitarium away from her Carmelite community for a while. Periodic absences for health reasons from her community would be repeated in later years as well.

On April 25, 1942, Jessica received the habit of the Carmelites in a clothing ceremony during a celebration of Mass with Monsignor

Albert G. Meyer presiding. She received her religious name from Monsignor Meyer in these words: "Miss Jessica Powers, you will henceforth be known as Sister Miriam of the Holy Spirit."[17] This seemed appropriate for Jessica: the name of Miriam, which means beloved of God in her favorite translation, and the title of the Holy Spirit because her "devotion to the Holy Spirit had long been a distinguishing mark of her poetry."[18] Afterwards Jessica visited with a group of friends and relatives in the convent parlor before beginning one year as a novice in the community.[19]

In spite of her bout with tuberculosis, Jessica was able to adjust to life in the Milwaukee Carmelite community, so that in August of 1946, she made final vows as a Carmelite nun there.[20] In this same year, Jessica published her second book of poetry, *The Place of Splendor*, which was well received by the general public and would eventually be translated into Italian in 1983. Jessica, who was known as Miriam in her religious community, kept her pen name of Jessica Powers whenever she published poetry.

As an active member of the community, Jessica's days were long and filled with multiple spiritual exercises and manual labor. The lifestyle of the group was austere, with meatless meals; eggs and milk-foods were limited as well. No games or musical instruments were permitted for recreation, just conversation and handiwork. Outside of recreation times, silence was the rule of the day, and reading was limited to a spiritual book read aloud at meals.[21]

During this period in her life, Jessica found herself in physical surroundings which appear to an outsider to be about as limiting as the internal mechanics of her day. The Milwaukee Carmel consisted of a two-story frame house and a backyard one hundred and thirty feet long by one hundred feet deep, enclosed by an eight-foot board wall. Inside the house, one of the first-story rooms was converted into a chapel measuring twenty-three feet long by thirteen feet wide, while the four bedrooms on the second-story were divided into eight small sleeping cubicles known as "the nuns' cells." The basement boiler-room was utilized as well: to the left was the laundry, to the right was the fruit-cellar, and straight ahead was the novitiate.[22]

Considering the above facts, it can easily be surmised that Jessica now lived within what Robert Morneau has described as "a rather limited external geography. Her natural habitat was interior, in those thousand of acres where God lay waiting."[23] Given the limits of her lifestyle, it is easy to understand why Jessica could not always find time to write poetry.

During the period from 1942 to 1953, the energies of the Milwaukee community were channeled into maintenance and expansion. After making inquiries and obtaining the proper permissions, Grace of the Eucharist moved to St. Paul, Minnesota in 1953 and began a daughter house of the Milwaukee community. The sisters from Milwaukee who transferred to the new Minnesota foundation were: Mother Grace of the Eucharist (Helene Mead), Sister Ann of Jesus (Susan Misera), Sister Paula of the Eucharist (Helen Szydlowski), Sister Mary of the Will of God (Beatrice Wempe), and Sister Maryanne of the Child Jesus (Mary Ann Kamen).[24]

In 1955 Jessica published a children's book, *The Little Alphabet,* and she was elected to her first term of office (1955-1958) as prioress of the Milwaukee community. She was to serve a total of three terms as prioress of the Discalced Carmelite Nuns in Wisconsin.[25] During her second term (1958-1961), two significant events took place: first, she supervised the move of the Milwaukee community to an new location in Pewaukee, Wisconsin; and second, she suffered from another bout with tuberculosis.

Even with the departures of members for the daughter house in Minnesota, by 1958 the Carmelites had outgrown their home on Wells Street; this necessitated a move to a larger site in Pewaukee, a suburb about twenty-five miles west of Milwaukee. The property, donated by Charles and Arlene Scholl, saw the rise of a modest chapel and spacious monastery which were dedicated by Bishop Roman Athielski on December 10, 1958. At this time the monastery, which was still under Jessica's leadership, consisted of eleven nuns and eight novices.[26] She and the other nuns supported themselves by alms and by funds gained through the sale of their handicraft which included bookbinding, woodcarving, fashioning rosaries, and sewing various articles.[27]

The move to the new monastery in Pewaukee provided the nuns with a wonderful seven acres behind their monastery. Jessica was delighted with the glorious countryside, the spectacular view of the lake, and the spaciousness of the monastery's interior rooms.[28] As prioress of the community, she did not have much time to devote to personal writing, but she felt her horizons expand in the new and scenic surroundings: "This is a place where one lives poetry rather than writes it."[29]

Toward the end of her second term as prioress (1958-1961), Jessica was sent by her doctor to the River Pines Sanitorium in Stevens Point, Wisconsin, to recover from a renewed bout of tuberculosis.

During her stay there in 1959-60, she wrote several poems including a melancholy piece entitled, "No Pity for Lovers," also preserved in the Marquette Archives under the alternate title of "The Parting of Lovers,"[30] and "Souvenir, Wisconsin River."[31] However, of her stay in the sanitorium, her sisters in Pewaukee have said:

> While she wrote no poetry during this period, she worked assiduously (to the concern of the medical staff) on *The Spiritual Realism of Saint Therese of Lisieux*, polishing the English of the sister translator and laboriously checking every word in a French dictionary to ensure accuracy (Sister did not know French).[32]

During an interview in 1960 for an article in *Spirit*, a Catholic magazine dedicated to the publication of poetry, Jessica shared some perceptive insights about the relationship between poetry and contemplation that she had formulated through her experience in these years. In her opinion, there was no reason why a nun "should not be a good poet like Holy Father St. John. No one lived the life of Carmel better than he did. His whole background reeks of poetry."[33] For Jessica, the writing and reading of poetry was an individual matter, but she cautioned that "for many great souls, poetry could be a great stumbling-block. Once you become conscious of self, you are taking yourself from contemplation. When self intrudes on the art, prayer is lost."[34] Prayer was the utmost concern, not poetry, in Jessica's estimation; and when she spoke of prayer, she spoke of humility as a necessary ingredient for progress in prayer. In the course of the interview, she stated:

> I don't think any human effort can make us humble, only the humiliations that God sends are of account. Our own are a little too gentle. No one else can humble us, either. It only hardens the soul when someone else tries. But the two (contemplation and poetry) should not be in conflict. . . . We are dealing with gifts of God, which God can give as He pleases, when He pleases, to whom He pleases. It is futile for us to lay down laws which say when or how God's gifts must be given.[35]

When asked to evaluate the state of the current poetry of the 1960s, Jessica replied: "Trying too hard to be unusual and intellectual, trying to impress, straining to publish, admiring one's own work—[these are] failures in poetic integrity,"[36] and she saw these factors, termed as lack of humility in the poet himself, as sometimes keeping much of the current poetry from maturing into true art. Her advice to aspiring younger poets consisted of these counsels:

> My only advice is that which I myself have been told. Perfect your technique as best you can. Read, study the best. Even copy the best until you find your medium. You will find your medium by studying theirs, and writing poetry. Remember that God made you an individual, that you are different. One day you will write poetry that is truly your own. But first learn to write well.[37]

The principles, which guided Jessica's poetic endeavors, were the practical ones which also guided her spiritual life. She studied the great Carmelite masters and followed their lead until God, who made her an individual, helped her to get in touch with her own different and unique experience of divine presence in her life, and until God lead her into a way of prayer that was truly her own.

Poetic Reflections Influenced by Carmelite Spirituality

The shifts in her poetry, which were noted in the New York period of her writing, continued to manifest themselves in the 1940s and 1950s as Jessica moved into an expanding inner landscape, the world of a Carmelite contemplative. Earlier themes are revisited but now they are recast in explicit biblical and classical Carmelite imagery as their lines unfold through the use of masterfully constructed extended metaphors. Moreover, a subtle new element appears, though scattered and undeveloped, to catch a reader by surprise: God and Spirit are cast as primal mother.[38]

"I Hold My Heart As A Gourd,"[39] which was published in 1942, begins with the speaker declaring an awareness of the powerful and overwhelming force of divine love entering into human relationships and re-ordering human vision: "I hold my heart as a gourd filled with love, / ready to pour upon humanity."[40] In claiming this new vision, the speaker rejects two motives for entertaining love:

> not that I see each one as my own neighbor
> though veiled with strangeness or with enmity,
> and not that it is my own self I see,
> my sins and virtues and my secret mind
> multiplied almost to infinity.[41]

In rejecting these two motives, the speaker does not deny their legitimacy; rather, the subject simply states:

> Though this to love a proper cause might be,
> not in these words is my true love defined.[42]

How then is the speaker's true love defined? The answer comes in the second stanza:

> I hold my heart as a gourd ready to pour
> upon all those who live.
> Not that I see each one as come from God
> and to my soul His representative,
> but that God inhabits what he loves
> and what His love sustains, and hence I see
> in each soul that may brush against my soul
> God Who looks out at me.[43]

The spirit within each living person is what speaks to the person who ultimately develops a mystical appreciation of God's presence in life. The distinction is carefully drawn between wanting to pour the heart upon all because each one comes from God as God's representative, and because "God inhabits what He loves and what His love sustains." Intoxicated with the second understanding, the speaker in the poem declares that "I see / in each soul that may brush against my soul / God Who looks out at me."

In 1945 Jessica published four noteworthy poems which are included in this study. In the poem "The Place of Splendor,"[44] a New York City subway terminal reappears as the setting for the encounter with the divine:

> Little one, wait.
> Let me assure you this is not the way
> to gain the terminal of outer day.
>
> Its single gate
> lies in your soul, and you must rise and go
> by inward passage from what earth you know.
>
> The steps lead down
> through valley after valley, far and far
> past the five countries where the pleasures are,
>
> and past all known
> maps of the mind and every colored chart
> and past the final outcry of the heart.

No soul can view
its own geography; love does not live
in places open and informative.

Yet, being true,
it grants to each its Raphael across
the mist and night through unknown lands of loss.

Walk till you hear
light told in music that was never heard,
and softness spoken that was not a word.

The soul grows clear
when senses fuse: sight, touch and sound are one
with savor and scent, and all to splendor run.

The smothered roar
of the eternities, their vast unrest
and infinite peace are deep in your own breast.

That light-swept shore
will shame the data of grief upon your scroll.
Child, have none told you? God is in your soul.[45]

The poem is addressed to a "Little one." The speaker of the poem offers to act as a guide to point out the way "to gain the terminal of outer day." The classic descriptions of the Carmelite masters, Teresa of Avila's journey through the mansions of the Interior Castle or John of the Cross' journey of the soul, are recast in the urban landscape of modern New York City with the narrow, single gate of a metaphorical terminal in the soul opening to an inward passageway of descending steps that lead through valleys and five countries, which represent the five senses, instead of Teresa's seven rooms in a mansion. There is no map or chart to mark the way, so the speaker must undertake John's journey, alone and at night. The speaker cautions that a guide and companion, "a Raphael,"[46] must be found for the journey, because it is foolhardy to undertake the journey alone and risk getting lost since "no soul can view / its own geography." When nearing the destination at the end of the journey, strange things will be experienced in "mist and night through unknown lands of loss." These strange experiences include: "light told in music that was never heard" and "softness spoken that was not a word." Passing through the dark night of the senses, the speaker comes to a place where:

The soul grows clear
when senses fuse: sight, touch and sound are one
with savor and scent, and all to splendor run.[47]

What the soul discovers is astounding:

The smothered roar
of the eternities, their vast unrest
and infinite peace are deep in your own breast.[48]

The journey's end is revealed as a "light-swept shore," and the parting question: "Child, have none told you?" is answered with the declaration: "God is in your soul."

The next poem, "The Garments of God,"[49] especially when read aloud, conveys a powerful thrust of emotion in response to the presence of God experienced as absence. The soul is cast in darkness, the speaker is "a child in the dark." God is not experienced without but as within sitting "on a chair of darkness" in the soul. The cry of the speaker is one of faith and of trust, coming not from sweet, fragile hands raised aloof, but from one who reaches out with "the fingers of [the] will" and "with a frantic hand to clutch," while declaring:

God sits on a chair of darkness in my soul.
He is God alone, supreme in His majesty.
I sit at His feet, a child in the dark beside Him;
my joy is aware of His glance and my sorrow is
                              tempted
to nest on the thought that His face is turned
                              from me.
He is clothed in the robes of His mercy,
                    voluminous garments—
not velvet or silk and affable to the touch,
but fabric strong for a frantic hand to clutch,
and I hold to it fast with the fingers of my will.
Here is my cry of faith, my deep avowal
to the divinity that I am dust.
Here is the loud profession of my trust.
I need not go abroad
to the hills of speech or the hinterlands of music
for a crier to walk in my soul where all is still.
I have this potent prayer through good or ill:
here in the dark I clutch the garments of God.[50]

Switching to a lighter theme, Jessica reflects on the beauty of snow-laden fir trees during a long Wisconsin winter and writes "The Cedar Tree," in which she compared the outer landscape, a fir tree decked with "cedar branches bending low" with the weight of the heavy snow, to the inner landscape within her mind and spirit, so heavy-laden with its trials:

> In the beginning, in the unbeginning
> of endlessness and of eternity,
> God saw this tree.
> He saw these cedar branches bending low
> under the full exhaustion of the snow.
> And since He set no wind of day to rising,
> this burden of beauty and this burden of cold,
> (whether the wood breaks or the branches hold)
> must be of His devising.
>
> There is a cedar similarly decked
> deep in the winter of my intellect
> under the snow, the snow,
> the scales of light its limitations tell.
>
> I clasp this thought: from all eternity
> God who is good looked down upon this tree
> white in the weighted air,
> and of another cedar reckoned well
> He knew how much each tree, each twig could bear.
> He counted every snowflake as it fell.[52]

Hence, God is pronounced "good," as the old maxim that "God never sends more than one can bear" is retold in snowbound imagery and rhyme.

Published in 1946, "The Legend of the Sparrow,"[53] explores a theme inspired by the scripture passage of the eagle inciting its nestlings forth and bearing them up on its pinions.[54] In doing this, Jessica follows the lead of John of the Cross[55] and Therese of Lisieux[56] who precede her in their comparisons of the flight of the soul in search of God to the flight of the bird in search of the sun. Whereas John writes of a bird of prey flying high and Therese visualizes herself as a little bird helped by her sibling eagles to soar aloft, Jessica limits herself to describing the flight of one small sparrow, who soars to the heights only when helped by the winds blowing "upward from the mountain peak" and the sun with its "magnetic rays." The union of the divine and the human are extolled in the last lines of this poem as miraculous, "only the sun knew, and the moving air / the miracle thereof," with love championing as the key factor in a movement which unites the divine and the human in this encounter, "a bird that wings itself with resolute love / can travel anywhere."

In the poem "There Is a Homelessness,"[57] Jessica begins with a description reminiscent of her New York days during the Great Depression:

> There is a homelessness, never to be clearly
> defined.
> It is more than having no place of one's own, no
> bed or chair.
> It is more than walking in a waste of wind,
> or gleaning the crumbs where someone else has
> dined,
> or taking a coin for food or clothes to wear.
> The loan of things and the denial of things are
> possible to bear.[58]

The experience of rootlessness encountered in traversing the exterior geography had impressed upon Jessica a metaphor for describing the interior homelessness encountered within the restless human heart. To be a stranger poised outside the doorway leading to lasting love is the human plight. The speaker of her poem explains:

> It is more, even, than homelessness of heart,
> of being always a stranger at love's side,
> of creeping up to a door only to start
> at a shrill voice and to plunge back to the wide
> dark of one's own obscurity and hide.[59]

Within this context, Jessica explores the great fundamental human dilemma, the mystery of life and death. Her speaker is conscious of possessing a "soul in the body sown" which only knows a brief life shrouded in mystery:

> It is the homelessness of the soul in the body
> sown;
> it is the loneliness of mystery:
> of seeing oneself a leaf, inexplicable and
> unknown,
> cast from an unimaginable tree;
> of knowing one's life to be a brief wind blown

down a fissure of time in the rock of eternity.
The artist weeps to wrench this grief from stone;
he pushes his hands through the tangled vines of
music,
but he cannot set it free.[60]

The speaker of this poem knows "the pain of the mystic" experienced
in the initial encounter with "the noon of" a God of infinity and in
the final realization of "the night of his own humanity." The last
stanza of the poem does not explain the encounter; it merely describes it. The noetic quality of the mystical experience prevails as
the human subject laments:

It is the pain of the mystic suddenly thrown
back from the noon of God to the night of his own
humanity.
It is his grief; it is the grief of all those
praying
in infinite words to an Infinity
Whom, if they saw, they could not comprehend;
Whom they cannot see.[61]

After grappling with the intricate complexities of the human experiences described in the preceding poems, the speaker is led into
the heart of the Christian contemplative vision, the Trinity. The following poem, published in 1946, makes an attempt to voice the mystery of the Triune love which animates the mystic:

Doxology

God fills my being to the brim
with floods of His immensity.
I drown within a drop of Him
whose sea-bed is infinity.

The Father's will is everywhere
for chart and chance His precept keep.
There are no beaches to His care
nor cliffs to pluck from His deep.

The Son is never far away from me
for presence is what love compels.
Divinely and incarnately
He draws me where His mercy dwells.

And lo, myself am the abode
of Love, the third of the Triune,
the primal surge and sweep of God
and my eternal claimant soon!
Praise to the Father and the Son
and to the Spirit! May I be,
O Water, Wave and Tide in One,
Thine animate doxology.[62]

Here the speaker praises the Trinity and addresses a request to God in the words: "O Water, Wave and tide in One," make of me, "Thine animate doxology." The incarnation of the Son is seen as a dynamic force which, through the action of the Holy Spirit, continues to draw and transform all humanity into "the abode of Love." In order to focus on the importance of this doxology in her theology, Jessica chose to end three of her books, *The Place of Splendor, The House at Rest*, and *Selected Poetry of Jessica Powers*, with this poem.

This ability to describe the presence of a living God in dynamic terms interacting with the human being through the action of the Holy Spirit, is characteristic of Jessica. In "The Wind of Pentecost,"[63] the speaker asks the questions: Whither, I ask, this rush of yearning / divinity?" and "dare I guess / that Love, the gale of God, is turning / towards acres of my nothingness?" Then the speaker calls upon God to "possess me as a hurricane."

The result of humanity's opening up to the Spirit of God is "the age of the Holy Spirit." Jessica wrote the poem, "This Is a Beautiful Time,"[64] with its first stanza employing the scriptural language of the Song of Songs:

This is a beautiful time, this last age, the age of the Holy
Spirit.
This is the long-awaited day of His reign in our
souls through grace.
He is crying to every soul that is walled:
Open to Me, My spouse, My sister.
And once inside, He is calling again:
Come to Me here in this secret place.
Oh, hear Him tonight crying all over the world
a last desperate summons of love to a dying race.[65]

In the second stanza, more scriptural imagery is used, the divine leaven[66] and the flattening of mountains and filling in of valleys.[67] Moreover, "acres," a metaphor appearing repeatedly in Jessica's poetry, sometimes to describe the locus of God, and other times to describe the locus of the human,[68] is used in this poem to describe all of humanity. Through grace the reign of God comes to souls "bought by blood, to their / Purchaser given," and so the poem concludes:

Acres we are to be gathered for God: He would pour
out His measureless morning
upon divinized lands, bought by blood, to their

     Purchaser given.
     Oh, hear Him within you speaking this infinite
                   love,
     moving like some divine and audible leaven,
     lifting the sky of the soul with expansions of
                   light,
     shaping new heights and new depths,
     and, at your stir of assent,
     spreading the mountains with flame, filling the
     hollows with heaven.[69]

Of the poems which Jessica published in 1947, three poems of interest are included in this study. The first poem, "The Masses," uses explicit language to address God as "the ancient primal mother." This poem also builds on the overwhelming helplessness of facing large numbers of people in need; perhaps, this is a reflection on the soup lines of unemployed in New York City or some similar scene experienced by Jessica during the Great Depression. This poem is noteworthy because it demonstrates Jessica's ability to weave multiple images into an extended metaphor in an effort to describe a real life situation, to unpack emotional baggage, to address a caring God immediately present to humanity, and to evoke a response on the part of the speaker.

The Masses

     My love had not the openness to hold
     so cumbersome a human multitude.
     People in bulk would turn the dials of my heart to Cold.
     The mind would bolt its doors and curtly vow
     to leave the crowded streets for awhile.
     And yet if there were patronage in heaven

my passion was to be
mother of the masses, claiming by some small right
                                    of anguish
this piteous and dear humanity.
Out of its need my heart began devising
ways to receive this breathing populace
without the warm oppression of its weight,
and the fastidious mind sought out as good
a multiplicity of motherhood
till the reluctant answer entered late:
I learned from God the ancient primal mother
whose hunger to create has brought forth these,
a multitude in lone nativities,
whose love conceived the numberless, and none
by twos and thousands; and with Him I bear them
in separate tenderness, one by one.[71]

While themes like God as mother are present and repeated in
Jessica's writings, they are not as frequent as those which refer to the
Holy Spirit, the figure of the Magdalen, or Carmelite favorites, such
as the figure of the prophet Elijah. The second poem chosen from
those published in 1947 for this study is "Night Prayer: To the
Prophet Elijah."[72] Here Jessica combines the scriptural references to
Elijah with her experience of star-gazing. Her speaker says:

This is the edge of time; this cliff encounters
the valleys of the measureless unknown
and the great surges of those outer seas
where swim Orion and the Pleiades.
I like to come here in the night alone.[73]

It is a restless love that drives the human subject out alone into the
night, but it is a link with the scriptural heritage of the past that
gives meaning to the human experience described here:

I like to seek this arched and alien window,
lean into night and life my restless love
to pastures where an ancient prophet tethered
horses of fire. I cry, "My father, my father,
the chariot of Israel and the driver thereof!"[74]

Like Elijah, who was forced to hide in the Wadi Cherith where he
drank from the stream while God sent ravens to bring him bread and
meat in the morning and evening, the speaker of the poem is fed with

heavenly food from the hand of God. When the speaker goes out alone into the night, a visitation or divine encounter takes place, and the Elijan experience is repeated:

> Where dwells this lonely eremite I know not,
> hid by what torrent, by what ravens fed;
> but when the moon suggests his solitude,
> my mind has taste of an unearthly food;
> where the night shines, my heart is visited.[75]

"God Is A Strange Lover"[76] is the third poem from 1947 publication chosen for this study. The figure of the Magdalen, which appeared in "Bird at Evening" in 1939, reappears. God is portrayed as "the strangest of all lovers" and the ways of God are described as "past explaining." God does not woo the soul with flowers, jewels, or music; rather, God "stalks the soul with sorrows" and "robs and breaks and destroys." At last, the divine encounter takes place when there is nothing left between the soul and God except love:

> Not till the great rebellions die . . . does He open the
> door of light and His tendernesses fall,/and then for what
> is seen . . . for what is heard in the heart, there is no
> speech at all.[77]

For centuries, the Carmelite masters of the spiritual life have written of the purging action of God that weans the soul from spiritual delight as its goal and re-orientates the soul to God alone. Jessica captures this "strange" action of God in the words "there is nothing at last but / her own shame, her own affliction, / and then He comes and there is nothing in the vast world but / Him and her love of Him." The closing lines of the poem personify in the figure of the Magdalen this course of purgation of a soul in prayer:

> God is a strange lover; the story of His love is
>   most surprising.
> There is no proud queen in her cloth of gold; over
>   and over again
> there is only, deep in the soul, a poor disheveled woman
> weeping . . .
> for us who have need of a picture and words: the
>   Magdalen.[78]

Back in the late 1930s, Jessica had argued with a New York editor for over two hours about whether truth or beauty was the

greater attribute of God. Now, in the late 1940s, Jessica had reached
a different opinion; she saw mercy as the greatest attribute of God.
"The Mercy of God" is a poem which explores the human journey
from self-righteousness to a righteousness that is God-given and
solely dependent on God's mercy alone. Through this process of
spiritual maturation, the speaker passes from fear to freedom. The
poem begins:

> I am copying down in a book from my heart's
> > archives
> the day that I ceased to fear God with a shadowy
> > fear.
> Would you name it the day that I measured my
> > column of virtue
> and sighted through windows of merit a crown that
> > was near?
> Ah, no, it was rather the day I began to see truly
> that I came forth from nothing and ever toward
> > nothingness tend,
> that the works of my hands are foolishness wrought
> > in the presence
> of the worthiest king in a kingdom that never
> > shall end.[80]

The speaker of the poem discovers God's peace and mercy only after
abandoning a false sense of self walled in by pride. Then the will of
God becomes easy to discern because it is experienced as that which
tends toward the greater expression of love. The poem concludes:

> I rose up from the acres of self that I tended
> > with passion
> and defended with flurries of pride;
> I walked out of myself and went into the woods of
> > God's mercy,
> and here I abide.
> There is greenness and calmness and coolness, a
> > soft leafy covering
> from the judgment of sun overhead,
> and the hush of His peace, and the moss of His
> > mercy to tread.
> I have naught but my will seeking God; even love
> > burning in me
> is a fragment of infinite loving and never my own.

> And I fear God no more; I go forward to wander
> forever
> in a wilderness made of His infinite mercy
> alone.[81]

Religious themes which center on scriptural passages or Carmelite figures predominate in the poetry which flowed from Jessica's pen during the years 1948-49. In 1948 she published: "The Flower of Love,"[82] a poem which has for its base the words of Saint John of the Cross: "Where there is no love, put love and you will find love"[83] linked with the Eden story; "The Book of Ruth,"[84] a poem drawing from the story of Ruth and Naomi, Old Testament figures, whom she juxtaposes with the quest of the soul for union with God; and "Renunciation,"[85] a poem which is based on the words of Saint Therese of Lisieux: "To compose the most sublime poetry is of less worth than the least act of self-renunciation."[86]

"Enclosure,"[87] published during this same period, merits a closer examination. Jessica has been living the life of a cloistered contemplative nun for more than half a decade. The honeymoon is over. Now the reality of living with a dozen or so women in close quarters with limited opportunities for outside contacts or excursions takes on a new dimension as the life itself is carefully re-examined. In this poem, Jessica uses the word "gypsy," which is one of her favorite nicknames for herself. Then her speaker tells of "madness" and links it with the life of enclosure, the cloistered life. The speaker of the poem poses the question: Was this "walling, barring, minimizing, shrinking" really what Saint Teresa of Avila was thinking of when she began the Discalced Carmelite reform movement? The answer to the puzzle of the cloistered contemplative life is teased out by the use of words like "clue" and "secret to outwit enclosure." The speaker abandons the outer landscape's invitation to roam its vast and open spaces and takes up the Elijan call, which resounds from Mount Carmel's heights,[88] to traverse the inner landscape instead. The heavy tone of the first stanza completely disappears in the last stanzas which bear traces of playfulness:

Enclosure

Gypsy by nature, how can I endure it—
This small strict space, this meager patch of sky?
What madness once possessed me to procure it?
And deed it to myself until I die?

What could the wise Teresa have been thinking
to set these bounds on even my little love?
This walling, barring, minimizing, shrinking—
how could her great Castilian heart approve?

And yet I meet the morrow with composure.
Before I made my plaint I found the clue
and learned the secret to outwit enclosure
because of summits and a mountain view.

You question, then, the presence of a mountain?
Yet it is here past earth's extravagant guess—
Mount Carmel with its famed Elian fountain,
and God encountered in its wilderness.

Its trails outrun the most adept explorer,
outweigh the gypsy's most inordinate need.
Its heights cry out to mystic and adorer.
Oh, here are space and distances indeed.[89]

The next poem, entitled "To Live with the Spirit,"[90] was published in 1949. It focuses on the receptive ability of the speaker to
"listen" and to "keep the vigil of mystery." Its lines are filled with
dynamic movement:

To live with the spirit of God is to be a listener.
It is to keep the vigil of mystery,
earthless and still.
One leans to catch the stirring of the Spirit,
strange as the wind's will.[91]

In the search for God, the speaker is blown and turned around continuously like a weather-vane. It is the movement of God's love that
draws the arrow of the human heart, whether one feels joyful like a
free-spirited wanderer or sorrowful like Job and Jeremiah. The
speaker is led along an unknown path lacking a compass to point out
"the whither and the why" of life's unexpected turns. The second
stanza continues:

The soul that walks where the wind of the Spirit
                              blows
turns like a wandering weather-vane toward love.
It may lament like Job or Jeremiah,
echo the wounded heart, the mateless dove.

It may rejoice in spaciousness of meadow
that emulates the freedom of the sky.
Always it walks in waylessness, unknowing;
it has cast down forever from its hand
the compass of the whither and the why.[92]

When the speaker gives up all to become listener and travel the unseen road in search of God, the Spirit of God transforms the human
listener into a lover.   Poised like the Trinity between "all activity"
and "all silence," the speaker is swept by a dynamic process upward
and onward into God, the ultimate goal; yet the speaker is sleeping in
peace in spite of "fire-sweep and water-rush and the wind's whim."
The poem concludes with the lines:

To live with the Spirit of God is to be a lover.
It is becoming love, and like to Him
toward Whom we strain with metaphors of creatures:
fire-sweep and water-rush and the wind's whim.
The soul is all activity, all silence;
and though it surges Godward to its goal,
it holds, as moving earth holds sleeping noonday,
the peace that is the listening of the soul.[93]

In this way, the speaker is transformed into a Christ-like lover and
listener.   The final stages of this transformation are marked by a profound peace which fills the human listener.
    Between 1950 and 1956, Jessica explores the same themes as in
earlier years with less frequency but with more depth.   Life settled
into a hard routine lived out in the cramped quarters of the Wells
Street Carmel in Milwaukee.   In the poem, "Not Garden Any More,"
Jessica writes:

God is not garden any more, to satiate the senses
with the luxuriance of full exotic wilderness.
Now multiple is magnified to less.
God has become as desert now, a vast unknown
                            Sahara
voicing its desert cry.[94]

    Having gone down so many pathways which lead to dead ends,
the speaker comes to the realization that to undertake the journey inward dependent on human strength alone is impossible; without
God's grace all amounts to defeat.   In "Israel Again," which was published in 1950, the speaker reflects:

Here I am, Israel dragging home from battle
with neither horse nor soldier at my side.
Where are the troops with which I sallied forth
and all the bright insignia of my pride?
I did not call on the Lord God of Hosts,
but rushed forth in my strength to meet the foe.
Here I lag home, a spectacle of wounds,
stripped of my armor, moaning as I go.

When will you learn, O witless Israel,
that he who clings to God in his distress
wins with the weapons of his nothingness?

I step outside myself in gay derision
to mock this torn one, but in sympathy.
I add, "Not all is lost! Oh, turn and see!
Borne after you by the divine forgiveness
is the rich booty of humility."[95]

The stripping and suffering experienced by the speaker is the result of pride and trust in self rather than in God. By returning to God, the "witless Israel" learns that nothing is lost. The speaker becomes conscious of possessing a weapon of nothingness and this realization opens the door for God to enter and restore the broken relationship. Then God bestows a "rich booty of humility" upon the speaker by means of divine forgiveness.

The following poem, "Counsel for Silence,"[96] demonstrates Jessica's awareness of creaturehood, poverty, and aloneness. She finds direction and comfort by meditating upon a favorite Carmelite theme, Elijah in the wilderness. Building upon poetic encounters with Elijah in her earlier writings and her continuous prayer based upon scripture, Jessica enters into this Old Testament scene so that once again Elijah's experience speaks to her in an effort to give meaning to her own experience. The scene is full of biblical imagery: the torrent of the Wadi Cherith, the prophetic hermit's anchorhold, and the ravens sent from God to supply bread and meat. These biblical elements are combined with echoes of John of the Cross' description of the soul departing in secret, secure past the grasp of human compulsions, and refreshed by grace of God flooding the soul once its motives have been purged and purified. Carefully weaving these two themes with modern day American street addresses, hints of farewell parties, and local town gossip of speculative nature, Jessica fashions a poem of subtle depth as demonstrated in the following masterful lines:

Counsel for Silence

Go without ceremony of departure
and shade no subtlest word with your farewell.
Let the air speak the mystery of your absence,
and the discerning have their minor feast
on savory possible or probable.
Seeing the body present, they will wonder
where went the secret soul, by then secure
out past your grief beside some torrent's pure
refreshment. Do not wait to copy down
the name, much less the address, of who might need
                              you.
Here you are pilgrim with no ties of earth.
Walk out alone and make the never-told
your healing distance and your anchorhold.
And let the ravens feed you.[97]

No matter how heavy the fortunes of life weigh upon her daily happenstances, Jessica manages, with a little help from her Gaelic wit, to let a wisp of humor break through in her poetry. "But Not With Wine,"[98] is a delightful example of sitting down to dine with God, and writing about it afterwards when one has sobered up a bit. The poem reads:

O God of too much giving, whence is this
inebriation that possesses me,
that the staid road now wanders all amiss
and that the wind walks much too giddily,
clutching a bush for balance, or a tree?
How then can dignity and pride endure
with such inordinate mirth upon the land,
when steps and speech are somewhat insecure
and the light heart is wholly out of hand?

If there be indecorum in my songs,
fasten the blame where rightly it belongs:
on Him who offered me too many cups
of His most potent goodness—not on me,
a peasant who, because a king was host,
drank out of courtesy.[99]

When a sober road "wanders all amiss" and the "wind walks much too giddily," it is no wonder that a condition of inebriation overtakes the speaker. This divine inebriation results, not from wine but from the goodness of God, a God of too much giving whose goodness is so potent that it overwhelms and makes the human heart light and full of song and mirth. This situation forces the speaker of the poem to conjure up a feeble defense blaming the king [God] for offering "me too many cups," which causes a peasant [like the subject] to drink "out of courtesy." The whole scene depicted in this poem is inspired by a passage from Isaiah: "You are drunk, but not with wine." Read aloud, "But Not With Wine"[100] is likely to bring a smile to the face of its audience.

Jessica does not expound any simplistic or sentimental solutions to life's questions in her poetry. As a cloistered Carmelite nun, she dived into the depths of human existence stripped of life's multitudinous trappings and surrounded by only bare necessities. In doing so, she found no solution except through the contemplation of the mystery of Christ. The poem, "Christ Is My Utmost Need," which was published in 1952, echoes the themes present in an earlier poem, "The Garments of God,"[102] but shifts the emphasis to the figure of Christ.

> Late, late the mind confessed:
> wisdom has not sufficed.
> I cannot take one step into the light
> without the Christ.[103]

In the opening lines of the poem, the speaker confesses that human wisdom has not been sufficient to provide the strength needed to undertake life's journey. It is impossible to advance one step, to gain one small fragment of enlightenment without the grace of Christ. The speaker in this poem does not possess a deistic god who acts as a clock-maker winding up his creation and then sitting on a cloud in the distant sky to see what will happen. Rather, the speaker is possessed by a living God who is incarnate in human flesh:

> Late, late the heart affirmed:
> wild do my heart-beats run
> when in the blood-stream sings one wish away
> from the Incarnate Son.
>
> Christ is my utmost need.
> I lift each breath, each beat for Him to bless,

knowing our language cannot overspeak
our frightening helplessness.[104]

In the next two stanzas, the subject of the poem reflects upon the past with its pride, power, and self-command. Nothing remains. A wreath hangs over the grave, the burial site of former days when the human subject bathed in the illusions of self-righteousness. However, going deeper into the labyrinth of the human psyche, the speaker is startled by the discovery of a hidden fear, "my steps surprised a dark Iscariot plotting in my own will." The potential to embrace evil is buried deep within the core of the individual human person. The poem continues:

> Here where proud morning walks
> and we hang wreaths on power and self-command,
> I cling with all my strength unto a nail-
> investigated hand.

> Christ is my only trust.
> I am my fear since, down the lanes of ill,
> my steps surprised a dark Iscariot
> plotting in my own will.[105]

The speaker recognizes only one way to entertain a hope of salvation: the cultivation of a radical trust in Christ. Faith, bordering on the frantic, steadies itself by the thought:

> Past nature called, I cry
> who clutch at fingers and at tunic folds,
> "Lay not on me, O Christ, this fastening.
> Yours be the hand that holds."[106]

The soul keeps its rhythm of seasons much the same as the earth does. Life's deserts are capable of blooming when visited by the Spirit of God. Jessica develops a sense of the mysterious interaction between consoling times and desolating times as manifested in scripture, in the stories of those who journey with her through life, and in her own life experiences. Published in 1952, "And Wilderness Rejoices," blends this understanding of human spiritual development with Carmelite themes and scriptural imagery and metaphors. Jessica writes:

And Wilderness Rejoices

Land that was desolate, impassable,
is forest now where secrets find their voices.
The desert is inhabited and blooms.
One with the meadow, wilderness rejoices.

Lebanon's glory is its green possession
and Carmel's beauty. Visited by love,
wastelands are pastures for the Lamb at midday,
And living solitudes to hold the Dove.

Never again will patriarch prefigure
or lean precursor walk or prophet call.
Here is fulfillment. One has come and given
the Spirit Who is flame and festival.

Sower and Sown are here. The bright groves
               flourish
and burn toward islands in the utmost sea.
Time has become a wilderness of presence
which too is essence of its jubilee.

Earth keeps its seasons and its liturgy,
as should the soul. Oh, come, green summer, blur
these wastes and let my soul in song declare
Who came by flesh and Who by fire to her.[108]

The poem echoes the words of Isaiah the prophet who speaks of Israel's restoration: "The desert and the parched land will exult . . . They will bloom with abundant flowers, and rejoice with joyful song. The glory of Lebanon will be given to them, the splendor of Carmel and Sharon."[109] The lamb and the dove are safe at midday in open pastures, because former times which called forth patriarchs and prophets are past. The image of "the Spirit Who is flame and festival" conjures up the Pentecost event[110] in the reader's mind, while "Sower and Sown are here"[111] announces the meeting of the divine and the human in the present moment.

In addition to their scriptural and Carmelite thematic content, Jessica's poems contain images of God that flow over into concrete images of landscape. For example, "Repairer of Fences,"[112] combines elements of Isaiah's prophetic descriptions of Yahweh, the "Repairer of the breach," and the "Restorer of ruined homesteads,"[113] with

traces of Robert Frost's "Mending Wall."[114] Published in 1952, the
poem sings of a God worth praising:

Repairer of Fences

I am alone in the dark, and I am thinking
what darkness would be mine if I could see
the ruin I wrought in every place I wandered
and if I could not be
aware of One who follows after me.
Whom do I love, O God, when I love Thee?
The great Undoer who has torn apart
the walls I built against a human heart,
the Mender who has sewn together the hedges
through which I broke when I went seeking ill,
the Love who follows and forgives me still.
Fumbler and fool that I am, with things around me
of fragile make like souls, how I am blessed
to hear behind me footsteps of a Savior!
I sing to the east; I sing to the west:
God is my repairer of fences, turning my paths
into rest.[115]

In this way, Jessica chronicles the human story which moves the
speaker from regions of aloneness, darkness, and ruin, into realms of
forgiveness and salvation forged by the hands of God, the Undoer of
walls, the Mender of fences, and the Love who follows and forgives.

   With the publication of "Ruah-Elohim"[116] in 1954, Jessica explores once more the theme of God as mother as well as Father and
Son. First, she reflects on the word for "spirit" in Hebrew which is
feminine in gender. Then she speaks of the mothering qualities of
God as "a goodness like maternity," and a "Love Who seeks to
mother." Lastly, Jessica links this feminine dimension in God to the
third person of the Trinity, the Holy Spirit. Her theological perspective concerning the feminine aspect of Godhood is simply developed
and relatively unsophisticated.

Ruah-Elohim

Spirit in Hebrew, feminine in gender
lifts my surmise to touch sweet certainty
that with a goodness like maternity
The Holy Ghost is tender.

Master and guide suppose a separation
should native weakness contravene their role,
but in event of mothering in the soul
hope fondles all creation.

Not as the newest infant who is bringing
no more than burden, I would to Him
yearling in grace and with the cherubim,
say all my love by clinging.

The elders must take conflict and distraction
from how and who and whither and the rest;
but always for children carried at the breast
love is the lone exaction.

Two are the Son and Father, but the Other
so shapes my will its dear theology.
Come but to kiss and cradle tenderly
is Love Who seeks to mother.[117]

Returning to poetic themes inspired by the writings Saint John
of the Cross, Jessica focuses on the human spirit, snow-paralyzed and
winter-bound by death's chill, longing for the springtime of God in
the consolation of resurrection. In *The Spiritual Canticle,* John of the
Cross refers to the north wind as deadening, but, when he writes of
the south wind, he says: "South wind come, you that waken love, /
Breathe through my garden."[118] John of the Cross gives the words
"south wind" a special meaning: "By south wind is meant the Holy
Spirit who awakens love."[119] In her poem, "Come, South Wind,"[120]
which was published in 1954, Jessica spins out this theme in great
detail:

Over and over I say to the south wind: come,
waken in me and warm me!
I have walked too long with a death's chill in the
air,
mourned over trees too long with branches bare.
Ice has a falsity for all its brightness
and so has need of your warm reprimand.
A curse be on the snow that lapsed from whiteness,
and all bleak days that paralyze my land.

> I am saying all day to Love who wakens love:
> rise in the south and come!
> Hurry me into springtime; hustle the winter
> out of my sight; make dumb
> the north wind's loud impertinence. Then plunge
>   me
> me into my leafing and blossoming,
> and give me pasture, sweet and sudden pasture.
> Where could the Shepherd bring
> his flocks to graze? Where could they rest at
>   noonday?
> O south wind, listen to the woe I sing!
> One whom I love is asking for the summer
> from me, who still am distances from spring.[121]

In 1955, Jessica published several poems whose contents merit consideration in this study. First, the poem "A Meadow Moreover," captures a remembrance of a meadow "out in undeeded lands, / past time, past even a need of name." The singing of a meadowlark in a city park conjures up this memory of the distant meadow with its singing birds. This mental picture is recast as a metaphor for picturing divine and human landscapes:

> God is a meadow in some high way,
> a meadow moreover revealed in ours
> where only the children find the flowers."[123]

This bright vision had a dark side smoldering underneath the surface of Jessica agile pen as demonstrated by her poem, "Take Your Only Son,"[124] which was published in 1956. This poem contains a vision of a possible conclusion to the speaker's quest for God that is quite the opposite of the one which Jessica paints for the children above. The subject of her poem reflects upon the story of Abraham which is recorded in the book of Genesis, relates it to the present state of human affairs, and records the despairing experience of God's absence:[125]

Take Your Only Son

> None guessed our nearness to the land of vision,
> not even our two companions to the mount.
> That you bore wood and I, by grave decision,
> fire and a sword, they judged of small account.

Speech might leap wide to what were best unspoken
and so we plodded, silent, through the dust.
I turned my gaze lest the heart be twice broken
when innocence looked up to smile its trust.

O love far deeper than a lone begotten,
how grievingly I let your words be lost
when a shy question guessed I had forgotten
a thing so vital as the holocaust.

Hope may shout promise of reward unending
and faith buy bells to ring its gladness thrice,
but these do not preclude earth's tragic ending
and the heart shattered in its sacrifice.

Not beside Abram does my story set me.
I built the altar, laid the wood for flame.
I stayed my sword as long as duty let me,
and then alas, alas, no angel came.[126]

In summary, several major theological themes are contained in
Jessica's poems published between 1941 and 1958. These developed
as a result of the guiding principles which were operative in her life:
she studied scripture and the great Carmelite masters; she followed
their lead until God, who made her an individual, helped her to get in
touch with her own different and unique experience of divine presence in her life; and, by means of her poetry, she chronicled the way
of prayer upon which God led her. Jessica's experience of God in
this period of her life is multi-faceted as she speaks of the Trinity,
God's Fatherhood and Motherhood, Christ, and the Holy Spirit.

Jessica documents in writing her awareness of the powerful and
overwhelming force of divine love entering into human relationships
and re-ordering human vision on a daily basis. In ordinary ways, the
meeting of the divine and the human is constantly replayed in the
present moment. For her the surest path to an awareness of the presence of God is the one leading through the ordinary events of daily
life, and not the one involving extraordinary phenomena.

Equally important, Jessica sees herself in relationship to a living
God who interacts in dynamic terms with her. Yet, in spite of the
fact that she recognizes the indwelling of the Holy Spirit at the core
of her being, Jessica can write of the presence of God experienced as
absence. She develops a sense of the rhythm and mysterious interaction between consoling times and desolating times as manifested in

scripture, in the stories of those who journey with her through life, and in her own life experiences. The purging action of God, which she learns to accept in times of spiritual darkness, weans her from spiritual delight and re-orientates her to God alone.

An additional characteristic of Jessica's poetry is her awareness of her human condition with its restlessness and sin. For her, sin is experienced as negation, not reality, and she recognizes that the potential to embrace evil is buried deep within the core of her own individual human person.

Jessica's hope for salvation comes through the cultivation of a radical trust in Christ. Through her own personal journey from self-righteousness to a righteousness that is God-given and solely dependent on God's mercy alone, Jessica comes to the conclusion that the greatest attribute of God is mercy. Only the grace of a loving and merciful God experienced as a living Christ incarnate in her flesh and as Holy Spirit indwelling in her every breath gives meaning to her daily life.

Jessica believes that listening in silence ushers in the final stages of transformation into a Christ-like lover and listener. She teaches that these final stages are marked by a profound peace which fills the human listener. Aware of her own continual struggles on this inner journey, Jessica calls herself a "gypsy." She had to learn a balancing act with the outer landscape's invitation to roam its vast and open spaces integrated with the Elijan call to traverse the inner landscape in a spirit of faith and trust. In doing so, Jessica acts as a discerning listener and as a spiritual guide for contemplatives journeying through the modern American landscape.

Jessica's pen produces few poems for several years following 1956. The reasons for this self-imposed silence are simple: ill health resulting from a renewed bout of tuberculosis, the added monastic duties and responsibilities following her election as prioress of the monastery, and the busy work necessitated by the move of the entire Carmelite community from Milwaukee to Pewaukee.

These events in Jessica's personal life are surrounded by major shifts in the cultural and theological context of her wider world. The relatively stable and ordered world of the United States in the 1950s and of the Roman Catholic Church in the period from Trent to 1960 begins to undergo radical paradigm shifts in cultural attitudes and religious thought in the early 1960s. As a new era is ushered into world affairs, so a new period begins in Jessica's life. She, too, must make radical changes in her thought and attitudes in order to survive and discover some semblance of meaning in the disorder and chaos dealt to her during this period of her life.

Chapter VI

The American Carmelite Vision of Jessica Powers (1958-1988)

❧

WITH THE COMMENCING OF THE SECOND VATICAN COUNCIL IN 1961, the Roman Catholic Church ushered in an era of change. Following the lead of the Council Fathers, the Roman Catholic Church in the United States began a program of adaptation and renewal in the mid 1960s. The first notable changes in the post-Vatican II Church were clearly visible in the liturgical renewal which swept the country. These liturgical changes were soon followed by other far-reaching and dramatic shifts in theology and spirituality.

Along with the larger Church, the Discalced Carmelite communities of women in the United States studied the documents of Vatican II and tried to implement their directives in the ordering of their daily life and prayer. Nuns representing the various communities of Discalced Carmelite in the United States gathered to discuss the possibilities for change in their way of life for the first time in a 1965 general meeting at De Mattias Hall on the grounds of Saint Louis University in St. Louis, Missouri. Jessica Powers was among these delegates.

The Spiritual Climate: Vatican II and Its Aftermath in Communities of Discalced Carmelite Nuns in the United States

After several years of experimentation and renewal, the Carmelite Communities Associated (CCA) emerged in 1970 as a spokesbody for the American communities of Discalced Carmelite Nuns who were committed to renewal and adaptation of their life according to the guidelines of Vatican II and in response to the needs of the Church.[1] A significant document produced by this group is entitled *Charter of Life*. Work on this document began as early as 1971 in

Richfield, Ohio, where the association had its first meeting. At this time, the focus of the nuns centered on the adaption and renewal of the Teresian charism in the historical and theological context of the United States in the second half of the twentieth century. Each member community of the CCA was asked to study and reflect on a particular aspect of the Teresian charism, record the results of their prayer and study, and report back to the main group the following year.

In 1972, a second meeting of the Carmelite Communities Associated was held in Richfield. This time the agenda included a discussion of the association's goals and objectives. Soon it became evident that a document was needed to express the lived experience of the Discalced Carmelite Nuns who were members of the Association. For three years, the delegates prayed, gathered information, and worked to formulate such a document.

Another meeting of the CCA took place in 1975 at Holyoke, Massachusetts. At this meeting the nuns discussed the history, tradition, and spirituality of the Discalced Carmelite Order. The result of their discussion was a renewed desire for a charter which would reflect their beliefs and lifestyle. The charter became the project of the chairperson and the coordinating committee who established a Charter of Life Task Force by August of 1975. Membership in this task force varied over the years, with Sister Teresa Hahn acting as chairperson from 1975-76 and Sister Joan Bourne acting as chairperson from 1977-79.[2] Through their communications with the co-operating members of the Association, this task force was able to produce *The Workbook*, a tool for intra-community dialogue and study in 1976. *The Workbook* became the basic tool for gathering information from the widespread communities of Discalced Carmelite Nuns in the United States. Reflecting upon this formative process, Sister Carol Sachse, OCD, who became the chairperson of CCA in 1979, writes:

> Each community sent in material, and everyone gave of herself in an effort to articulate our experience of Carmel today. A communal expression evolved through prayer, study, dialogue, and growth. The deeper mutual understanding which resulted from the involvement of the communities was one of the finest fruits of this endeavor. Thus, the Charter manifests our unity, trust, and love.[3]

The *Charter of Life* contains noteworthy shifts in emphasis and understandings on the part of the Carmelites who drafted it, especially when compared with earlier documents, such as the one produced by the Wells Street Carmel of Milwaukee in the 1940s. The writers of the *Charter of Life* attempt to document the essence of their contemplative life in terms that are dynamic and relational. In addition to this, the document challenges its readers to go beyond the written word, to envision beyond the limits of the present, and to move forward in an ever continuing search for the face of God.

Printed and distributed in 1979, *Charter of Life: A Contemporary Statement of the Teresian Charism* by the Carmelite Communities Associated CCA begins with the recognition of the Christian roots of the Carmelite contemplative lifestyle by saying: "We have been baptized into Christ, sealed by his Spirit, and joined to his body the Church where we share the heritage of children who dare to say: Our Father."[4] Thus, the Christocentrism of Teresian spirituality receives a central position in this document. The following of Jesus Christ is described as a life of love spent in solitary prayer with guiding principles gleaned by Saint Teresa of Avila from the Carmelite Rule of Saint Albert of Jerusalem. These principles, which expound a balanced daily rhythm of solitary prayer and communal Eucharistic celebration linked with manual labor in a simple lifestyle, characterize the contemplative spirituality of the Discalced Carmelites. Moreover, the *Charter of Life* explains:

> For, from within the ancient Carmelite tradition imaged in the figures of Elijah and the Virgin Mary, [and] Teresa, daughter and doctor of the Church, evolved a distinctive style of contemplative life and a spirit of prayer infused with her own remarkable sense of the Risen Christ and the Church.[5]

Further on in the document, silence, solitude, and contemplative prayer are emphasized and described in terms that are relational. Solitude is explained as "a desert of time and space for uncluttered attention to [God]; our silence, a climate of peace for listening."[6] Both are extolled as necessary for making up the environment of prayer. For this reason, each Carmelite is allotted her own room apart:

> Our room is for us a place both sacred and familiar, a desert where we are at home. We reserve two hours each day for solitary prayer, but the same spirit of prayer

overflows into the hours of reading, study, and work, gracing each as we take it up with a quality of unhurried attention and esteem. This spirit of prayer and leisure, nurtured in solitude but all-pervasive, gives to the successive moments of our life a contemplative dimension and draws them together into a unity.[7]

The daily hours of prayer in solitude and silence are balanced by daily communal worship in Eucharist, community meetings, and common meals as "daily in the Eucharist Christ calls forth from us the deepest personal response, only to transform this gift of ourselves into a communion of life."[8] In this document, Carmelites call themselves solitaries bound to community with Christ as the unity of their lives. The same love of Christ which leads them into solitary prayer leads them together in community, and is explained in these words:

> These two lofty and compelling ideas [solitary and communal] mark our way as Carmelites, a way which is the Paschal journey of our Christian life. Between fidelity to solitary prayer and commitment to creating a community of love, our days move in a rhythm of creative tension, not without its stress and demands, but sweetened always by a joyful gratitude for the abundance of life and the beauty of the calling which is the portion of our heritage.[9]

The challenge which these contemporary Carmelites take up is one that seeks to form a relationship which is both relevant and meaningful to their wider world, while preserving their particular Christian heritage. In their efforts to outline this dynamic process, the Carmelites produce one especially inspiring passage in their document which celebrates the Risen Christ, living and incarnate in all times and places:

> We are children of our time. We acknowledge its history, its culture, its greatness, its sin. What we are by inheritance, we choose in love, for we believe that the God whose face we seek comes to meet us in each unfolding moment of the human story. At the same time, we believe that Carmel's life of prayer is a vital part of the Christian response to the Gospel imperative that we redeem the times. And so we have fashioned our life of prayer in ways appropriate to itself yet new, in order to

become within the local church and community a more
visible and accessible presence of the universal love to
which we aspire. Whatsoever things are just, noble, gra-
cious and true, these we ponder and hold fast, while our
lives proclaim that the Lord Jesus is near.[10]

In spite of this vivid vision of themselves as children of their
time engaged in the process of redeeming the times, Carmelites recognize that their life is ultimately one lived in the darkness of faith
centered on "One whom we love but do not see," and subject to a
barren appearance because the "fruitfulness of our prayer is the unseen work of grace in the secret places of the human spirit."[11]
Within this call to contemplative life in the Carmelite tradition, there
lies the seeds of the paradox of life. The human spirit is endowed
with an ability to transcend the visible reality of earthly existence and
the seemingly finality of death; consequently, the human spirit can
envision a timeless life with a divine Creator, Savior, and Lover.
Carmelites contemplate this mystery continually. Their human response is one of trust in a loving God who saves. Their witness
helps to lift the heavy burden of doubt and despair which plagues human lives and encourages others to live in hope. The *Charter of Life*
builds on these convictions and concludes with the passage:

We believe that our life, though ordinary as ourselves,
speaks of more than ourselves. For when we are present
in the neighborhoods and cities of the human community, we are a prophetic presence of the Church pointing
beyond ourselves to the very mystery of God . . . . At
the same time, like the prophets of old, we are free to
move in those narrow places on the frontiers of society
and culture, to live and to speak the truth as we increas-
ingly come to see it. . . . we keep our eyes on Jesus. His
love impels us, and zeal for God's reign consumes like
fire. Yet we go our way with a quiet heart, having a
common care for unity and for the peace which binds us
together, praying continually in the power of the Holy
Spirit, and giving thanks to the Father whatever may
come, always and everywhere.[12]

In the Pewaukee Carmelite community, Jessica and her sisters
were challenged to examine their lives by this process of renewal and
adaption. Both their prayer and lifestyle came under close scrutiny as

they sought to be faithful to the spirit of the Second Vatican Council and their Carmelite heritage.

Notwithstanding, the communication process initiated to articulate a common expression of Carmelite spirituality in the United States and to produce the document, *Charter of Life*, failed to unite the Discalced Carmelite Nuns of the United States into one national union. Instead, four associations were formed with their membership drawn from Latin Rite and Byzantine Rite Discalced Carmelite communities of nuns in the United States: the Association of Saint Joseph, the Carmelite Communities Associated, the Association of Saint Teresa, and the Association of Mary Queen of Carmel, which is important for this study of Jessica Powers because the Carmelite community of Pewaukee is one of its members.[13]

Jessica Powers and Her Final Passages

Jessica rejoiced in the scenic beauty of her new and spacious surroundings in Pewaukee, but the rhythm of life brought many major changes following the Second Vatican Council. In 1965, an optimistic Jessica attended a general meeting of Discalced Carmelite Nuns in St. Louis, Missouri. Hopes were high for implementing the documents of Vatican II, but the changes were too fast paced for many of the conservative nuns who took a preservationist stance and refused to change. On the other hand, these same changes were too slow paced for others, who opting for a more radical transformist position and liberal attitudes, chose to depart from their Carmelite communities in disillusionment. Subsequently, many Carmelite communities, like other communities, dwindled in number as a result of departures and the abrupt decline of incoming vocations which followed in the wake of Vatican II.

In 1968, the members of the Carmelite community in Albuquerque, New Mexico, began the process for transferring to the Pewaukee Carmel in hopes that the two communities might form a viable community by joining resources and personnel. The Albuquerque foundation had been a daughter house of the Santa Fe, New Mexico that was founded in 1955 by four professed sisters of the Santa Fe Carmel, a sister in temporary vows, and an extern novice. Helen Marie of the Infant Jesus of Prague was prioress of this community and Oklahoma-born Bernadette of the Immaculate Conception (Louise Ranallo) was the sub-prioress. Bernadette was among these nuns from the southwest who transferred to Pewaukee in 1969 and lived

with Jessica from this time until the end of Miriam's life.[14] The joining of the two communities seemed to alleviate temporarily some of
the more pressing financial and personnel problems of both groups.

In 1971 Jessica left Pewaukee for a while to travel west. Her
biographer, Dolores Leckey, hints that she was debating whether or
not to stay in the community in Pewaukee, Wisconsin.[15] Others say
it was a routine medical leave.[16] Whatever may be the case, after
spending some time with her sick brother in Arizona, Jessica headed
for San Diego and the Carmelite Monastery there. Her diary records
some of the highlights of her journey: her long soul-searching talks
with a counselor and spiritual director; her outings to parks and the
zoo, the movies, sightseeing, and dinners. This source also includes
a collection of poems and several pieces of haiku which she referred
to as her "West Coast Poems." Jessica was now in her sixties and
still filled with a sense of being on a journey. On one hand, her lat-
est series of travels could be likened to a biblical pilgrimage looking
for "a promised land" in the west or meaning to life's surprising and
unexpected turns; on the other hand, this final outing could be seen
as a bit of "wanderlust" with the old "gypsy," as she sometimes
called herself, once more dictating the moves.[17]

Eventually, Jessica felt herself ready to return to Pewaukee.
Both her physical health and her spirits were greatly improved by her
west coast stay. The warm southern sun had sparked an interest in
her to renew her poetry writing, which resulted in a new collection of
poems entitled *The Mountain Sparrow*, an artistic edition of poems
which Jessica printed in collaboration with her sisters in Reno, Nevada in 1972. Later in 1980, the Carmelite supplement of Proper Offices was published with an appendix of hymns, which Jessica had
spent a great deal of time collecting, editing, and writing.[18] Besides
this, she printed a small collection of Advent poems entitled *Journey
to Bethlehem* during this same year (1980). An Italian translation of
The Place of Splendor was published in 1983, and the following year
(1984), a book of her poetry called *The House at Rest* was published.
Then, from 1986 to her death in 1988, she worked with Sister Regina
Siegfried, ASC of St. Louis, and Bishop Robert Morneau of the
Green Bay Diocese, on a book of her poems entitled *Selected Poetry*,
published posthumously in 1989.

Finally, the long years of work and prayer, marked with several
battles of tuberculosis, took their toll on Jessica. In addition to this,
she had been suffering from osteoporosis, from a hiatal hernia, and
from a number of other complications during the last two years of

her life. Still, she was able to participate in community events and work with business connected with her poetry, although her body seemed to be giving out.

To the end of her life, Jessica remained mentally alert, but often she complained "of her memory not performing as she wished."[19] Then on August 17, 1988, Jessica suffered a stroke; the following day, she died at age 83.[20] In remembering Jessica's life with them, her Carmelite sisters in Pewaukee wrote:

> These bare chronological facts hardly capture the delight of Sister Miriam's personality, or the depth of her spirituality, as those who had the joy of her friendship know. She was full of fun, loving to tell jokes (of which she had a good stock) and telling them extremely well with her Irish sense of humor and twinkling eyes.[21]

The Final Years: Poetic Reflections on Passages in Life

In her final years Jessica seems to reach complete freedom in expression of mystical insight and in poetic versification. First, she adopts more theological themes played out in contemporary settings employing universal language. Secondly, her verse frees itself of all the traditional poetic devices of rhyme and measured rhythm; regular line or stanza patterns are abandoned; and she presents "primarily an interior topography."[22] As a result, a number of her later poems are in modern verse form, but "even in the most loosely structured poem she often gently strikes a rime, as if the tendency were innate, a prompting not to be denied of what she would call her Gaelic ear." Now she makes the shift complete from specific imagery to less specific language. Robert Boudreau theorizes that:

> These shifts occur because the new freight the more general terms carry becomes more and more religious as she moves deeper and deeper into contemplative life, into her reading of the Bible, of St. John of the Cross, and of St. Teresa of Avila.[24]

The poetic results of these shifts are reflected in the way she moves away from the use of the extended metaphor and into the use of symbol and allegory in her later poems.

Reflecting her early experiences in life, Jessica's poems of the 1920s ask the fundamental questions raised by life itself which concern the mystery of God, of love, of suffering, of death, and of resurrection. In the middle period of her life, she explores both the inner and outer landscapes of her world in an effort to find the answers to these questions; in her later years, Jessica realizes that she has found meaning in life in spite of the fact that she cannot answer all of the questions which life has asked of her.

Jessica's mature theological insights can be gleaned from her poems written between the period 1961 and 1988. They can also be found in a few scattered pieces of brief prose slipped into her journal or published in Carmelite newsletters, which were circulated privately among the Carmelite communities.

Eight poems chosen for this study fall into the category of those published in the 1960s. For the most part, their themes are familiar replays of material found in the poems of earlier years. However, if arranged in chronological order, these nine poems yield a definite pattern which is characteristic of authentic spiritual development documented in past theological studies of religious figures. A running analysis of these poems uncovers the following components of Jessica's progressive development in the spiritual life and in her insights into mystical theology.

First, through the means of her poetry, Jessica confirms that the entrance into a vibrant spiritual life is gained by faithfulness to and perseverance in prayer regardless of a desert-like aridity experienced in the rhythm of daily life. The poem, "Pure Desert," which was published in 1961, speaks vividly of this spiritual dryness in prayer:

> This is pure Gobi desert, you declare;
> I see, past sandstorms (of exaggeration)
> and rage of flesh at ghostly motivation,
> pink health invade your prayer.

Having run the gauntlet of prayer for many years, Jessica is able to write words of encouragement, of sympathy, and of gentle guidance for her readers. She prophesies that "pink health [will] invade your prayer," and reassures with the words: "I coax you onward." In sympathy, she says:

> Pure desert, you complain, though now you walk
> who once had shuffled through the arid miles.
> Sighting a day of flight, I shelve my smiles
> and share your pilgrim talk.[26]

As a spiritual guide, Jessica aptly outlines the journey unfolding before her fellow pilgrim on the road. With stark realism, she describes the hardness of the path:

> All true ascesis as a desert lies:
> hot wind, hot sand, no water, and no way.
> The ego agonizes through each day.
> Freedom is when it dies.[27]

After passing through this place of purgation, Jessica offers the welcomed assurance that the weary traveler will experience comfort and rest. The final stage of the spiritual journey ends in a place of rebirth:

> I coax you onward: soon, first breeze of bliss;
> soon, sun that scorches cooled to sun that warms.
> Your youth will dance when shady lanes lock arms
> with each green oasis.[28]

The second component of this progressive development in the spiritual life is the ripening of a Christocentric mystical vision. Once past this trial of spiritual aridity, the redeemed world opens up to let in a vision of the hidden Christ seen everywhere. Published in 1963, "The Hidden Christ"[29] is a poem cast in a Christmas scene which contains an ox and ass, straw and stable, but no Child. Immersed in traditional Christmas surroundings, the human subject has come upon a dead end in the search for God. The poem continues:

> I sought His stable where He gave
> His goodness in the guise of bread.
> Emptiness came to me instead.
>
> Filled with my Father's words, I cried
> "Where have You hid Yourself?" and all
> The living answered to my call.[30]

Forced to go beyond the standard religious symbols in the search for the divine presence, the speaker enters deeper into the realization of the presence of God in all living creatures everywhere. Returning to the Christmas scene fortified by this mystical insight, the speaker is filled with joy and sees the Child. The next stanzas read:

> I found Him (and the world is wide)
> dear in His warm ubiquity.
> Where heart beat, there was Christ for me.

I went back to the Christmas cave,
glad with the gain of everywhere.
And lo! the blessed Child was there.[31]

The conclusion of the poem ends with the human subject participating in the transforming power of the Risen Christ incarnate in humanity: "He multiplied His good / and fed in me the multitude."[32] Two theological insights reside in these lines: first, the doorway to the divine is the human person of Jesus Christ; and secondly, whatever the mystic receives in the divine embrace is gift for all humanity.

Besides this vision of Christ hidden everywhere which enters once the trials of spiritual purgation are past, there is a third component often noted in authentic spiritual development, a breaking down of barriers between the sacred and the secular in the Christian mystic's experience of the redeemed world. Like the previous poem, this poem entitled "In Too Much Light,"[33] begins with a Christmas scene. Moreover like the previous poem, it goes beyond this concrete religious scenario to make a theological statement about the mystical insight to be gained when the speaker risks going "out past the loss of perishable sun." The poem reads:

The Magi had one only star to follow
a single sanctuary lamp hung low,
gold ornament in the astonished air.
I am confounded in this latter day;
I find stars everywhere.

Rumor locates the presence of a night
out past the loss of perishable sun
where, round midnight, I shall come to see
that all the stars are one.

I long for this night of the onement of the stars
when days of scattered shining are my lot
and my confusion. Yet faith even here
burns her throat dry, cries: on this very spot
of mornings, see, there is not any place
when the sought Word is not.
Under and over, in and out this morn
flawlessly, purely, wakes the newly born.
Behold, all places which have light in them
truly are Bethlehem.[34]

Trapped in a time when "days of scattered shining are my lot / and my confusion," the speaker in the poem longs for "this night of the onement of the stars." Yet, even in this scattered state of confusion, the speaker confesses that, in the light of faith, it is possible to see that God is everywhere.

The fourth component of Jessica's progressive development in the spiritual life encompasses a robust vision of the world alive with the presence of God. This vision allows the speaker to reject the idea of suffering, one of human existence's inherent components, as something to be feared. In the words of Therese of Lisieux: "All is a grace"[35] for the Christian mystic. Jessica had a first-hand knowledge of sickness and suffering; she knew the devastating effect it can have on the human spirit. Like mystics before her, Jessica learned to embrace suffering as a grace, and she turns this experience around with another bit of her Gaelic humor in a clever poem entitled, "Suffering,"[36] published in 1965:

All that day long I spent the hours with
                suffering.
I woke to find her sitting by my bed.
She stalked my footsteps while time slowed to
                timeless,
tortured my sight, came close in what was said.

She asked no more than that, beneath unwelcome,
I might be mindful of her grant of grace.
I still can smile, amused, when I remember
how I surprised her when I kissed her face.[37]

Pain and suffering give a new dimension to the passing of time; days grow long when the hours are filled with suffering and "time slow[s] to timeless." Likewise, spoken words are weighted differently when suffering comes "close in what was said." Eyes tend to close out sight for suffering "tortured my sight," and ears do the same for sound. In this way, pain and suffering seem to reorder all relationships with the inner and the outer world. New insights can be gleaned and owned if the speaker is willing to risk the embrace of "her grant of grace."

In regard to the spiritual life, the next component of Jessica's progressive development is concerned with the relationship between the nature of God and human nature. Having transversed this far on the spiritual journey, Jessica has gained an understanding of the glory of God and the true state of human nothingness. God takes the initiative to invite the speakers of her poetry to enter into a relationship with the divine. In answering this divine call, the speakers are forced to take a humble stance of gratitude and praise before God. The efforts of Christian theology in past times to explain the components of this relationship between the divine and human in exact language have proven futile. In the poem, "Encounter of Love," also known by the alternate title of "One Answer," which was published in 1965, Jessica does not try to explain the relationship in theories; rather, she celebrates its components in song. The poem contains a single stanza:

> Downfalls of goodness on her barren life
> brought peaks of praise. She stood on the cool
> > ledge
> of lauds and made her total melody
> effective answer. But the rains came on
> in shameless mercy and her throat went dry.
> Silence alone could wear the reverence
> that dares to worship. Once, in too much light,
> she glanced aside and saw her inch of worth,
> a mind too small, a heart too small where sky
> and trees and even soil and rubbish shone.
> Silence cried out and crumbled at her feet.
> Nothing but pain could go to meet this love.[39]

When the speaker is willing to go forth and meet God playing by God's rules, sudden and unexpected wisdom coupled with sheer delight follows the encounter. An important component of Jessica's spiritual legacy is the primacy given in her poems to this encounter and its aftermath, especially as played out in the biblical narratives and juxtaposed with her own life experience. For Jessica, Sacred Scripture contained the guidelines for this encounter with God. As the years passed, more and more she found her story contained in the Bible's sacred pages. For example, an editors' note in her book of *Selected Poetry* states that she [Jessica Powers] was baptized during Sexagesima week [on February 26, 1905]. Using this as a reflective beginning point, Jessica's poem, "Sign at Sexagesima,"[40] which was published in 1965, contain understanding of the relationship between the human and God recast in words reminiscent of the biblical narrative of Noah and the rainbow-signed covenant:

I entered the kingdom in Noah's week
at the sign of the rainbow,
out of black waters into the waters of life.
I know my place; I can find my page in the ancient
    Scripture
as all can: prefigurement, a call
to pattern and fulfillment in the new.
With love I bow, with reverence bow before
my sacramental beginnings.

My darkness was always rain and turbulent waters,
a troubled world held in a crowded place.
My light was always rest on a mountaintop
in a new christened innocence of morning
with all the world washed clean.
The earth blushing with youth, dressed herself
in flowers and leaves,
and over all the sign of the sacred rainbow,
covenant like a poem one could read
over and over again and relish meaning,
itself arched doorway and a sudden entrance
to unexpected wisdom and delight.[41]

Likewise, Jessica understood that resolute pilgrims, who risk leaving all and undertaking the search for God, were on a journey like the Old Testament figure of Abraham.[42] There are no trustworthy maps to mark out the exact route a pilgrim will follow on this journey. Faith leads the pilgrim on a way unmarked and beyond the known landmarks of the familiar world of kin and neighbor. When traveling with nothing but faith in God for a guide, the pilgrim can end up in "far and lonely" places like the human subject in the following poem, which was published in 1967:

Abraham

I love Abraham, that old weather-beaten
unwavering nomad; when God called to him,
no tender hand wedged time into his stay.
His faith erupted him into a way
far-off and strange. How many miles are there
from Ur to Haran? Where does Canaan lie,
or slow mysterious Egypt sit and wait?
How could he think his ancient thigh would bear
nations, or how consent that Isaac die,
with never an outcry nor an anguished prayer?

> I think, alas, how I manipulate
> dates and decisions, pull apart the dark,
> dally with doubts here and with counsel there,
> take out old maps and stare.
> Was there a call at all, my fears remark.
> I cry out: Abraham, old nomad you,
> are you my father? Come to me in pity.
> Mine is a far and lonely journey, too.[43]

Old and weather-beaten, this nomad has left the safe and familiar to travel the far, the strange, and the lonely road into the mysterious territory of God. The result of this restless and relentless pursuit of God is seen in the countenance of the aged traveler whose face reflects the lines of time. It would have been less trouble to opt for an early demise, to court a death wish and "pull apart the dark," rather than to run life's race to an ancient end. In playing out life to its fullest edge, two thoughts break into the speaker's consciousness. First, a wonder sparked by the forces of creativity, which has been given birth by the speaker's "ancient thigh," gives rise to the realization of the human capacity for acting as a participant in co-creation. This thought is given counterpoint by a second realization, the human capacity for giving silent and passive consent to participation in death dealing: "how consent that Isaac die, with never an outcry nor an anguished prayer?" The uselessness of trying to "manipulate dates and decisions," or trying to control and chart one's own course and path, becomes evident. Faith in an ancient promise fulfilled in a distant land is the only recourse to sustain the speaker through the daily paradoxes of life's journey. Thus, Abraham functions as a prophetic guide for the speaker.

In the final analysis, Jessica's theology is one that speaks an affirmation of life to all who have the heart to listen. She understood the effects of Pentecost in the human soul. A personal Pentecost produces singing and dancing, harbingers of faith in a God who is living and loving all humanity into grace-filled existence.[44] Published in 1967, "Only One Voice,"[45] is a poem which captures the joy of one human being's personal Pentecost:

> Only one voice,
> but it was singing
> and the words danced and as they danced
> > held high —

oh, with what grace! — their lustrous bowls of
                                                joy.
Even in dark we knew they danced, but we —
none of us — touched the hem of what would
                                        happen.
Somewhere around a whirl, swirl, a pirouette,
the bowls flew and spilled,
and we were drenched, drenched to the dry bone
in our miserable night.

Only one voice,
but morning lay awake in her bed and listened,
and then was out and racing over the hills
to hear and see.
And water and light and air and the tall trees
and people, young and old, began to hum
the catchy, catchy tune.
And everyone danced, and everyone, everything,
even the last roots of the doddering oak
believed in life.[46]

Although she was too busy with the details of monastic admini-
stration to produce her usual output of poetry during much of the sixties, these were fruitful years for Jessica. Her physical being was en-
joying the spaciousness of the Pewaukee monastery and its scenic
grounds; her spiritual being was well along in its journey inward on
the quest for God.

However, as the sixties rolled by and the seventies rolled in,
things would change. What began as a joyful embrace of life would
be thrown back into a dark night guided by a blind faith in God
alone.

For this study, six poems have been chosen to represent Jessica's thoughts and insights recorded in the seventies. During portions of this period of time, her life was filled with inner chaos and
turmoil which illustrates that, while on earth, even the mystic must
walk in faith. Recorded in chronological order, the themes of these
poems are varied. She begins the next decade of her life with this
poem published in 1970, which celebrates the wonderfulness of being
alive and in a race with all of creation towards God, as she extends
the following invitation to her readers:

Everything Rushes, Rushes

The brisk blue morning whisked in with a thought:
everything in creation rushes, rushes
toward God—tall trees, small bushes,
quick birds and fish, the beetles round as naught,

eels in the water, deer on forest floor,
what sits in trees, what burrows underground,
what wriggles to declare life must abound,
and we, the spearhead that run on before,

and lesser things to which life cannot come:
our work, our words that move toward the Unmoved,
whatever can be touched, used, handled, loved—
all, all are rushing on **ad terminum**.

So I, with eager voice and news-flushed face,
cry to those caught in comas, stupors, sleeping:
come, everything is running
        flying,
         leaping,
hurtling through time!
    And we are in this race.[47]

    The speaker in the poem above is in the midst of a glorious celebration of life. In the lines of the poem, creation is envisioned as a dynamic on-going force with humanity acting as "the spearhead" of it all. Poems like "Everything Rushes, Rushes," fulfill Jessica's heartfelt desire to awaken "those caught in comas, stupors, sleeping" amidst modern day materialism and consumerism, which spawns depression and meaninglessness. In her last years, Jessica voiced the desire "to draw people to God through her poetry."[48] Bishop Robert Morneau received a letter from Jessica written on Palm Sunday, 1987, which gives the following explanation of her motivation for writing during the last part of her life as well as the current state of affairs in her "poetry department":

> My poetry department hasn't been tended to in years and
> is in disorder: I haven't found time to straighten it out,
> nor the ambition right now. My only purpose in writing
> is that these are things I would like to say to everyone,
> especially those who are turning from God. But I do not
> know if they would find grace in any words of mine.[49]

The cause of the disorder and turmoil in her life, which became somewhat evident in the early seventies, is a matter of speculation, a guarded secret that only tentative future inquiries and investigations can unlock. Whatever compelled her to undertake her West Coast journey in 1971 also affected her writing. The jubilation chronicled in her poem "Everything Rushes, Rushes," is quietly shelved for a while. Perhaps this was the natural result of aging and sickness that dampened her spirits; or the quiet grief at the sobering thought of family and friends passing on before her; or the strain of seeing a beloved and stable world of Roman Catholicism and Carmelite cloistered life, which she had known and supported whole-heartedly for so many years, appear to crumble in the aftermath of Vatican II with its sweeping changes and radical shifts in theological perspective.

In regard to the trials of spirit brought on by sickness, Jessica's health had been precarious most of her life due to her repeated bouts of tuberculosis. She had plenty of practice in reflecting upon the meaning of life while in ill health. Published in 1970, "Siesta in Color,"[50] was written from her sick bed. In its lines, she records the ability of an ordinary experience to open up into memories of bygone days. Hence, her life is flooded with renewed meaning as she remembers the love of her Gaelic grandmother, which enables her to experience the presence of those she loves and by whom she is loved and to recall the promise of the covenant between God and humanity symbolized by the rainbow of color splashed upon her sickroom wall.

In her poem, "For a Proud Friend, Humbled,"[51] a reader seems to find an eulogy for a beloved friend who has gone before Jessica in death. Her mourning is accompanied by words that set a gentle tone: "that least place to which all mercies come"; or "on your face / only response of love lies"; or "to see you humbled into gentleness."

For a Proud Friend, Humbled

In that least place to which all mercies come
I find you now, settled in peace, at home,
poor little one of Yahweh. On your face
only response of love lies, with no trace
or drifting hint of what had brought you low.
Down steps of like unworthiness I go
weighted with heart (and how heart can oppress!)
to see you humbled into gentleness
(and into innocence) so utterly.
Pray me, my blessed, into your company.[52]

Another eulogy came from her pen in 1971. She wrote the poem, "Los Angeles Earthquake,"[53] in response to the earthquake in the San Fernando Valley on February 9, 1971, that took the lives of sixty-nine people.[54] This time the eulogy is for a beloved humanity preceding her in death, but it is linked to personal dreams that "spilled debris across my sleep, / trapped me in rubble, hemmed me in with ruin / not too unlike what San Fernando Valley yielded at sunrise." The poem begins:

> There was a mystery abroad that night.
> I, too, was restless in my bed; I turned
> and tossed. Dreams spilled debris across my
> > sleep,
> trapped me in rubble, hemmed me in with ruin
> not too unlike what San Fernando Valley
> yielded at sunrise. How could my just wrath
> fall on that restless giant lain still so long,
> shifting for arm's ease or a shoulder rest,
> soothing a muscle spasm or a foot
> asleep, or racked by some disordered dream?
>
> I wonder was he seeing what I saw:
> not too much left of time which out at sea
> was sinking and with none to rescue her?
> Or of his waking eye did he discern
> how soon the sands run out for both of us?
> Anyway, he turned over and his weight
> of bedding moved with him, and houses fell.[55]

Next, she makes the promise to her "restless giant," as she calls her "brother" on the journey, that death is not the end of life: "new earth, new heaven. See, the end is sweet." She reassures her "brother" that there is "a later rising in some glorious dawn." The poem concludes:

> If I could find him, wakeful still with pain,
> harried by dreams, discomfited by fear,
> I think that I could reassure him now:
> new earth, new heaven. See, the end is sweet.
> My brother, sleep. You'll need your whole great
> > strength
> for later rising in some glorious dawn.[56]

In an interview after her death, the Pewaukee nuns remarked that Jessica possessed a great love for the Church, the Pope, and her Carmelite community. However, some of the changes in the Church following Vatican II were hard for her. Without saying what these problematic changes were, her sisters testify that Jessica always went along in the spirit of obedience with the changes in the Church which followed Vatican II.[57] An analysis of Jessica's poems does not produce any sure evidence that aging or illness, or that the death of family and friends, or that the changes of Vatican II caused her to re-examine her life in the Pewaukee Carmel and question if God had called her there. Rather her last physical journey across the great western countryside of the United States seems to follow the ever-searching rhythm established earlier in her life. Like a pilgrim on a biblical journey, Jessica could leave no stirring unexplored and no road untraveled in her search for God. The intrinsic nature of her quest, the search for God, necessitates an inherent restlessness which acts as a driving force that always pushes its participant outward and onward beyond the seeming normal patterns of human activity.

After a while on the West Coast, Jessica appears to have come to terms with whatever the needs were that prompted her journey. Having regained her footing once again, she felt ready to take up her cloistered life in the Pewaukee Carmel with renewed fervor. As a result, the next poem, "The Mystical Sparrow,"[58] which was published in 1972, returns to a theme based on the Carmelite experience of religious life inspired by the small, mystical bird of Saint John of the Cross' *Spiritual Canticle*. The speaker of the poem reflects on John of the Cross' words: "Lost in the fathomless abyss of God"[59] and compares human life with the flight of a bird:

Distantly pure and high, a mountain sparrow
is solitary in transfigured sky.
A ball of bird melodious with God
is lightsome in its love.
Not to dear mate or comrade do I cry
but to my own remote identity
who know my spirit as divinely summoned
to gain that perch where no horizons lie.

Here is the king's secret scattered when I focus
unworthy song on one small eremite
lost in infinities of airy desert
where love is breathed out of the breast of light.

For call, for meeting-place, good end and rest
each has a symbol; each invokes a sign.
I take a bird in vastness and on height
to mark my love. It sings its jubilation
alone upon the housetop of creation
where earth's last finger touches the divine.[60]

In 1979, Jessica published another thought-provoking poem entitled, "Wanderer."[61] Inspired by a reading of Saint Hildegarde of
Bingen's *Scivias*,[62] Jessica begins her poem with the question:
"Where did I dwell?" or what is the state of the human condition
when it is not referenced to God? The answer is given: "I dwelt in
the shadow of death." Depression and meaninglessness which lead to
death are the lot of those estranged from God. The next question
asks: "Where did I walk?" or what course does a human life take if it
has no spiritual foundations? The answer to this question goes: "I
walked on the primitive pathway of error." This points to the reality
of countless lives acted out in superficial terms without ever discovering the truth of their inheritance from God. "What did I hold for
ease against my breast?" is the third question posed. The answer to
this question is: "The flimsy comfort of a wanderer / for whom there
is no rest." Compulsive desires for change and novelty, for new
faces and experiences, force the human subject to seek comfort and
forgetfulness in wandering from place to place, always searching. A
dual question ends the poem: "How did I ever come then to the
light?" and "How did I ever, blind with self, discover the small strict
pathway to this shining place[?]" This dual question can be reduced
to the terms "How is the human person saved?" Her answer to this
question is simple: God saves. No traces of a theology of works or
self-righteousness lurk in the lines of her poetry. She writes:

Where did I dwell: I dwelt in the shadow of death,
as did a mystic anciently aver.
Where did I walk? I walked on the primitive
pathway of error, was a child of earth
(and down the years my speech betrayed by birth).
What did I hold for ease against my breast?
The flimsy comfort of a wanderer
for whom there is no rest.

Two nestlings vied for life in me: I fed
the greedy one whose talent was to beg

(no one had warned me of the cowbird's egg).
I let the little one grow thin and pale
and put a blame on life that she was frail.

How did I ever come then to the light?
How did I ever, blind with self, discover
the small strict pathway to this shining place,
I who betrayed the truth over and over,
and let a tangle of dark wood surround me?
Simple the answer lies: down cliffs of pain,
through swamps and desert, thicket and terrain,
oh, Someone came and found me.[63]

At length, the seventies passed with Jessica growing older, wiser, and more settled. She gardened less and bird-watched more; she wrote less and prayed more. Reflecting on the lessons taught to her by life, she formed her final vision of God as she entered the eighties.

Of the eleven poems published in the eighties and chosen for this study, nine of them appeared in her 1984 publication, *The House at Rest*. These poems reveal several important theological insights gleaned by Jessica's thorough perseverance in pursuing her steadfast quest for God.

For Jessica, her vision of God is one of a merciful God, who triumphs over darkness and thereby saves humanity from its own "loveless embrace of folly." Her poem, "The Vision,"[64] opens with the request of an anonymous speaker who commands that the vision of her human subject be put into writing:

and I wrote what I saw.
I saw the world kissing its own darkness.[65]

The speaker in this poem rose to meet the sunrise but there was no sunrise, strained to see a path but there was no path. Fighting to go forward on the journey, the speaker encounters many obstacles:

and the long-armed brambles cried in a strident
voice:
never through here!
But I struggled on, fumbling my beads of no.[66]

Then the speaker comes to a place which holds the promise of pleasure through partaking the opium of forgetfulness. It is a city like that of Babylon described by James Weldon Johnson in "The Prodigal

Son," one of a group of black dialect sermons in verse contained in Johnson's most famous work, *God's Trombones*; or, it is a dance hall, like the one described long years ago in her poem, "Petenwell Rock," published in 1926. The poem, "The Vision," continues:

> I came to a dark city were nobody knew
> that there was darkness.
> And strange! though there was no light I still
> > could see
> What I did not want to see:
> people who moved to the loveless embrace of folly.
> They ate her gourmet foods; they drank her wine,
> danced to her music that was crazed with rhythm,
> were themselves discord though they knew it not,
> or if they knew, cared less.[69]

The longing to "court the darkness" is strong within the speaker. In the mystical encounter, the most frightening experience of evil is not to be found outside the human person but within the confines of one's own inner capacity for evil if abandoned by love's guiding force. Although gripped by temptation's "frightening urge," the speaker is constrained by fear and, like Moses, wanders out into the desert to encounter a "burning bush."[70] The poem proceeds:

> Outside the city wall I stood in thought,
> parried a moment with a frightening urge
> to court the darkness;
> but I held back, fearing the face of love.
>
> Crossing a field I wandered through a desert
> when suddenly behind a rock I found
> a little sagebrush where a fire was burning,
> shining and dancing. After my first amazed
> worship of silence I was loud with praise.
>
> I watched with fear the darkness circling it,
> lunging against it, swirling a black cloak
> to suffocate the light,
> until the shades broke loose and one by one
> in terror fled.
>
> The flame burned on, innocent, unimperiled.
> There was no darkness that could put it out.[71]

Over and over again, the speaker is forced to walk in faith as long as the feet of the body remain on mortal soil. Assured salvation is not the lot of a Christian on this spiritual journey. One year's peak experience in the spiritual life can give way to an experience of barren wilderness in the following year. For sixty years, Jessica testifies to this in her poetry. Yet, she never gives up hope, for no darkness can put out the flame.

For Jessica, the pathway to God is a never-ending one which unwinds through desert and wilderness. In the process of wandering, the speaker is instructed by the Spirit in the way of wisdom, which heightens the awareness of the hidden presence of God within the human person. Published in 1984, "This Trackless Solitude,"[72] traces the journey of the pilgrim lover led on by the Spirit in the search for God. Jessica's familiar use of "acres" in this poem refers to the inner world of the speaker. She teaches that God "is here" in the soul and that the soul is "in God." The poem reads:

> Deep in the soul the acres lie
> of virgin lands, of sacred wood
> where waits the Spirit. Each soul bears
> this trackless solitude.
>
> The voice invites, implores in vain
> the fearful and the unaware;
> but she who heeds and enters in
> finds ultimate wisdom there.
> The Spirit lights the way for her;
> bramble and brush are pushed apart.
> He lures her into wilderness
> but to rejoice her heart.
>
> Beneath the glistening foliage
> the fruit of love hangs always near,
> the one immortal fruit: **He is**
> or, tasted: **He is here**.
>
> Love leads and she surrenders to
> His will, His waylessness of grace.
> She speaks no word save His, nor moves
> until He marks the place.
>
> Hence all her paths are mystery,
> presaging a divine unknown.
> Her only light is in the creed
> that she is not alone.

The soul that wanders, Spirit led,
becomes, in His transforming shade,
the secret that she was, in God,
before the world was made.[73]

Back in 1926, Jessica had written a poem, "Cabaret,"[74] whose opening lines spoke of "a penny of love." Now, in her last years, it seems as if she is unconsciously revisiting those beginning experiences, those first awkward attempts at formulating life's questions, those first delvings into the mystery of God. The poem, "This Paltry Love," which was published in 1984, contains in its opening lines, one of her now ancient phrases, "a penny [match] of love." Suddenly the momentum of life renewed breaks and catches the simply laid opening words, "I love you, God," with a fiery breath. The time of youth is past, and the youthful dreams of glory gone, but such musings matter not to the subject of this poem who declares:

I love you, God, with a penny match of love
that I strike when the big and bullying dark of
                               need
chases my startled sunset over the hills
and in the walls of my house small terrors move.
It is the sight of this paltry love that fills
my deepest pits with seething purgatory,
that thus I love you, God—God—who would sow
my heights and depths with recklessness of glory,
who hold back light-oceans straining to spill on
                               me, on
me,
stifling here in the dungeon of my ill.
This puny spark I scorn, I who had dreamed
of fire that would race to land's end, shouting
                               your worth,
of sun that would fall to earth with a mortal
                               wound
and rise and run, streaming with light like blood,
splattering the sky,
soaking the ocean itself, and all the earth.[76]

Caught up in the mystery of human lowliness in relationship to God's glory, Jessica is not depressed by the weight of her own limitations; rather, she burns with zeal reminiscent of the words of the prophet Elijah: "I have been most zealous for the Lord, the God of hosts."[77] The peace, which she sought throughout all her life with its inner and outer journeys, comes to her in these last years rather unexpectedly. Jessica finds the inspiration to write about her passage into this peace in the poetic lines of Saint John of the Cross:

> On a dark night
> Kindled in love with yearnings—
> Oh, happy chance!—
> I went forth unobserved,
> My house being now at rest.[78]

Published in 1984, "The House at Rest"[79] chronicles this stage of her journey as she juxtaposes John's lines with imagery gleaned from her own American landscape:

> How does one hush one's house,
> each proud possessive wall, each sighing rafter,
> the rooms made restless with remembered laughter
> or wounding echoes, the permissive doors,
> the stairs that vacillate from up to down,
> windows that bring in color and event
> from countryside or town,
> oppressive ceilings and complaining floors?

> The house must first of all accept the night.
> Let it erase the walls and their display,
> impoverish the rooms till they are filled
> with humble silences; let clocks be stilled
> and all the selfish urgencies of day.

> Midnight is not the time to greet a guest.
> Caution the doors against both foes and friends,
> and try to make the windows understand
> their unimportance when the daylight ends.
> Persuade the stairs to patience, and deny
> the passages their aimless to and fro.
> Virtue it is that puts a house at rest.
> How well repaid that tenant is, how blest
> who, when the call is heard,
> is free to take his kindled heart and go.

In the opening lines of the poem, the speaker asks the question: "How does one hush one's house?" or "How does one come to possess inner peace, quiet prayer, and the presence of God?" A simple answer is not possible, so the speaker begins to construct a familiar scene as a transition point. The concreteness of the typical American dwelling place, the house with its walls, rafters, doors, stairs, windows, ceilings, floors, and rooms, functions as an allegorical framework for the inner mansions of the human spirit. The first requirement for entering into this spiritual state is not couched in terms of "doing something;" rather, this first requirement is laid out as an interior disposition, an attitude of acceptance: "The house must first of all accept the night." To facilitate this spiritual state, it is necessary to live simply: "erase the walls and their display, / impoverish the rooms"; to live in truth and silence: "with humble silences"; and to reorder time and priorities so that a paradigm shift takes place in which the speaker becomes God-centered instead of self-centered: "let clocks be stilled / and all the selfish urgencies of day."

The last stanza lays bear the most subtle of all compulsive-obsessive behavior, relationship addictions: "Midnight is not the time to greet a guest. / Caution the doors against both foes and friends."[80] In this process of spiritual development, the speaker must face squarely the fact that relationships with others must be reorientated and regrounded, not in one-sided need or want, but in celebration of gift and mutual realization of the God-centeredness of each human individual with the unique contribution that entails in relationship to the incarnation of Christ. Years are needed to persuade "stairs that vacillate from up to down" in human relationships "to patience" and not to give up the process. The breaking of old patterns, healing of the ruptures, and restoration of relationships takes a lifetime, or at least, many years for most. God dictates the timing for this process; it cannot be rushed on an artificially manufactured and controlled time scale. In the end, God will initiate the call:

> How well repaid that tenant is, how blest
> who, when the call is heard,
> is free to take his kindled heart and go.[81]

For eighty years, Jessica had been sounding to God her "yes" as an affirmation of the life which God had given to her. It had not always been easy to do so, for grief and pain had haunted her since childhood in spite of the delicate surprises and delights which life had offered along the way. In her poem, "Yes,"[82] which was published in 1984, she writes that heaven will be realized in a last neverending "yes" to God:

Yes

Yes to one   is often no to another
here walks my grief   and here has often been
my peak of anguish   yes is the one need
of my whole life   but time and time again
law forces no   up through my heart and lips
spiked leaden ball   rending as it arises
leaving its blood and pain   yes is the soft
unfolding of petals   delicate with surprises
curve and caress   and billowing delight
out to the one or many   I would guess
heaven for me   will be an infinite
flowering of one species   a measureless sheer
beatitude of yes

Jessica's deepest yearning was for God. Sometimes this is expressed as a longing for heaven as in the poem, "The Homecoming," where, like the prodigal in the gospel parable, Jessica sees herself arriving home in eternity and being welcomed royally:

By naught foretold could she have guessed
such welcome home: the robe, the ring,
music and endless banqueting
these people hers; this place of rest
known, as of long remembering
herself a child of God and pressed
with warm endearments to His breast.[84]

At the end of her own personal journey, Jessica, the aged poet, places her meager savings on the betting board of life. In the poem, "The Great Mystery,"[85] which was published in 1984, she shares with her readers a comment which she remembers as having been spoken by her uncle at funeral gathering in her childhood: "Well, he (or she) has, he would say, solved the great mystery." In response to his words, Jessica pictures herself as a child trying to reach a keyhole in the door of death to see what is on the other side. Now, as an adult, she finds:

the keyhole still too high,
though now I can surmise that it will be
light (and not darkness) that will meet the
eye.[86]

Indomitable as ever, Jessica refuses to choose anything but the promise of life, and therefore, acts as an eloquent spokesperson for a Christian faith witnessing to belief in resurrection.

Although she had never had the opportunity to be formally schooled in theology, Jessica possessed a keen and open mind. Her broad understanding of God and humanity coupled with her simplicity and realism bestows a timeless and universal quality upon her poetry. Her use of Julian of Norwich's image of God as Mother[87] in the poem, "Millet's 'Feeding Her Birds'"[88] is a good example of these characteristic qualities. Published in 1984, its closing lines read: "Or if there must be words, to speak none other / than: O my Mother God, my God and Mother."[89] This use of poetic language to depict God as Mother, which has reoccurred periodically in Jessica's poetry since the 1940s, is noteworthy and marks her as a woman in touch with threads of Christian tradition lost in the past, attuned to the mystical insights of her historicity, and simultaneously, ahead of her times.

Added to the characteristics mentioned above, there is another important element present throughout Jessica's poetry: many of her themes are biblically based. Like the writers of ancient Carmelite documents and the great Carmelite poets before her, Jessica draws her main source of reflection from the Sacred Scriptures. In the poem, "The Leftovers," which was published in 1986, scriptural references to the Old Testament, such as Elisha feeding the multitude with the twenty loaves of bread,[91] as well as the New Testament, in lines like Jesus feeding the multitude with the five small barley loaves and two dried fish,[92] are linked with a realization that even the smallest fragments of daily life are miracles of love.[93] Likewise, her poem, "The Rock Too High for Me,"[94] conjures up biblical figures of Moses, Job, and Jeremiah, and juxtaposes them with the present day plight of her human subject. In spite of God's forgiveness and love, the human subject tries to go it alone, gets discouraged, and would be totally lost without God's grace. The poem reads:

> Up toward the rock too high for me, too tall
> for my small reach, I clambered, but in vain.
> I was cast down to sober earth again.
>
> Who would believe me if I cared to tell
> that love wrought this undoing, that love's hand
> dashed me from heights, then kindly offered me
> wit to have peace in shadows where I stand?

Who would believe me if I said that grace
devised this lodging in a lowly place?

Though bathed in an immeasurable forgiveness,
a blinding love that wakes the furthest trust,
Yet I am Moses straining his eyes on Pisgah;
I am Job, stopping his mouth with ashes;
· I am Jeremiah, face in the dust.[95]

If theology is defined as the study of the nature of God and religious truth or as an organized body of opinions concerning God and
humanity's relationship to God, then Jessica is a theologian. Her
whole life was caught up in a firsthand study of the nature of God
and religious truth with her poems outliving her as an organized body
of opinions concerning God and humanity's relationship to God.

The final poem included in this study of Jessica Powers' life
and works is one of the last ones she wrote in the 24 months preceding her death in 1988. "God is Today,"[96] begins and ends in the simplest of words spoken by an aged poet, an old lady with twinkling
eyes and a smile playing around her lips, and it contains a summary
of eighty years of questioning and answering cast in these insightful
lines:

God is today.
He is not yesterday.
He is not tomorrow.

God is the dawn, wakening earth to life;
the first morning ever,
shining with infinite innocence; a revelation
older than all beginning, younger than youth.
God is the noon, blinding the eye of the mind
with the blaze of truth.
God is the sunset, casting over creation
a color of glory
as He withdraws into mysteries of night.

God is today.
He is not yesterday.
He is not tomorrow.
He never is night.

In summary, Jessica's poems dating from the 1958 to 1988 period yield a definite pattern which is characteristic of authentic spiri-

tual development. Through the means of her poetry, she confirms that the entrance into a vibrant spiritual life is gained by faithfulness to and perseverance in prayer regardless of the aridity experienced in the rhythm of daily life. She sees the mission of the Christian as one of participating in the transforming power of the Risen Christ incarnate in humanity: the door way to the divine is the human person of Jesus Christ, and whatever the mystic receives in the divine embrace is gift for all humanity. The barrier between the sacred and the secular breaks down, even the barrier of inner and outer, as dualities move to unities. A certain single-mindedness, simplicity, and wholeness evolves which allows Jessica to take the next step as she moves closer to God on this journey. This gypsy finds her match in God and her identity as a "still gypsy" emerges.

Next, Jessica explores the divinely-initiated relationship between the nature of God and human nature: the glory of God and the true state of human nothingness. In answering this call to enter into a conscious relationship with God, she is forced to take a humble stance of gratitude and praise before God. When she goes forth to meet God on God's terms, sudden and unexpected wisdom coupled with sheer delight follows the encounter. An important component of Jessica's spiritual legacy is the primacy given in her poems to this encounter and its aftermath, especially as played out in the biblical narratives which she carefully juxtaposes with her own life experiences in her poetry. For her, Sacred Scripture contained the guidelines for this encounter with God. At length, Jessica found her story contained in the Bible's sacred pages, and she understood that resolute pilgrims, who risk leaving all and undertaking the search for God, were on an uncharted journey guided by faith alone. Jessica's theology, which is based upon an affirmation of life, enables her to constantly renew her vision of a loving and merciful God. She has known a personal Pentecost and a faith in a God who is living and loving all humanity into grace-filled existence. But Jessica does not formulate her theological positions in the context colored by a continual spiritual high like a mystical Cinderella. What begins as a joyful embrace of life will be thrown back again and again into a dark night guided by blind faith in God alone. Throughout her life, Jessica dodged repeated occurrences of restlessness and inner chaos, outer turmoil and serious illness. Her life demonstrates that earthly existence is continually lived out as a journey in faith toward God.

The ever-searching rhythm established earlier in her life is mirrored in Jessica's last physical journey across the western United

States. Like a biblical pilgrim, she leaves no stirring unexplored and no road untraveled in her search for God. The "gypsy" in her is well suited to the demands of this quest's intrinsic nature, which seem to necessitate a quality of inherent restlessness capable of pushing her beyond the established confines of her earlier farm-cloistered and later monastic-cloistered world. As a result, Jessica becomes lost in the abyss of God, in a solitary life marked by the mysterious driving forces of divine love in which God is experienced as both Father and Mother, immanent and transcendent, near yet far. Ultimately, she speaks of God as a merciful God, who triumphs over darkness and saves her from the abyss with its most frightening evil, aptly described by her as the evil lurking within the confines of her own inner capacity for choosing death if abandoned by love's guiding force.

Caught in the mystery of human lowliness in relationship to God's glory, Jessica learns not to be depressed by the weight of her own limitations and capacity for turning from God. For her, the first requirement for entering into the presence of God is not couched in terms of doing something; rather, this first requirement is laid out as an interior disposition, an attitude of acceptance. She teaches that it is necessary to live simply; to live in truth and silence; and to reorder time and priorities so that a paradigm shift takes place in which God becomes center instead of self. In addition to this, Jessica addresses the most subtle of all compulsive-obsessive behavior, relationship addictions. In this process of spiritual development, she faces squarely the fact that relationships with others must be reorientated and regrounded in God.

Jessica refuses to choose anything but God's promise of life. She believes that, when the contemplative is stripped to the core of nothingness as a result of having given all to undertake the quest, God will initiate the call to enter into the fullness of divine presence. In the end, Jessica speaks of the peace, which she sought throughout her life with its inner and outer journeys, coming to her in these last years rather unexpectedly. At last, she finds herself ready to enter fully into the presence of God.

Chapter VII

Conclusion

DURING HER LIFE SPAN, JESSICA POWERS WAS HEAVILY INVOLVED IN numerous changes: rural to urban migration, prosperity to depression economics, war to post-war philosophy, and pre-Vatican II to post-Vatican spirituality. In her early writings, Jessica explored traditional Carmelite themes which eventually opened up and re-vitalized her in a later period of American life ushered in after the 1960s. Her spiritual legacy is profound enough to be in tune with the best of the classical spiritual writers who precede her, and it holds the promise of capturing the attention of a new generation of spiritual pilgrims who can identify with this American Carmelite and her "gypsy" spirit.

Jessica Powers was able to successfully integrate her spiritual and cultural heritage. Thus, her unique contribution to historical theology is a viable poetic expression of Carmelite spirituality in the historical context of the United States in the twentieth century. In her early years of writing, Jessica asked crucial and significant questions of life as she experienced it while growing up in rural Wisconsin. She asked the right questions, but they were dangerous questions for they aroused in her a spirit of wanderlust. No longer was Jessica content to remain on the farm, to settle down and raise a family, or to work in a small circle of acquaintances with limited experiences and contacts. Her life became one long search, one continual crossing of outer and inner landscapes. What were these questions which she asked of life? What was the object of her search? What method did she use to relentlessly track down and chart the working of her human experience, the inner journey and the passages of her "gypsy" spirit? And most important of all, what spiritual insights and theological positions inform her guiding legacy to later travelers on similar pilgrimages across their inner landscapes?

To begin with, the questions Jessica asked were couched in terms related to the paradoxes of life, suffering, death, and resurrection, which she experienced in her early life. Basically, these questions about the meaning of existence were laid out in her significant poems, "Petenwell Rock" and "Cabaret," both published in 1926 as initial expressions of her conversion which orientated her life toward a continual quest for God. In the poem, "Petenwell Rock," the paradox of human existence unfolds as the speaker goes through life amid dancing, laughter, lights, and music, only to be confronted in the end with anger, grief, loneliness, madness, and death. All this takes place "beneath the silver of the moon" with some elements of nature responding sympathetically and others reacting indifferently to the human plight. In the companion poem, "Cabaret," Jessica sketches a scene in which each element, both animate and inanimate, has a double meaning, a paradoxical twist. When "the black door beyond all revelry" is opened by God or the keeper of this cabaret, the speaker of the poem will be lost in meaninglessness and darkness if God is revealed in the end to be a God of death and not a God of life. A choice is given to the speaker, who sits in the cabaret of life poised on a chair that is tipped: to spend a penny cautiously from the sidelines and see what happens or to spend all one owns to participate fully in the dance of life. Jessica chooses to risk all she owns to join in this dance called life. The initial result of her choice is a series of long physical journeys which she takes across the United States, eventually from coast to coast.

In the process of her physical journeys across outer landscapes, the object of Jessica's search is translated into an inner quest for God and narrowed down by her spiritual yearnings to a desire for entrance into the presence of God. At length, she finds that her heart's desire excludes her from active engagement with a wide and wonderful world and compels her to embrace a life-time commitment to cloistered contemplation of this same beloved world. Her goal was not to fashion for herself an easy life or a life of consolations, but a life built on truth and meaning grounded in an experiential knowledge of the presence of God as mediated through the everyday circumstances of her life. For Jessica, the surest path to an awareness of the presence of God is the one leading through the ordinary events of daily life, and not one involving extraordinary phenomena.

The method, which Jessica used to relentlessly track down and chart the working of God in her life was a close reading of the experiences which she encountered daily in her own life, coupled with the diligent study of Sacred Scripture and the great Carmelite masters of the spiritual life, Teresa of Avila, John of the Cross, and Therese of Lisieux. She combined this study and reflection with a genius for using simple lyrics to describe familiar and ordinary things as she speaks about her relationship with God. As a happy by-product, she discovers that humor is a necessary ingredient for keeping her balance in this process. Jessica's genius revolves around her skill and fidelity in using the medium of poetry to chronicle the rhythms, cycles, seasons, and inner landscapes which her "gypsy" spirit encountered as she journeyed Godward. Thus, her legacy is made up of a rich portfolio of spiritual insights and theological positions gleaned throughout an active writing career of over sixty years and recorded in her poetry.

Jessica Powers' spiritual insights and theological positions contribute to the study of spirituality and theology in the modern American context. She holds that the entrance into the deeper realms of the spiritual life is gained by embracing a daily rhythm of prayer in spite of dryness and aridity. Jessica sees herself in relationship to a living God whom she encounters at the core of her being through the action of the Holy Spirit and whom she struggles to recognize in each and every person and event of her daily life. In spite of this, Jessica can write of the presence of God experienced as absence. She develops a sense of the rhythm and mysterious interaction between consoling times and desolating times as manifested in scripture and in her own life experiences. The purging action of God, which she learns to discern in times of spiritual darkness and aridity, leads her away from striving after spiritual delight and evaluating her life by its terms. This same purging action enables her to set her sights, like a compass, on God alone.

Jessica teaches that those travelers who risk going beyond the familiar guideposts of standard religious symbols cannot fail to enter into the realization of the presence of God in all creation, if they are faithful to the call of God in continuous prayer. God is not a deceiver. A sincere searcher will find the door swinging open if knocked upon, and it will be a door to life, not a door to death. The breaking down of the barrier between the sacred and the secular is part of her religious experience of her world alive with presence of a living God waiting to be discovered everywhere. As a result, Jessica is able to record mystical sightings and soundings of God in the creeping Charlie plants in her own backyard or the birds at twilight outside her window pane.

For Jessica, the doorway to the divine is the humanity of Jesus Christ. She believes that whatever she has been given by God is a gift, freely given and meant to be shared by all humanity in the mystery of Christ. Jessica does not expound any simplistic or sentimental solutions to life's questions. The contemplation of the mystery of Christ is the only solution she finds plausible. Human wisdom has not provided her with the sufficient resources to undertake her life's journey. Only the grace of a loving creator-God experienced as a living Christ Incarnate in her flesh and as Holy Spirit indwelling in her every breath gives meaning to her daily life. Having gone down too many pathways that lead to dead ends, Jessica realizes that to undertake the journey inward dependent on human strength alone is impossible; without God's grace all amounts to defeat. The stripping and suffering which she experiences is the result of her pride and trust in self rather than in God. Through all of this, Jessica becomes conscious of her own nothingness, and this realization opens the door for God to enter and restore the broken relationships in her life. Through her own personal journey from estrangement to intimacy with God, Jessica comes to the conclusion that the greatest attribute of God is mercy. Therefore, faith and trust in a loving, merciful God are necessary prerequisites for entry into the spiritual life because all comes as a free gift from God.

Jessica explores at length the relationship between the nature of God and human nature. God takes the initiative to invite her into a relationship. In order to answer this call, Jessica finds herself in a position of humility and gratitude before God. Accepting God on God's terms in the encounter of the human with the divine, releases an outpouring of wisdom and delight, a radical shift in centeredness, and a profound understanding of reality. An important component of Jessica's spiritual legacy is the primacy given in her poems to this encounter and its aftermath. For Jessica, Sacred Scripture contains the guidelines for this encounter with God, especially as played out in the biblical narratives which she carefully juxtaposes with her own life experiences in her poetry. Wherever she turned, Jessica found her story contained in the stories of the Bible's sacred pages. She understood that she was a spiritual gypsy, who risked losing all in her search for God. She discovered the necessity of being guided by faith alone since no single uniform map exists to mark out the exact route on this inward journey. Even when traveling with faith in God for a guide, a spiritual gypsy can end up in lonely places. Yet, Jessica offers a faith in an ancient promise fulfilled in God's presence beyond place and time, near yet far, as the only recourse to sustain one through the daily paradoxes of life's journey.

Lost in the abyss of God, Jessica experiences God as both Father and Mother, immanent and transcendent, near yet far. Her experience of God is not one-sided; rather, it is multi-faceted as she speaks of the Trinity, God's Fatherhood and Motherhood, Christ, and the Holy Spirit. Jessica sees herself in relationship to a living God who interacts in dynamic terms with her being through the indwelling action of the Holy Spirit.

In her poems, Jessica speaks of God as a merciful God bridging the abyss and saving her from the most terrifying darkness of all, the evil lurking within herself and beckoning her to choose death instead of the life promised to those who persevere in faith to the end. Realizing her own human limitations and capacity for turning from God's love, Jessica came to understand the weight of sin and evil, depression and human suffering. Contemplating the mystery of good and evil on a new and broader level, Jessica developed a realization of the human capacity for acting as a participant in the co-creative process and the human capacity for giving silent and passive consent to participation in death dealing. Hounded by the specter of evil raised in the inner depths of her own being, Jessica turns toward God like a homing pigeon.

In addition to this, Jessica experiences sin as negation, choosing the lie that God is death instead of life. Armed with this theological position and spiritual insight, she is capable of enticing suffering to her bedside and surprising her with a kiss. The world alive with the presence of God is a vision which allows Jessica to reject the idea of suffering, one of human existence's inherent components, as something to be feared. She learned how to accept suffering as an inescapable part of life. Consequently, she is able to explain that suffering gives a new dimension to the passing of time and reorders all relationships with the inner and outer world so that new insights can be gleaned about the relationship of the nature of God with human nature.

With her characteristic vigor and passionate longing for entry into the presence of God, Jessica chronicles her spiritual insights and charts her way as she gropes down narrow passages in her own inner landscape. In the course of time, Jessica reaffirms that her salvation does not consist in doing something on her part; rather, it consists in an interior disposition, an attitude of acceptance of God's love and grace as actively lived out in the ordinary circumstances of her daily life. She teaches that it is necessary to live simply, to live in truth and silence, and to reorder time and priorities so that a paradigm shift takes place in which God becomes center instead of self.

Furthermore, Jessica addresses the most elusive of all compulsive-obsessive behavior, relationship addictions. In this process of spiritual development, she discovers that relationships with others must be reorientated and regrounded, not in one-sided need or want, not in personal attraction or repulsion, but in celebration of gift and mutual realization of the God-centeredness of each human individual with the unique contribution that entails in relationship to the Incarnation of Christ. Years are needed to undertake this process. The breaking of old patterns, healing of the ruptures, and restoration of relationships takes many years. God dictates the timing for this process which cannot be rushed.

Repeatedly, Jessica focuses her energy on choosing God's promise of life. She believes that, when the contemplative is stripped to the core of nothingness as a result of having given all to undertake the quest, God will initiate the call to enter into the fullness of divine presence. In the end, Jessica speaks of the peace, which she sought throughout all her life with its inner and outer journeys, coming to her unexpectedly in her last years.

Jessica believes that listening in silence ushers in the final stages of Christian transformation. She teaches that these final stages are marked by a profound peace which fills the human listener who learns to balance and integrate the outer landscape with the Elijan call to traverse the inner landscape. In doing so, Jessica acts as a listener and as a spiritual guide for contemplatives journeying through the modern American landscape.

The spiritual legacy of Jessica Powers, an indomitable "gypsy" for eighty-three years, is rich because her poetry documents the repeated rhythms and recurrent cycles of spiritual aridity and spiritual consolation experienced by human beings bound by the limitations of earthly existence while engaged in an authentic relationship with a living and loving God. Jessica Powers has influenced a wide audience of American Catholic and non-Catholic readers on a popular level in newspapers, magazines, and other periodicals for over sixty years. Through her writings, Americans have been introduced to biblical and Carmelite themes set in a language and context which they could identify and integrate into their own personal lives. In this way, the writings of Jessica Powers have influenced the formation of American spirituality in the twentieth-century, and as she wished, her poetry has been used by others in their search for God. The tracks of this mystic have endured.

Bibliography

I. Primary Sources

Books:

Powers, Jessica. *The Lantern Burns.* New York: Monastine, 1939.

_____. *The Place of Splendor.* New York: Cosmopolitan Science and Art Service, 1946.

_____. *The Little Alphabet.* Printed privately, 1955.

_____. *Mountain Sparrow.* Reno, Nevada: Published by Carmel of Reno, 1972.

_____. *Journey to Bethlehem.* Printed privately, 1980.

_____. *The House at Rest.* Privately printed, 1984.

_____. *Selected Poetry of Jessica Powers.* Edited by Regina Siegfried and Robert Morneau. Kansas City, Mo.: Sheed & Ward, 1989.

II. Italian Sources

Powers, Jessica. "Poesie: Il medicante; Fortitudo et Decor; Il pensiero della morte; Promessa di gioia; E bello il nostro tempo." Traduzione e inedite di Margherita Guidacci. *Città di Vitta* 25 (Firenze 1970): 581-85.

_____. "Poesie." Traduzione e introduzione di Margherita Guidacci. *Città di Vitta* 35 (Firenze 1980): 31-38.

_____. *Luogo di splendore: Poesie.* Traduzione di Margherita Guidacci, illustrazioni di Fausta Beer. Città del Vaticano: Libreria Editrice Vaticana, 1983.

III. Secondary Sources

Andersen, Joy, gen. ed. *American Catholic Who's Who 1978.* Vol. 22. Washington, D.C.: National Catholic News Service/A Division of the U.S. Catholic Conference, 1978. S.v. "Powers, Jessica."

Baldwin, S. M. Luke. "Burns the Great Lantern." *Catholic World* 168 (February 1949): 354-61.

_____. "Wisconsin Poet Integrates Rural Upbringing, City Life, Monastery." *(LaCrosse, WI) Times Review*, 2 January 1986, 8-9.

Berlingeri, Francesca. "Una nuova voce poetica dal Carmelo: Jessica Powers." *Humanitas* 7 (Luglio 1958): 536-42.

Boudreau, Richard. "A Meadow Moreover: The Wisconsin Poems of Jessica Powers." In *Jessica Powers Symposium: Proceedings of the Symposium in Milwaukee, Wisconsin, August 26, 1989*, by Marquette University, 1989, 8-13.

Brunini, John. "Of Love and Peace." *Spirit* 14 (1947): 57.

The Discalced Carmelite Nuns of the Association of Mary, Queen of Carmel. *Carmel in the United States, 1790-1990)*. Eugene, Oregon: Queen's Press, 1990.

"Father Danihy's Poetry Class Student Has Book Published." Newspaper clipping taken from Jessica Powers Collection (Box 7: Scrapbook), Department of Special Collections and University Archives, Main Library, Marquette University, Milwaukee, WI.

Flanagan, Mary Jo. "Jessica Powers: Contemplative, Carmelite, Poet." *(Milwaukee) Catholic Herald*, 29 December 1983, 1.

"Friends Crowd Small Chapel For Investiture At Carmel." *(Milwaukee) Catholic Herald Citizen*, 2 May 1942.

Garza, Melita Marie. "Nun's Collected Poems Resurrected Since Death." *Milwaukee Journal*, 5 August 1989, 4 (A).

Geigel, Winifred F. "A Comparative Study of the Poetry of Jessica Powers and St. John of the Cross." Unpublished thesis, St. John University, 1960.

Grace, William and John O'Connor. "Literary Cavalcade: Presenting Jessica Powers." *Tablet*, 7 June 1941.

Hopkins, J. G. E. "A Modern Poet with a Medieval Ideal." *America* 61 (September 2, 1939): 498-99.

Kavanaugh, Kieran. "Jessica Powers in the Tradition of St. John of the Cross: Carmelite and Poet." *Spiritual Life* 36 (Fall 1990): 161-76.

_____. "Jessica Powers in the Tradition of St. John of the Cross: Carmelite and Poet." In *Jessica Powers Symposium: Proceedings of the Symposium in Milwaukee, Wisconsin, August 26, 1989*, by Marquette University, 1989, 26-33.

Kiley, Paul J. "Bright Dream: Jessica Powers' *The Lantern Burns*." *Magnificat* 68 (June 1941): 75-79.

K. L. "The Lantern Burns." *The Protestant Digest* 3 (1940): 346-48.

"Lake Site Is Donated for Nuns' Community." [Unspecified newspaper clipping], 6 December 1956, 10. Newspaper clipping taken from the Jessica Powers Collection (Box 3: Folder 3), Department of Special Collections and University Archives, Main Library, Marquette University, Milwaukee, WI.

"Laube Lauds Woman Poet: Spare-Time Publisher Produces Second Volume." *New York Times Book Review*, 8 October 1939.

Leckey, Dolores. "Jessica Powers: Out of Silence, Music." *Commonweal* 15 (September 1988): 485.

————. "Jessica Powers: Notes on a Poet's Life." In *Jessica Powers Symposium: Proceedings of the Symposium in Milwaukee, Wisconsin, August 26, 1989*, by Marquette University, 1989, 1-7.

————. "Notes on a Poet's Life." *Spiritual Life* 36 (Fall 1990): 137-49.

Mary Francis. "Poetry and the Contemplative." *Spirit* 22 (1955): 83-86.

Mary Immaculata, C.S.J. "The Lantern Burns." *Magnificant* 72 (1940): 121-22.

Mary Joseph of Divine Providence. "But God Is Singing!" *Spiritual Life* 36 (Fall 1990): 132-36.

Mary Therese, Sor.D.S. "Jessica Takes the Veil." *Magnificat* 81 (1949): 168.

Mary Timothy, S.S.N.D. "The Silent Poet." *Spirit* 27 (May 1960): 52-57.

McDonnell, Thomas P. "The Nun As Poet." *Spirit* 26 (March 1959): 20-26.

McGarty, Bernard. "An Emily Dickinson From Juneau County." *Carmelite Digest* 4 (Summer 1989): 13-15.

————. "An Emily Dickinson From Juneau County." *(Milwaukee) Times Review*, 1 September 1988, 8.

————. "Powers, Like Emily Dickinson, Seeks Life's Inner Meaning." *(LaCrosse, WI) Times Review,* 2 January 1986, 9.

————. "Various Poets Have Influenced Powers." *(LaCrosse, WI) Times Review*, 2 January 1986, 8.

Miller, Marilynn. "Jessica Powers." *Mount Mary Quarterly* 17 (March 1941): 7-13.

"Miss Powers, Poet, to Take Order's Vows." *Milwaukee Journal*, 9 August 1946.

Morneau, Robert F. "Come Is the Love Song." *Emmanuel* 91 (December 1985): 546-51.

————. "Contemplation and Poetry: Jessica Powers." In *Carmel 200—Contemplation and the Rediscovery of the American Soul: Proceedings of the Carmelite Bicentennial Symposium in Baltimore, Maryland, August 12-18, 1990,* by the Carmelites of the Ancient Observance, the Carmelite Communities Associated, and by the Discalced Carmelite Friars, 1990. Photocopied.

————. "An Experience of God: Reflections of a Poet's Journey." *Emmanuel* 93 (November 1987): 486-93.

————. "The Garments of God." *Emmanuel* 92 (June 1986): 264-267/287.

————. Introduction to *Selected Poetry* by Jessica Powers. Kansas City, MO: Sheed & Ward, 1989.

————. "Jessica Powers: Landscapes of the Sacred." Summer Seminar on Carmelite Spirituality: Proceedings of the Seminar in Notre Dame, Indiana, June 16-28, 1991, by The Center for Spirituality of Saint Mary's College, 1991. Photocopied.

————. *Jessica Powers: Mantras from a Poet.* Kansas City, Mo.: Sheed & Ward, 1991.

————. "Poetry and Health." *Vision* 2 (January-February 1992): 3.

————. "A Refugee God." *Emmanuel* 92 (December 1986).

————. "The Spirituality of Jessica Powers." *Spiritual Life* 36 (Fall 1990): 150-60.

————. "The Spirituality of Jessica Powers." In *Jessica Powers Symposium: Proceedings of the Symposium in Milwaukee, Wisconsin, August 26, 1989,* by Marquette University, 1989, 14-19.

————. *Theologicans and Poets.* A Dialogue by Bishop Robert F. Morneau. Credence Cassettes AA9127. Kansas City, MO, 1988.

New Catholic Encyclopedia. 1966 ed. S.v. "Religious Orders, Literary Influence of Carmelites," by Wilhelm Grenzmann.

Noonan, James E. "Your Parish—Lyndon Station: St. Mary's & Irish Settlers." Newspaper clipping taken from Jessica Powers Collection (Box 10: Folder 13), Department of Special Collections and University Archives, Main Library, Marquette University, Milwaukee, WI.

Nuns of the Pewaukee Carmel, WI. "Sister Miriam of the Holy Spirit, OCD." *Carmelite Digest* 4 (Summer 1989): 8-12.

O'Hearn, Catherine. "Of Interest to Women." *Torch* (February 1940): [no pp.]. Taken from Papers in the Jessica Powers Collection (Box 7, Scrapbooks), Department of Special Collections and University Archives, Main Library, Marquette University, Milwaukee, WI.

Payne, Steven. "Editoral." *Spiritual Life* 36 (Fall 1990): 130-31.

"Plans Are Made to Publish Works of Local Poet." *Mauston (Wisconsin) Juneau Co. Chronicle*, 17 March 1939.

"Poet Will Publish Verses of a Former Milwaukeen." *Milwaukee Journal*, March 1939.

Schaeverling, Margaret. "Sister Miriam of the Holy Spirit." *Magnificat* 83 (February 1949): 169-72.

Scully, Doris Trainer. "Family History: Pewaukee." Papers donated on 26 August 1989 to the Jessica Powers Collection (Box 3: Folder 5), Department of Special Collections and University Archives, Main Library, Marquette University, Milwaukee, Wisconsin.

"Services Set For Pegis, 72, Ex-Pro at MU." *(Milwaukee)*, 1978. Unspecified and undated newspaper clipping taken from Jessica Powers Collection (Box 10: Folder 3), AMU.

Siegfried, Regina. "Jessica Powers: The Paradox of Light and Dark." *Studia Mystica* 7 (Spring 1984): 28-45.

_____. "Write Me Down As A Small Adjective Attending Light, The Archangelic Noun." In *Jessica Powers Symposium: Proceedings of the Symposium in Milwaukee, Wisconsin, August 26, 1989,* by Marquette University, 1989, 20-25.

_____. "Write Me Down The Archangelic Noun: The Brightening Words of Emily Dickinson and Jessica Powers." St. Louis, Mo.: Aquinas Institute of Theology Lecture Series on Spirituality and the Arts, 27 September 1991. Photocopied.

Shufletavski, Dorothy. "Fosterling of Night." *Labarum* (Clarke College of Dubuque, Iowa, 1945): 252.

"So He Printed His Own Lines: Clifford Laube Then Found He Was a Publisher Too." *New York Sun*, 9 March 1939.

"The Story of Jessica Powers and Her Search for Happiness." *(Milwaukee) Catholic Herald Citizen,* 1942, 41-42.

Tracy, Carroll. "Juneau County and the World: The Small Account." *Mauston (Wisconsin) Star,* 8 August 1958, 3.

Weakland, Rembert. "Homily on Trinity Sunday Delivered by the Archbishop of Milwaukee." Milwaukee, Wisconsin, 17 June 1984. Photocopied.

_____. "A Spiritual Journey," *Wisconsin: Milwaukee Journal Magazine* (Milwaukee), 15 April 1990.

"Wisconsin Poet Enters Carmel Here." *(Milwaukee) Catholic Herald Citizen*, 18 April 1942.

IV. Interviews

Jagoe, Bede. Director of Campus Ministry at Saint Louis University. Interview by author, 4 October 1991, tape recording, St. Louis, Missouri.

Leckey, Dolores. Executive director of the Secretariat on Laity and Family Life for the National Conference of Catholic Bishops in Washington, D.C. and biographer of Jessica Powers. Interview by author, 1 November 1991, telephone conversation, Washington, D.C.

Sister Miriam of the Holy Spirit (Jessica Powers). Interview by Sister Regina Siegfried, RSM and Bishop Robert Morneau of Green Bay, WI, 1987. Transcripts of tape in the Jessica Powers Collection, Department of Special Collections and University Archives, Main Library, Marquette University, Milwaukee, Wisconsin. AMU.

Ranallo, Bernadette and Mary Joyce King, members of the Carmelite Monastery of the Mother of God in Pewaukee, Wisconsin. Interview by author, 23 October 1991, Pewaukee, Wisconsin.

Womack, Carmen, member of the Carmelite Monastery of Saint Joseph in Piedmont (Oklahoma City), Oklahoma. Interview by author, 10 January 1992, telephone conversation, Oklahoma City, Oklahoma.

V. Book Reviews

Reviews of *The Lantern Burns:*

Barret, Alfred, in *Messenger of the Sacred Heart* 75 (1940): 107-8.

_____, in *Thought* 15 (September 1940): 530-31.

Binsse, Harry, in *Commonweal* 32 (May 1940): 107-108.

Boggs, Tom, in *The Forum* (September 1939).

Catholic Worker (May 1940).

Feeney, Leonard, in *America* 63 (May 1940): 192.

Kolars, Mary, in *Spirit* 6 (November 1939): 152-53.

New York Times Review (22 October 1939).

O'Hearn, Catherine, in *Torch* (February 1940).

Reilly, Joseph, in *The Catholic World* 151 (May 1940): 252.

Salesianum [This book review, written by J.J.B., is taken from the Official Bulletin of the Alumni Association of St. Francis Seminary, Published quarterly by The Salesianum Publishing Co., St. Francis, Wisconsin, n.d.: [no page given]. A copy of it can be found in the Jessica Powers Collection (Box 7, Scrapbook), Department of Special Collections and University Archives, Main Library, Marquette University, Milwaukee, WI.]

Sign 19 (December 1939): 312-13.

Reviews of *The Place of Splendor:*

Brunini, John G., in *Spirit* 14 (May 1947): 57-59.

Freemantle, Anne, in *Commonweal* 46 (July 1947): 361.

Hughes, Josephine N., in *America* 77 (August 1947): 584.

Laube, Clifford J., in *Thought* 22 (June 1947): 246-48.

Sign 26 (July 1947): 57.

Reviews of *The House at Rest:*

Howell, Olga M., in *St. Anthony Messenger* (June 1987).

Morneau, Robert F., in *Emmanuel* 92 (December 1985): 591-92.

Reviews of *Mountain Sparrow:*

Stone, John Colm, in *Spiritual Life* 19 (Winter 1973): 276.

Reviews of *Selected Poetry of Jessica Powers:*

Fischer, Philip C., in *Review for Religious* 50 (May/June 1991): 465.

Shah, Bernard, in *Carmelus: Commentarii ab Instituto Carmelitano Editi* 38 (Rome, 1991): 268-69.

VI. Carmelite Publications (Privately Printed)

A. From *Encounter: An Inter-Monastery Quarterly of the Discalced Nuns of the United States.* Oklahoma City, OK: Privately printed, 1971-76.

Madden, Marie Celeste. "Mountain Sparrow: A Community Experience in Work and Play." *Encounter* 8 (Winter 1973): 39-41.

Powers, Miriam. "The One Who Hears." *Encounter* 9 (Autumn 1974): 2-3.

"Meeting of Father Finian OCD with 57 U.S. Carmels, 5-9 October 1974." *Encounter* 10 (Spring 1975): 67.

"Meetings of Contemplative Nuns with Most Rev. Augustine Mayer, Secretary of the Sacred Congregation for Religious and Secular Institutes." *Encounter* 11 (Summer 1976): 45-59.

B. From *Mary: Aylesford Carmelite Newsletter* (Winter 1988-89): 3. Death notice of Sister Miriam Powers.

C. From *Pewaukee Carmel:*

"Christmas Letter." 1988.

"Christmas Letter." 1989.

"Circular Letter for Sister Miriam." Customary notice of the events surrounding the life of a nun circulated throughout Discalced Carmelite communities at the time of death.

D. From *The Queen's Inter Com: Newsletter of the Association of Mary Queen of Carmel:* (pages concerning Jessica Powers)

Vol. 7, no. 1 (Summer 1986): 8.   Pewaukee Carmel
            2 (Autumn 1986): 9.
            3 (Winter 1986-87): 8.
Vol. 8, no. 1 (Summer 1987): 10.
            2 (Autumn 1987): 15.
            3 (Winter 1987-88): 9.   Piedmont Carmel
            "   "   "   "   8.   Pewaukee Carmel
            4 (Spring 1988): 6.
Vol. 9, no. 1 (Summer 1988): 6
            2 (Autumn 1988): 9.   Miriam's death
            3 (Winter 1988-89): 9.
            4 (Spring 1989): 10.
Vol. 10, no. 1 (Summer 1989): 9.
            2 (Autumn 1989): 11.

VII. Anthologies

Adventures in American Literature. Cardinal Newman Edition. Chicago: Harcourt, Brace, 1954.

From One Word. Selected Poems from *Spirit* (1944-49). Edited by John G. Brunini. NY: Davin-Adair, 1950.

Joyce Kilmer's Anthology of Catholic Poets. Edited by James Tobin. Garden City, NY: Image Books, 1953.

Poetry Out of Wisconsin. Edited by August Derleth and Raymond E. F. Larsson. NY: Henry Harrison, 1937.

Sealed Unto The Day. Selected Poems from *Spirit* (1944-49). Edited by John G. Brunini. NY: Devin-Adair, 1950.

The Second America Book of Verse (1930-1955). NY: America Press, 1955.

VIII. Related Literature

A. Carmelite Studies and Christian Monasticism:

Abel, Felix Marie. *Histoire de la Palestine.* Paris: J. Gabalda, 1952.

Albert of Jerusalem. "The Rule of Saint Albert." The Latin text with an English Translation by Bede Edwards. In *The Rule of Saint Albert,* ed. Hugh Clarke and Bede Edwards, 73-93. Aylesford & Keningston: Carmelite Book Service, 1973.

Anne of St. Bartholomew. *Autobiography of the Blessed Mother Anne of St. Bartholomew*. Edited by Marcel Bouix. Translated by a Religious of the Carmel of St. Louis. St. Louis, Mo.: Privately printed, 1916. ·

Ballestrero, Anastasius. *The Spirit of the Rule of Carmel*. Buffalo, NY: Carmelite Press, 1963.

Balthasar, Hans Urs von. *Therese of Lisieux: The Story of a Mission*. Translated by Donald Nicholl. NY: Sheed & Ward, 1954.

Bielecki, Tessa. "Bridal Mysticism." In *Speaking of Silence: Christian and Buddhists on the Contemplative Way*, ed. Susan Walker, 38-47. NY: Paulist, 1987.

Bird, T. "Saint Theresa and the Scriptures." In *Christian Simplicity in Saint Therese:The Place of Saint Therese of Lisieux in Christian Spirituality*, ed. Michael Day, 123-33. Westminster, Maryland: Newman, 1953.

Buckley, Michael. "Perpetual Inspiration for Carmelites: The Rule of St. Albert." *Carmelite Digest* (Winter 1988): 47-58.

Carmel of the Mother of God. Edited by Discalced Carmelite Nuns [of Milwaukee, WI]. Milwaukee, WI: Privately printed, 1942.

Carmelite Directory of the Spiritual Life. Translated from the Latin. Chicago, Illinois: The Carmelite Press, 1951.

Carmelite Nun. *The Nun's Answer*. Chicago: Henry Regnery, 1958.

Chitty, Derwas J. *The Desert a City: An Introduction to the Study of Egyptian and Palestinian Monasticism Under the Christian Empire*. Oxford: Blackwell, 1966.

Cicconetti, Carlo. *The Rule of Carmel: An Abridgement*. Translated by Gabriel Pausback. Edited and abridged by Paul Hoban. Darien, Illinois: Carmelite Spiritual Center, 1984.

Cousin, Patrice. *Précis d'histoire monastique*. Belgium & Paris: Bloud & Gay, 1956.

Currier, Charles Warren. *Carmel in America: A Centennial History of the Discalced Carmelites in the U.S.* Darien, Illinois: Carmelite Press, 1989.

Day, Dorothy. *Therese*. Springfield, Illinois: Templegate, 1979.

Deeney, Aloysius. "The History of the Carmelite Rule." Oklahoma City, OK: Villa Teresa Lecture Series, 9 November 1991. Tape recording.

Dickens, C. W. Trueman. "Teresa of Avila and John of the Cross." In *The Study of Spirituality*, ed. Cheslyn Jones, Geoffrey Wainwrght, and Edward Yarnold, 363-376. NY: Oxford University, 1986.

Discalced Carmelite Nuns of the Association of Mary, Queen of Carmel. *Carmel in the United States of America (1790-1990)*. Eugene, Oregon: Queen's Press, 1990.

Discalced Carmelites of Boston & Santa Clara. *Carmel: Its History, Spirit, and Saints*. New York: Kenedy & Sons, 1927.

Doyle, Sharon. "Carmelite Spirituality." In *Spiritual Life Institute's NADA Network: Connecting Monastery and Marketplace* 9 (July-August 1989): 1-2.

Edwards, Bede. "Introduction to the Rule of Saint Albert." In *The Rule of Saint Albert*, ed. Hugh Clarke and Bede Edwards, 11-41. Aylesford & Keningston: Carmelite Book Service, 1973.

Egan, Harvey D. *What Are They Saying About Mysticism?* New York, NY: Paulist, 1982.

FitzGerald, Constance. *Carmelite Adventure: Clare Joseph Dickinson's Journal of Trip to America and Other Documents*. Baltimore, MD: Carmelite Sisters, 1990.

Fitzgerald, Hubert. "History of the Order from the Reformation to the Present Time." In *Carmel's History: Proceedings of the Fourth Regional Third Order Congress Southwestern Province Held in San Antonio, Texas 3-5 October 1958*, 20-39. N.p.: Privately printed, 1958.

Friedman, Elias. *The Latin Hermits of Mount Carmel: A Study in Carmelite Origins*. Rome: Teresianum, 1979.

Gorres, Ida F. *The Hidden Face: A Study of St. Therese of Lisieux*. Translated by Richard and Clara Winston. NY: Pantheon, 1959.

Hardman, Anne. *English Carmelites in Penal Times*. London: Burns Oates and Washbourne, 1936.

_____. *Life of the Venerable Anne of Jesus: Companion of St. Teresa of Avila*. With a Preface by Father Benedict Zimmerman. St. Louis, MO: Herder, 1932.

Healy, Augustine. "Primitive Rule of Our Lady of Mount Carmel." In *Carmel's History: Proceedings of the Fourth Regional Third Order Congress Southwestern Province Held in San Antonio, Texas, 3-5 October 1958*, 14-19. N.p.: Privately printed, 1958.

Healey, Kilian. "The Carmelite Rule After Vatican II." *Ascent* 2 (1970): 51-67.

Hellwig, Monkia. "St. Teresa's Instpiration for Our Times." In *Centenary of St. Teresa: Catholic University Symposium, 15-17 October 1982*, ed. John Sullivan, 212-24. Carmelite Studies, no. 3. Washington, D.C.: Institute of Carmelite Studies, 1984.

Hendrix, Rudolf. "The Original Inspiration of the Carmelite Order as Expressed in the Rule of Saint Albert." In *The Rule of Saint Albert*, ed. Hugh Clarke and Bede Edwards, 67-72. Aylesford & Keningston: Carmelite Book Service, 1973.

Hennesey, James. "Several Youths Sent From Here: Native-Born Priests and Religious of English America, 1634-1776." In *Studies in Catholic History in Honor of John Tracy Ellis*, ed. Nelson H. Minnich, Robert B. Eno, and Robert F. Trisco, 1-26. Wilmington, Delaware: Michael Glazier, 1985.

Hoffman, Joseph. "From Hermits to Friars: Carmelite Renewal in the Middle Ages." *Carmelite Digest* (Winter 1988): 33-38.

Hostie, Raymond. *Vie et mort des ordres religieux: Approches psychosociologiques*. Bibliothèque d'études psycho-religieuses. Paris: Desclée de Brouwer, 1972.

Jamart, Francois. *The Spirit and Prayer of Carmel*. Translated by E.J. Ross. Westminster, MD: Newman, 1951.

John of the Cross. *The Collected Works of St. John of the Cross*. Translated by Kieran Kavanaugh and Otilio Rodiguez. Washington, D.C.: Institute of Carmelite Studies, 1979.

_____. *The Complete Works of Saint John of the Cross*. Translated by E. Allison Perrs from the critical Spanish edition by P. Silverio de Santa Teresa. Vol. 1, *General Introduction, Ascent of Mount Carmel, and Dark Night of the Soul*. Vol. 2, *Spiritual Canticle, Poems*. Vol. 3, *Living Flame of Love, Cautions and Counsels, Spiritual Sentences and Maxims, Letters and Documents, and Indices*. Westminster, MD: Newman Press, 1935; reprint, 1959.

_____. *Living Flame of Love*. Translated and edited by E. Allison Peers from the critical Spanish edition by P. Silverio de Santa Teresa. Garden City, NY: Image Books, 1962.

_____. *Spiritual Canticle*. Translated and edited by E. Allison Peers from the critical Spanish edition by P. Silverio de Santa Teresa. Garden City, NY: Image Books, 1961.

Kelley, Laurence. *A Carmelite Shrine in Maryland*. N.p.: Privately printed, 1957.

Latimer, Christopher. "The Prayer of St. Teresa Today." *Spiritual Life* (Spring 1968): 91-97.

Leroy, Jules. *Moines et monastères du Proche-Orient*. Paris: Horizons de France, 1958.

"The Liturgy as the Source and the Summit of Carmelite Life." Papers from Secretariatus Pro Monialibus, X:1-19. Roma: Curia Generalis O.C.D., 1971.

Madden, Richard. *Men in Sandals*. Milwaukee: Bruce, 1954.

Martin, Rose L. *Elizabeth: The Story of a Nun*. New York: Twin Circle, 1968.

Merton, Thomas. "Carmelite Sanctity." *Ascent* 2 (1969): 39-44.

Murphy, Roland E. "The Figure of Elijah in the Old Testament." *Ascent* 1 (1969): 8.-15.

New Catholic Encyclopedia. 1966 ed. S.v. "Carmelite Nuns, Discalced," by Peter Thomas Rohrbach.

_____. S.v. "Spirituality," by Kieran Kavanaugh.

Paschal of the Blessed Sacrament. "Saint Elias, Prophet and Father of Carmel." In *Carmel's History: Proceedings of the Fourth Regional Third Order Congress Southwestern Provice Held in San Antonio, Texas, 3-5 October 1958*, 1-7.

Rodriguez, Otilio. *A History of the Teresian Carmel: An Abridgement of Its Origins and Development 1562-1979*. Lectures given first to Carmelite Fathers in the "Courses of Renewal" on Mount Carmel (1976-1977) and later to some of the communities of Carmelite Sisters in the U.S.A. Printed at Darlington Carmel and circulated privately.

Rohrbach, Peter Thomas. *Journey to Carith: The Story of the Carmelite Order*. Garden City, NY: Doubleday, 1966.

Sachse, Carol. Introduction to *Charter of Life: A Contemporary Statement of Teresian Charism* by Carmelite Communities Associated. Reno, Nevada: Carmelite Press, 1979.

Saggi, Louis and Valentine Macca. *Saints of Carmel: A Compilation from Various Dictionaries*. Translated by Gabriel N. Pausback. Rome: Carmelite Institute, 1972.

Sheppard, Lancelot. *The English Carmelites*. London: Burns Oates, 1943.

_____. *Barbe Acarie: Wife and Mystic*. NY: David McKay, 1953.

Smet, Joachim. *The Carmelites: A History of the Brothers of Our Lady of Mount Carmel*. 4 vols. Darien, Illinois: Carmelite Spiritual Center, 1975-1985.

This is an important source for Carmelite history in the Medieval period. After the sixteenth-century, the work deals with the history of the Calced Carmelite Order and not the Discalced Order. In addition, there is a noteworthy section on Calced Carmelite history and spirituality and in the United States in Vol. 4, *The Modern Period, 1750-1950*. Darien, Illinois: Carmelite Spiritual Center, 1985.

_____. *Cloistered Carmel: A Brief History of the Carmelite Nuns*. Rome: Institutum Carmelitanum, 1986.

Stratton, Robin. *The Carmelite Sisters of Baltimore and the Education of Young Ladies (1831-1851)*. Baltimore, Maryland: Privately printed, n.d.

Teresa of Avila. *The Collected Works of St. Teresa of Avila*. Vol. 1, *The Book of Her Life, Spiritual Testamonies, and Soliloquies*. Translated by Kieran Kavanaugh and Otilio Rodriguez. Washington, D.C.: Institute of Carmelite Studies, 1976.

_____. *The Collected Works of St. Teresa of Avila*. Vol. 2, *The Way of Perfection, Meditation on the Song of Songs, and The Interior Castle*. Translated by Otilio Rodriguez and Kieran Kavanaugh. Washington, D.C.: Institute of Carmelite Studies, 1980.

_____. *The Collected Works of St. Teresa of Avila*. Vol. 3, *The Book of Her Foundations and Minor Works: The Constitutions, On Making the Visitation, A Stairical Critique, Response to a Spiritual Challenge, and Poetry*. Translated by Kieran Kavanaugh. Washington, D.C.: Institute of Carmelite Studies, 1985.

Therese of Lisieux. *Her Last Conversations*. Translated by John Clarke. Washington, D.C.: Institute of Carmelite Studies, 1977.

_____. *Letters of St. Therese of Lisieux: General Correspondence (1980-1897)*. Translated by John Clarke. Vol. 2, *General Correspondence (1890-1897)*. Washington, D.C.: Institute of Carmelite Studies, 1988.

_____. *Story of a Soul: The Autobiography of St. Therese of Lisieux*. Translated by John Clarke. Washington, D.C.: Institute of Carmelite Studies, 1975.

Thomas, Catherine. *The Story of a Carmelite Nun*. Garden City, NY: Image Books, 1959.

Valabek, Redemptus M. *Prayer Life in Carmel: Historical Sketches*. Rome: Institutum Carmelitanum, 1982.

Wilderink, Vitalis. "The First Carmelite Sisters." *Ascent* 2 (1969): 77-86.

Williams, Michael. *High Romance*. NY: MacMillian, 1951.

_____. *The Little Flower of Carmel*. NY: Kenedy & Sons, 1925.

B. American Catholicism and Religious History:

Blantz, Thomas. "George N. Shuster and American Catholic Intellectual Life." In *Studies in Catholic History: In Honor of John Tracy Ellis*, ed. Nelson H. Minnich, Robert B. Eno, and Roberst F. Trisco, 345-66. Wilmington, Delaware: Michael Glazier, 1985.

Blied, Benjamin J. *The Catholic Story of Wisconsin.* Milwaukee: Family Friend, 1948.

_____. *Three Archbishops of Milwaukee: Michael Heiss (1818-1890), Frederick Katzer (1844-193), Sebastian Messmer (1847-1930).* Milwaukee, Wisconsin: n.p., 1955.

Chinnici, Joseph P. "The History of Spirituality and the Catholic Community in the United States: An Agenda for the Future." In *Studies in Catholic History: In Honor of John Tracy Ellis,* ed. Nelson H. Minnich, Robert B. Eno, and Robert F. Trisco, 392-416.

_____. *Living Stones: The History and Structure of Catholic Spiritual Life in the United States.* The Bicentennial History of the Catholic Church in America Authorized by the National Conference of Catholic Bishops, gen. ed. Christopher Kauffman. NY: Macmillian, 1989.

Clements, Robert B. "Michael Williams and the Founding of *The Commonwealth,*" *Records of the American Catholic Historical Society* 84 (1974): 163-173, as found in *Modern American Catholicism (1900-1964),* ed. Edward Kantowicz, 137-147. New York: Garland, 1988.

Dolan, Jay P. *The American Catholic Experience: A History from Colonial Times to the Present.* Garden City, NY: Image Books, 1985.

Eliade, Mircea, ed. *The Encyclopedia of Religion.* New York: MacMillan, 1987. S.v. "Gurdjieff, G. I.," by Michel de Salzmann.

Ellis, John T. *American Catholicism.* 2d revised ed. Chicago History of American Civilization, ed. Daniel J. Boorstin. Chicago: University of Chicago, 1969.

Fogarty, Gerald. "American Catholic Approaches to the Sacred Scripture." In *Studies in Catholic History: In Homor of John Tracy Ellis,* ed. Nelson H. Minnick, Robert B. Eno, and Robert F. Trisco, 91-126. Wilmington, Delaware: Michael Glazier, 1985.

_____. *American Catholic Biblical Scholarship: A History from the Early Republic to Vatican II.* Forward by Roland E. Murphy. San Francisco: Harper & Row, 1989.

Franklin, R. William, and Robert L. Spaeth. *Virgil Michel: American Catholic.* Collegeville, MN: Liturgical Press, 1988.

Kantowicz, Edward K., ed. *Modern American Catholicism (1900-1964).* The Heritage of American Catholicism, ed. Timothy Walch. NY: Garland, 1988.

This work contains twenty selected historical essays of which the following six provide helpful background material for understanding the life and times of Jessica Powers: [98-115] David J.

O'Brien, "Catholicism and Americanism," from *American Catholics and Social Reform* (New York 1968): 212-27, 273-74; [116-36] Philip Gleason, "In Search of Unity: American Catholic Thought, 1920-1960," *The Catholic Historical Review* 65 (1979): 185-205; [137-147] Robert B. Clements, "Michael Williams and the Founding of *The Commonwealth*," *Records of the American Catholic Historical Society* 85 (1974): 163-173; [352-371] Vincent P. DeSantis, "American Catholics and McCarthyism," *The Catholic Historical Review* 51 (1965): 1-30; [382-98] Philip Gleason, "Catholicism and Cultural Change in the 1960s," *The Review of Politics,* 34 (1972): 91-107; [399-417] John Tracy Ellis, "American Catholicism, 1953-1979: A Notable Change," *Thought* 54 (1979): 113-131.

Kennelly, Karen. *American Catholic Women: A Historical Exploration.* The Bicentennial History of the Catholic Church in America Authorized by the National Conference of Catholic Bishops, gen. ed. Christopher Kauffman. NY: Macmillian, 1989.

Kkuzniewski, Anthony J. *Faith and Fatherland: The Polish Church War in Wisconsin (1896-1918).* Notre Dame Studies in American Catholicism, No. 3. Notre Dame, Indiana: University of Notre Dame, 1980.

Lane, Belden. *Landscapes of the Sacred: Geography and Narrative in American Spirituality.* NY: Paulist, 1988.

Liptak, Dolores. *Immigrants and Their Church.* The Bicentennial History of the Catholic Church in America Authorized by the National Conference of Catholic Bishops, gen. ed. Christopher Kauffman. NY: Macmillian, 1989.

Meagher, Timothy J., ed. *Urban American Catholicism.* Heritage of American Catholicism, ed. Timothy Walch. NY: Garland, 1988.

Messbarger, Paul R. "The Failed Promise of American Catholic Literature." *U.S. Catholic Historian* 4 (1985): 143-58.

Michel, Virgil. *The Social Question: Essays on Captialism and Christianity.* Edited by Robert L. Spaeth. Introduction by William Franklin. Collegeville, MN: St. John's University, 1987.

Murphy, Roland E. "Reflections on the History of the Exposition of Scripture." In *Studies in Catholic History: In Honor of John Tracy Ellis*, ed. Nelson H. Minnich, Robert B. Eno, and Robert F. Trisco, 489-499. Wilimington, Delaware: Michael Glazier, 1985.

New Catholic Encyclopedia, 1966 ed. S.v., "American Literatrue: Poetry," by Joseph Schwartz.

_____. S.v., "Literary Associations, Catholic," by Redmond Ambrose Burke.

NAB (New American Bible). Nashville, TN: Nelson, 1987.

O'Brien, David. *Public Catholicism*. The Bicentennial History of the Catholic Church in America Authorized by the National Conference of Catholic Bishops, ed. Christopher Kauffman. NY: Macmillian, 1989.

_____. *The Renewal of American Catholicism*. NY: Oxford University Press, 1972.

Portier, William L., ed. *The Inculturation of American Catholicism (1820-1900)*. Heritage of American Catholicism, ed. Timothy Walch. NY: Garland, 1988.

Reher, Margaret Mary. *Catholic Intellectual Life in America*. The Bicentennial History of the Catholic Church in America Authorized by the National Conference of Catholic Bishops, ed. Christopher Kauffman. NY: Macmillian, 1989.

Rummel, Leo. *The History of the Catholic Church in Wisconsin*. Madison, WI: Wisconsin State Council Knights of Columbus, 1976.

C. Religious-Literary Studies and Related Literary Works:

Barnet, Sylvan. *A Short Guide to Writing About Literature*. 4th ed. Boston: Little, Brown & Co., 1979.

Biddle, Arthur W., and Toby Fulwiler. *Reading, Writing, and the Study of Literature*. NY: Random House, 1989.

Bossis, Gabrielle. *He and I*. Translated by Evelyn M. Brown. Sherbrooke, Quebec, Canada: Editions Paulines, 1969.

Brooks, Cleanth, and Robert Penn Warren. *Understanding Poetry*. NY: Holt, Rinehart, & Winston, 1976.

Burke, Kenneth, and Stanley Romaine Hopper. "Mysticism as a Solution to the Poet's Dilemma." In *Spiritual Problems in Contemporary Literature*. ed. Stanley R. Hooper, 95-116. NY: Harper & Bros, 1957.

Daiches, David. "Theodicy, Poetry, and Tradition." In *Spiritual Problems in Contemporary Literature*. ed. Stanley R. Hooper, 73-95. NY: Harper & Bros, 1957.

Detweiler, Robert. *Breaking the Fall: Religious Readings of Contemporary Fiction*. San Francisco: Harper & Row, 1989.

Dickinson, Emily. *Poems*. Edited by George Monteiro. Gainesville, Florida: Scholars' Facsimiles & Reprints, 1967.

Eagleton, Terry. *Literary Theory: An Introduction*. Minneapolis: University of Minnesota, 1983.

Edel, Leon. *Writing Lives: Principia Biographica.* NY: W. W. Norton, 1984.

Edwards, Michael. *Towards A Christian Poetics.* Grand Rapids, MI: Wm. B. Eerdmans, 1984.

Encyclopedia Britannica: Micropaedia, 15th ed., 1983. S.v. "Jean Toomer."

Fitzgerald, Sally. "Rooms With a View." *Katallagate* 8 (Summer 1982): 4-11.

Frost, Robert. *Poetry and Prose.* Edited by Edward Connery Lathem and Laurence Thompson. NY: Holt, Rinehart, and Winston, 1972.

Griffith, Kelley, Jr. *Writing Essays About Literature.* 2d ed. San Diego: Harcourt, Brace, Jovanovich, 1986.

Heilbrun, Carolyn G. *Writing a Woman's Life.* NY: W. W. Norton, 1988.

Hildegarde of Bingen. *Scivias.* Translated by Bruce Hozeski with a Forword by Matthew Fox and Adelgundis Fuhrkotter. Santa Fe, NM: Bear, 1986.

Hopkins, Gerard Manley. *The Poems of Gerard Manley Hopkins.* 4th ed. Edited by W. H. Gardner and N. H. Mackenzie. London: Oxford University, 1967.

Johnson, James Weldon. *God's Trombones: Seven Negro Sermons in Verse.* New York: Viking, 1968.

Julian of Norwich. *Showings.* Translated and an Introduction by Edmund Colledge, with a Preface by Jean Leclercq. The Classics of Western Spirituality. NY: Paulist, 1978.

Kermode, Frank. *An Appetite for Poetry.* Cambridge, Mass.: Harvard University, 1989.

Martin, Robert Bernard. "The Poet, the Nun, and the Daring Young Man." In *Leon Edel and Literary Art*, ed. Lyall H. Powers, 29-42. Studies in Modern Literature, gen. ed. A. Walton Litz, no. 84. Ann Arbor, Michigan: UMI Research Press, 1988.

Noon, William. *Poetry and Prayer.* New Brunswick, NJ: Rutgers University, 1967.

Ruland, Vernon. *Horizons of Criticism: An Assessment of Religious-Literary Options.* Chicago: American Library Association, 1975.

Sewall, Richard B. "In Search of Emily Dickinson." In *Extraordinary Lives: The Art and Craft of American Biography,* ed. William Zinsser, 63-90. NY: American Heritage, 1986.

_____. *The Life of Emily Dickinson.* Vol. 2. NY: Farrar, Straus, and Giroux, 1974.

Schwartz, Delmore. "The Vocation of the Poet in the Modern World." In *Spiritual Problems in Contemporary Literature.* ed. Stanley R. Hooper, 59-69. NY: Harper & Bros, 1957.

TeSelle, Sallie McFague. *Literature and the Christian Life.* New Haven, Conn.: Yale University, 1966.

Thompson, Francis. *Poetical Works.* London: Oxford University, 1969.

Thoreau, Henry David. *Annotated Walden.* Edited with Introduction, Notes, and Bibliography by Philip Van Doren Stern. Ink, NY: Clarkson N. Potter, 1970.

Wylie, Elinor. *The Collected Poems of Elinor Wylie.* New York: Alfred A. Knopf, 1954.

D. Twentieth-Century American Studies:

Allen, Frederick Lewis. *Only Yesterday: An Informal History of the 1920s.* NY: Harper & Row, 1964.

Doan, Edward Newell. *The LaFollettes and the Wisconsin Idea.* NY: Rinehart, 1970.

Eigo, Francis, ed. *Christian Spirituality in the U.S.: Independence and Interdependence.* Proceedings of the Theological Institute of Villanova University. Pennsylvania: Villanova University, 1979.

Gara, Larry. *A Short History of Wisconsin.* Madison: State Historical Society, 1967.

Hoffman, Frederick J. *The Twenties: American Writing in the Postwar Decade.* NY: Collier, 1962.

Hofstadter, Richard. *The Age of Reform: From Bryan to F.D.R.* NY: Vintage Books, 1955.

James, Janet Wilson, ed. *Women in American Religion.* Pennsylvania: University of Pennsylvania, 1980.

Jordan, Winthrop D., Leon F. Litwack, et al. *The United States: Combined Edition.* 6th ed. Englewood Cliffs, NJ: Prentice-Hall, 1987.

Lapham, Increase Allen. *Wisconsin.* NY: Arno, 1975.

Leighton, Isabel, ed. *The Aspirin Age (1919-1941).* NY: Simon & Schuster, 1963.

Nesbit, Robert Carrington. *Wisconsin: A History.* Madison, WI: University of Wisconsin, 1973.

O'Brien, Michael. *McCarthy and McCarthyism in Wisconsin.* Columbia & London: University of Missouri Press, 1980.

Sklar, Kathryn Kish, and Thomas Dublin. *Women and Power in American History: A Reader Vol. II from 1870.* Englewood Cliffs, NJ: Prentice-Hall, 1991.

Tallack, Douglas. *Twentieth-Century America: The Intellectual and Cultural Context.* Longman Literature in English Series, gen. ed. David Carroll & Michael Wheeler. London: Longman, 1991.

White, Ronald C., and C. Howard Hopkins. *The Social Gospel: Religion and Reform in Changing America.* With an essay by John C. Bennett. Philadelphia: Temple University, 1966.

IX. Archival Material

The Jessica Powers Papers, Department of Special Collections and University Archives, Main Library, Marquette University, Milwaukee, Wisconsin. AMU. The papers are processed only on a preliminary basis. As the collection grows it is likely that box and folder numbers for specific documents will change.

Endnotes

Chapter 1

1. Regina Siegfried, "Write Me Down As A Small Adjective Attending Light, The Archangelic Noun," in *Jessica Powers Symposium: Proceedings of the Symposium in Milwaukee, Wisconsin, August 26, 1989*, by Marquette University (Milwaukee, WI: Marquette University, 1989), 23.
2. Ibid., 24.

Chapter 2

1. 1 Kings 17-21; 2 Kings 2 NAB (New American Bible). For a discussion of Elijah in the spirituality of Carmelites see Peter Thomas Rohrbach, *Journey to Carith: The Story of the Carmelite Order* (Garden City, NY: Doubleday, 1966), 18-19, 33; Discalced Carmelites of Boston and Santa Clara, *Carmel: Its History, Spirit, and Saints* (New York, NY: P. J. Kenedy & Sons, 1927), 5-6, 1; Roland E. Murphy, "The Figure of Elijah in the Old Testament," *Ascent* 1 (1969): 15; and Pascal of the Blessed Sacrament, "Saint Elias, Prophet and Father of Carmel," in *Carmels History: Proceedings of the Fourth Regional Third Order Congress Southwestern Province Held in San Antonio, Texas, 3-5 October 1958* (N.p.: Privately printed, 1958), 6.
2. For a discussion of Camelite spirituality and bridal mysticism, see Tessa Bielecki, "Bridal Mysticism," in *Speaking of Silence: Christian and Buddhists on the Contemplative Way*, ed. Susan Walker (NY: Paulist, 1987), 38-47. For a brief survey of mysticism with a special reference to bridal mysticism, see Harvey D. Egan, *What Are They Saying About Mysticism?* (New York: Paulist, 1982), 118. For a brief survey of spiritual marriage in the "Seventh Mansion" of Teresa of Avilas writings, see pages 207-11 the introduction to *The Song of Songs* and pages 276-78 of the introduction to *The Interior Castle* in Teresa of Avila, *The Collected Works of St. Teresa of Avila* (Washington, D.C.: Institute of Carmelite Studies, 1980), vol. 2, *The Way of Perfection, Meditation on the Song of Songs, The Interior Castle*, intro. and trans. by Otilio Rodriquez and Kieran Kavanaugh. For examples of the manner in which spiritual marriage is treated in John of the Cross writings, see John of the Cross, *The Collected Works of St. John of the Cross*, trans. Kieran Kavanaugh (Washington, D.C.: Institute of Carmelite Studies, 1979), 393-94, 402, 517-19.

3. For a brief account of Teresa of Avilas understanding of the Rule of Saint Albert, see Hugh Clarke and Bede Edwards, *The Rule of Saint Albert* (Aylesford & Kensington: Carmelite Book Service, 1973), 35-36. For a brief discussion of the Teresian reform of sixteenth-century Spain, see Rohrbach, "The Reform," chap. V in *Journey to Carith*, 137-169. For an additional account of the life and influence of Teresa of Avila, see the introduction to Teresa of Avila, *The Collected Works of St. Teresa of Avila*, vol. 1, *The Book of Her Life*, trans. Kieran Kavanaugh and Otilio Rodriguez (Washington, D.C.: Institute of Carmelite Studies, 1976), 1-26.

4. Rohrbach, "The Struggle for Existence," chap.VI, in *Journey to Carith*, 172-228.

5. Monika Hellwig, "St. Teresa's Inspiration for Our Times," in *Centenary of St. Teresa: Catholic University Symposium, 15-17 October 1982*, ed. John Sullivan, 21-24, Carmelite Studies, no. 3 (Washington: D.C.: Institute of Carmelite Studies, 19), 217.

6. Ibid., 224.

7. Teresa of Avila, *The Collected Works of St. Teresa of Avila*, vol. 2, *Meditations on the Song of Songs*, trans. Otilio Rodriguez and Kieran Kavanaugh (Washington, D.C.: Institute of Carmelite Studies, 1980), 208-210.

8. Aloysius Deeney, "The History of the Carmelite Rule," Oklahoma City, OK: Villa Teresa Lecture Series on Carmelite Studies, 9 November 1991, tape recording.

9. For translations of her poetry, see Teresa of Avila, *The Collected Works of St. Teresa of Avila*, vol. 3, *The Book of Her Foundations; Minor Works* (Washington, D.C.: Institute of Carmelite Studies, 1985), 375-410.

10. For descriptions of the two kinds of dark nights, see Juan de la Cruz, "The Ascent of Mount Carmel," and "The Dark Night," in *Collected Works*, trans. Kieran Kavanaugh and Otilio Rodriguez (NY: Doubleday, 1964), 66-290 and 295-388.

11. Bielecki, "Bridal Mysticism," 44,46.

12. Aloysius Deeney, "The History of the Carmelite Rule," Oklahoma City, OK: Villa Teresa Lecture Series on Carmelite Studies, 9 November 1991, tape recording.

13. For examples of Americans influenced by Therese of Lisieux, see Joseph P. Chinnici, "James Keller," chap. 17 in *Living Stones: The History and Structure of Catholic Spiritual Life in the United States* (NY: Macmillian, 1989), 198. Also see Dorothy Day, *Therese* (Springfield, Illinois: Templegate, 1979). For Thereses influence on Michael Williams, see Robert B. Clemens, "Michael Williams and the Founding of *The Commonwealth*," *Records of the American Catholic Historical Society* 84 (1974): 168-69, as found in *Modern American Catholicism*, ed. Edward Kantowicz (NY: Garland, 1988), 142-43.

14. For a discussion of the role scripture played in the spirituality of Therese of Lisieux, see T. Bird, "St. Therese and the Scriptures," in *Christian Simplicity in St. Therese: The Place of St. Therese of Lisieux in Christian Spirituality*, ed. Michael Day (Westminster, MD: Newman, 1953), 123-33.

15. For descriptions of the worldwide appeal of Therese of Lisieux, see Ida F. Gorres, *The Hidden Face: A Study of St. Therese of Lisieux*, trans. Richard and Clara Winston (NY: Pantheon, 1959), 2-5; and Rohrbach, *Journey to Carith*, 322, 325-26.

16. See Peter Thomas Rohrbach, "Expansion," in chap. 7, *Journey to Carith: The Story of the Carmelite Order* (Garden City, NY: Doubleday, 1966), 248-51.

17. Charles Warren Currier, *Carmel in America: A Centennial History of the Discalced Carmelites in the U.S., 1790-1890* (Darien, Illinois: Carmelite Press, 1989), 26; and Rohrbach, *Journey to Carith*, 237-48.

18. See Constance FitzGerald, ed., *The Carmelite Adventure: Clare Joseph Dickinson's Journal of "A Trip to America" and Other Documents* (Baltimore, MD: Carmelite Sisters, 1990), 9; and Peter Thomas Rohrbach, *Journey to Carith*, 248-50.

19. Rohrbach, *Journey to Carith*, 242-49.

20. See Currier, *Carmel in America*, 27-34; and Lancelot C. Sheppard, *The English Carmelites* (London: Burns Oates, 1943), 81-84.

21. See Constance FitzGerald, ed., *The Carmelite Adventure*, 21. In footnote 41 on page 39, FitzGerald states: "I am indebted to Joseph Chinnici for sharing by telephone some of the conclusions he has reached from researching the papers of the Carmelite founders and Charles Neale in the Archives of the Carmelite Monastery in Baltimore."

22. James Hennesey, "Several Youth Sent from Here: Native-Born Priests and Religious of English America, 1634-1776," in *Studies in Catholic History: In Honor of John Tracy Ellis*, ed. Nelson H. Minnich, Robert B. Eno, and Robert F. Trisco (Wilmington, Delaware: Michael Glazier, 1985), 15-17, 20.

23. These two American-born women were members of the Brent family and Matthews family, important Catholic families in the history of Maryland. The Brent family was related to the Carroll family of whose sons were Charles Carroll, a signer of the Declaration of Independence, and John Carroll, the first bishop of the United States. The Brent family, Matthews family, and Neale family were also related by common ancestors and by marriage. Several members of these families figure in Jesuit as well as Carmelite American Catholic History. See Constance FitzGerald, *The Carmelite Adventure*, 10-19.

24. See Constance FitzGerald, *The Carmelite Adventure*, 10-13; and Currier, *Carmel in America*, 34, 42.

25. FitzGerald, *The Carmelite Adventure*, 21-23.

26. Ibid., 23. In this quote, Ignatius refers to Ignatius of Loyola. This spiritual tradition also influenced the spirituality of John Carroll, the first bishop of the United States.

27. Ibid., 24.

28. See Rohrbach, *Journey to Carith*, 332-33; and FitzGerald, *The Carmelite Adventue*, 13-19.

29. FitzGerald, *The Carmelite Adventure*, 30-31. Also see John Tracy Ellis, *American Catholicism*, 2d revised ed., Chicago History of American Civilization, ed. Daniel J. Boorstin (Chicago: University of Chicago, 1969), 134.

30. See Hennesey, "Several Youths Sent From Here," 21-22; Currier, *Carmel in America*, 52-54; and FitzGerald, *The Carmelite Adventure*, 19-21.

31. FitzGerald, *The Carmelite Adventure*, 29.

32. Ibid., 5.

33. Ibid., 7.

34. See Currier, *Carmel in America*, 55; and FitzGerald, *The Carmelite Adventure*, 24-26.

35. FitzGerald, *The Carmelite Adventure*, 24. In footnote 49 which accompanies this passage on page 24 of *The Carmelite Adventure*, Constance FitzGerald notes that she is indebted to Joseph Chinnici for much of this analysis of the spirituality of the American Carmelite founders.

36. FitzGerald, *The Carmelite Adventure*, 28-30.

37. Martin, *Elizabeth: The Story of a Nun* (New York: Twin Circle, 1968), 9.

38. Hennesey, "Youths Sent From Here," 22-23.

39. Martin, *Elizabeth*, 11-17.

40. Ibid., 4.

41. Martin, *Elizabeth*, 26.

42. See Rohrbach, *Journey to Carith*, 333; Currier, "Lawsuits," chap. 16 in *Carmel in America*, 150-165; and Robin Stratton, *The Carmelite Sisters of Baltimore and the Education of Young Ladies (1831-1851)* (Baltimore, MD: Privately printed, n.d.), 3-4.

43. Stratton, *The Carmelites of Baltimore and the Education of Young Ladies*, 3-5, 8.

44. The Discalced Carmelite Nuns of the Association of Mary, Queen of Carmel, *Carmel: In the United States of America, 1790-1990* (Eugene, Oregon: Queens Press, 1990), 11.

Chapter 3

1. Melita Marie Garza, "Nun's Collected Poems Resurrected Since Death: Marquette Plans Seminar on Her Work," *The Milwaukee Journal*, 5 August 1989, citing Dolores Leckey.

2. A brief description of the Wisconsin landscape around the Powers family farm can be found in Richard Boudreau, "A Meadow Moreover: The Wisconsin Poems of Jessica Powers," in *Jessica Powers*

Symposium: Proceedings of the Symposium in Milwaukee, Wisconsin, August 26, 1989, by Marquette University (Milwaukee, WI, 1989), 9. For a more detailed description of the physical geography of central Wisconsin, see Increase Allen Lapham, *Wisconsin* (NY: Arno, 1975).

3. Garza, "Nun's Collected Poems Resurrected Since Death," citing Dolores Leckey.

4. Dolores Leckey, "Notes on a Poet's Life," *Spiritual Life* 36 (Fall 1990): 142, citing Jessica Powers, Letter to Christopher Powell.

5. Papers from Jessica Powers Papers (Box 3: Folder 2), AMU. James Trainer, Jessica's great-grandfather, was born on May 30, 1826, in Castle Douglas, Dumfriese, near the Bridge of Dee, Parish of Balmaghie, Kirkcudbright, Scotland. He died at Lyndon Station, Wisconsin, on 11 October 1888.

6. "The Family of James Trainer and Anne Dalling: Family Genealogy," taken from Jessica Powers Papers (Box 3: Folder 2), AMU. Daniel Trainer died in Lyndon Station, WI on 18 November 1872 and is buried in Lyndon Cemetery. Another brother Robert Trainer came to America, returned to Scotland to marry Margaret Curran, and they moved back to Lyndon Station. Robert and James, Jessica's grandfather, were converts to the Catholic faith.

7. Carroll Tracy, "Juneau County and the World: The Small Account," *The Mauston Star*, 8 August 1958. This newspaper clipping contains the story of how James Trainer, Jessica's grandfather, helped to save General Sherman and the Union Army during the Civil War in their march across the Carolinas. He suggested the strategy of saving the swamp-bogged army by building corduroy roads and under his direction the Wisconsin "Pioneer Corps" built miles of them. He and his division were cited for gallantry and ingenuity.

8. Papers taken from Jessica Powers Papers (Box 3: Folder 2), AMU. Jessica Powers' great-grandmother was Catherine Keena. She was born 19 May 1835 in Ballitore, County Kildare, Ireland and died 24 August 1910 at Lyndon Station, Wisconsin. Jessica was ten years old at the time of her death.

9. See Dolores Leckey, "Notes On A Poet's Life," *Spiritual Life* 36 (Fall 1990), 142; and Jessica Powers, *Selected Poetry of Jessica Powers*, ed. Regina Siegfried and Robert Morneau (Kansas City, MO: Sheed & Ward, 1989), 192.

10. Sister Miriam of the Holy Spirit (Jessica Powers), Interview by Sister Regina Siegfried ASC and Bishop Robert Morneau of Green Bay, WI, 1987, taken from transcript p. 1, tape 1: side 1, in Jessica Powers Papers (Box 4: Folder 7), AMU.

11. Although Jessica's parents named her Agnes Jessika Powers, she preferred to be known as Jessica because this spelling was the same as that of a singer, Jessica Dragonet whom she admired. See Dolores Leckey, "Notes on a Poet's Life," *Spiritual Life*, 147.

12. Powers, *Selected Poetry,* 192.

13. Jessica Powers, "West Coast Poems: Prayer for My Family," *Diary/Journal*, 12 March 1971, in Jessica Powers Papers (Box 3: Folder 8), AMU.

14. Larry Gara, *A Short History of Wisconsin* (Madison, WI: The State Historical Society of Wisconsin, 1962), 184.

15. Ibid., 200. For a more detailed discussion of the Progressive Era in Wisconsin history, see Edward Newell Doan, *The LaFollettes and the Wisconsin Idea* (New York: Rhinehart, 1970).

16. Miriam of the Holy Spirit, Interview by Siegfried and Morneau, transcript p. 1, tape 1: side 1. AMU.

17. Dolores Liptak, *Immigrants and Their Church* (New York: Macmillian, 1989), 76, citing Bernard Smith Papers, Propagation of the Faith Collections, Archives of University of Notre Dame (microfilm), originals in the archives of the Benedictine Abbey of Saint Paul's Outside the Walls.

18. For a more detailed discussion of Irish religious history in the United States, see Dolores Liptak, "The Irish Take Charge," chap. 5 in *Immigrants and Their Church*, 76-91.

19. For an excellent summary of these ideas in a chart form, see Chinnici, *Living Stones*, 120.

20. For a detailed discussion of these ideas, see Chinnici, "The Immigrant Vision, 1830-1866," part 2 in *Living Stones,* 35-86.

21. Chinnici, "The Crisis of Americanism and the structures of Catholic Spiritual Life," chap. 11 in *Living Stones*, 120.

22. Ibid.

23. For a discussion on the influence of Isaac Hecker and his vision of the Holy Spirit's interior action within human beings, see Jay P. Dolan, *The American Catholic Experience: A History from Colonial Times to the Present* (Garden City, NY: Image Books, 1985), 235-36; and Chinnici, *Living Stones*, 97-98.

24. See Virgil Michel, *The Social Question: Essays on Capitalism and Christianity*, ed. Robert L. Spaeth and intro. R. William Franklin (Collegeville, MN: St. John's University, 1987); R. William Franklin and Robert L. Spaeth, *Virgil Michel: American Catholic* (Collegeville, MN: Liturgical Press, 1988), Ellis, *American Catholicism*, 137-38; and Chinnici, "Virgil Michel and the Priesthood of the Faithful," chap. 15 in *Living Stones*, 177-85.

25. For more details on the Americanist vision, see Chinnici, "The Spirituality of Americanism, 1866-1900," part 3 in *Living Stones*, 87-134.

26. See Chinnici, "A Fractured Inheritance, 1900-1930," part 4 in *Living Stones,* 135-74.

27. See Mary Luke Baldwin, "Wisconsin Poet Integrates Rural Upbringing, City Life, Monastery," The Times Review (Milwaukee), 2 January 1986; and Powers, Selected Poetry, 192.

28. See Powers, *Selected Poetry*, 192; Baldwin, "Wisconsin Poet," *Times Review*, 2 January 1986; and Powers, Interview by Siegfried and Morneau, transcript p. 1, tape 1: side 1, AMU.

29. Powers, *Selected Poetry*, 192.

30. See Richard Boudreau, "A Meadow Moreover: The Wisconsin Poems of Jessica Powers," 8; and Dolores Leckey, Executive Director of the Secretariat on Laity and Family Life for the National Conference of Catholic Bishops in Washington, D.C. and biographer of Jessica Powers, interview by author, 1 November 1991, telephone conversation, Washington, D.C.

31. "Father Danihy's Poetry Class Student Has Book Published," unidentified newspaper clipping, taken from Jessica Powers Papers (Box 7, Scrapbook), AMU.

32. "The Story of Jessica Powers and Her Search for Happiness," *(Milwaukee) Catholic Herald Citizen*, undated article from 1942, taken from Jessica Powers Papers (Box 2:11), AMU.

33. Powers, *Selected Poetry*, 193.

34. Leckey, "Notes on a Poet's Life," *Spiritual Life*, 144.

35. See Jessica Powers, "Dreams of You," in *Selected Poetry*, 147; and *American Poetry* 7 (March/April 1924): 19.

36. Leckey, "Jessica Powers: Notes on a Poet's Life," in *Jessica Powers Symposium: Proceedings of the Symposium in Milwaukee, Wisconsin, August 26, 1989,* by Marquette University (Milwaukee, Wisconsin: Marquette, 1989), 5; and Powers, *Selected Poetry,* 193.

37. Mary Luke Baldwin, "Wisconsin Poet Integrates Rural Upbringing, City Life, Monastery," in *(Milwaukee) Times Review*, 2 January 1986, 9.

38. Dolores Leckey, "Jessica Powers: Notes on a Poet's Life," in *Jessica Powers Symposium*, 5.

39. Richard Bourdeau, "A Meadow Moreover: The Wisconsin Poetry of Jessica Powers," 11; Thomas P. McDonnell, "The Nun as Poet," *Spirit* 26 (March 1959): 24; and Regina Siegfried, "Write Me Down the Archangelic Noun: The Brightening Words of Emily Dickinson and Jessica Powers," 11-13.

40. Bernard McGarty, "Jessica Powers, an Emily Dickinson from Juneau County," *The Times Review* (Milwaukee), 2 January 1986, quoted in Regina Siegfried, "Write Me Down the Archangelic Noun: The Brightening Words of Emily Dickinson and Jessica Powers," 11.

41. Boudreau, "A Meadow Moreover," 11.

42. Siegfried, "Write Me Down the Archangelic Noun: The Brightening Words of Emily Dickinson and Jessica Powers," 12.

43. Ibid.

44. Ibid.

45. See Jessica Powers, "Petenwell Rock," in *Selected Poetry*, 103; *Forge* 2 (Summer 1926): 12; and in *The Lantern Burns* (NY: Monastine, 1939): 50.

46. See Jessica Powers, "Cabaret," in *Selected Poetry*, 42; and *The Forge* 11 (1926): 13.

47. John of the Cross, "The Dark Night," in The Collected Works of Saint John of the Cross, trans. Kieran Kavanaugh and Otilio Rodriguez, with introductions by Kieran Kavanaugh (Washington, D.C.: Institute of Carmelite Studies), 711.

48. See Jessica Powers, "Robin at Dusk," in *Selected Poetry*, 187; and *Columbia* 6 (April 1927): 23. Also published in Italian under the title, "Pettirosso al Crepuscolo," in *Luogo di splendore: Poesie*, trans. Margherita Guidacci (Citta del Vaticano: Libreria Editrice Vaticana, 1983), 28-29. For a discussion of this poem, see Winifred F. Geigel, "A Comparative Study of the Poetry of Jessica Powers and St. John of the Cross" (M.A. thesis, St. John's University, 1961), 34, 59; Paul J. Kiley, "Bright Dream: Jessica Powers' *The Lantern Burns*" *Magnificant* 68 (June 1941): 76; and "The Story of Jessica Powers and Her Search for Happiness," *(Milwaukee) Catholic Herald Citizen*, 1942, 42.

49. Francis Thompson, "Hound of Heaven," in *Poetical Works* (London: Oxford, 1969), 89-94.

50. Gerard Manley Hopkins, "God's Grandeur," in *The Poems of Gerard Manley Hopkins*, 4th ed., ed. W. H. Gardner and N. H. Mackenzie (London: Oxford Press, 1967), 66.

51. See Jessica Powers, "Celestial Bird," in *Selected Poetry*, 31; *Poetry* 33 (December 1928): 124; and in *Place of Splendor* (NY: Cosmopolitan Science and Art Service, 1946), 54.

52. See Jessica Powers, "Lo Spirito Santo," in *Selected Poetry*, 32; *Commonweal* 11 (December 4, 1929): 139; and in *The Lantern Burns*, 16-17. Also translated in Italian under the title, "Lo Spirito Santo," in *Luogo di splendore*, 10-11. For a discussion of this poem, see Mary Timothy, S.S.N.D., "The Silent Poet," *Spirit* 27 (May 1960): 52.

53. John of the Cross, "The Living Flame of Love," in *Collected Works*, trans. Kieran Kavanaugh, 717.

54. Elinor Wylie, "The Velvet Shoes," in *The Collected Poems of Elinor Wylie* (New York: Alfred A. Knopf, 1954), 40.

55. See Jessica Powers, "The Granite Woman," in *Selected Poetry*, 62; *Commonweal* 9 (January 3, 1929): 350. For a discussion of this poem, see Dolores Leckey, "Jessica Powers: Notes on a Poet's Life," in *Jessica Powers Symposium: Proceedings of the Symposium in Milwaukee, Wisconsin, August 26, 1989*, by Marquette University (Milwaukee, Wisconsin: Marquette University, 1989), 4.

56. Henry David Thoreau, *Annotated Walden*, edited with introductory notes and bibliography by Philip Van Doren Stern (Ink, NY: Clarkson N. Potter, 1970), 442.

57. See Jessica Powers, "Michigan Boulevard, Chicago," in *Selected Poetry*, 82; *Commonweal* 17 (December 21, 1932): 208. For a discussion of this poem, see Geigel, 34, 37; Marilynn Miller, "Jessica Powers," *Mount Mary Quarterly* 17 (March 1941): 10; Kiley, "Bright Dream," 77-78; and Francesca Berlingeri, "Una nuova voce poetica dal Carmelo: Jessica Powers," Humanitas 7 (Luglio 1958): 538.

58. Matthew 2:1-12.

59. Jessica Powers' book *The Lantern Burns* was reviewed and praised by Dorothy Day and Peter Maurin in *The Catholic Worker* VII, 8 (May 1940). Individual poems of Jessica Powers appeared in their publication as well.

60. See Jessica Powers, "The Uninvited," in *Selected Poetry*, 10; published in 1935; and in *The Lantern Burns*, 30. Also translated into Italian under the title, "Gli esclusi," in *Luogo di splendore*, 26-27. For a discussion of this poem, see Robert Morneau, "The Spirituality of Jessica Powers," in *Jessica Powers Symposium: Proceedings of the Symposium in Milwaukee, Wisconsin, August 26, 1989*, by Marquette University (Milwaukee, Wisconsin: Marquette University, 1989), 18; and Miller, 9.

61. See Matthew 22:1-14; and Luke 14:7-24.

62. See Jessica Powers, "Track of the Mystic," in *Selected Poetry*, 135; published in 1932; and in *The Lantern Burns*, 14. For a discussion of this poem, see Regina Siegfried, "Write Me Down As a Small Adjective Attending Light, the Archangelic Noun," in *Jessica Powers Symposium: Proceedings of the Symposium in Milwaukee, Wisconsin, August 26, 1989*, by Marquette University (Milwaukee, Wisconsin: Marquette University, 1989), 24; and Geigel, 39.

63. See Jessica Powers, "Shining Quarry," in *Selected Poetry*, 30; *Spirit* 1 (November 1934): 139; in *Place of Splendor*, 42. For a discussion of this poem, see Timothy, "The Silent Poet," 57; Geigel, 63, 69.

64. Exodus 3:1-3.

65. See Matthew 4:19; Mark 1:16-17; and Luke 5:1-11.

66. Powers, *Selected Poetry*, 193.

67. Richard Boudreau, "A Meadow Moreover: The Wisconsin Poems of Jessica Powers," 8. Also see clipping from *Milwaukee Journal* [undated] in Jessica Powers Collection (Box 7: Scrapbook), AMU.

Chapter 4

1. Powers, *Selected Poetry*, 193.

2. Miriam of the Holy Spirit, Interview by Siegfried and Morneau, transcript p. 2-3, of tape 1: side 1.

3. "Notes on a Poets Life," *Spiritual Life*, 145.

4. Winthrop D. Jordan, Leon F. Litwack, et al., "The Great Depression and the New Deal," chap. 28 in *The United States: Combined Edition*, 6th ed. (Englewood Cliffs, NJ: Prentice-Hall, 1987), 631.

5. Jordan, "The Harlem Renaissance," in *The United States*, 609-11.

6. Miriam of the Holy Spirit, "Diary/Journal," entries from 1971 while on West Coast, taken from Jessica Powers Collection (Box 3: Folder 8), AMU.

7. Jordan, "The Harlem Renaissance," in *The United States*, 610.

8. Ibid., 611.

9. In 1926 Jean Toomer left the United States and took up a studies in France at the Gurdjieff Institute. Later Toomer returned to the United States and founded a similar establishment at Portage, Wisconsin, that was dedicated to expansion of consciousness and meditation. See *Enclyclopedia Britannica: Micropaedia*, 15th ed. 1983. S.v. "Jean Toomer." For a more detailed discussion of Gurdjieff, Georgii Ivanovich Gurdzhiev (1877-1949), and his school of methodology for the development of consciousness, see Mircea Eliade, ed. *The Encyclopedia of Religion* (New York: MacMillian, 1987), s.v. "Gurdjieff, G. I.," by Michael de Salzmann.

10. Richard Hofstadter, *The Age of Reform: From Bryan to F.D.R.* (NY: Vintage Books, 1955), 302.

11. Ibid., 308.

12. J.M. Keynes, "The United States and the Keynes Plan," *New Republic* 103 (29 July 1940): 158, quoted in Hofstadter, *The Age of Reform*, 309.

13. Ibid.

14. Jordan, *The United States*, 658.

15. Dolores Leckey, "Notes on a Poets Life," *Spiritual Life*, 139.

16. John Tracy Ellis, *American Catholicism*, 2d revised ed., Chicago History of American Civilization, ed. Daniel J. Boorstin (Chicago: University of Chicago, 1969), 129.

17. Jay P. Dolan, *The American Catholic Experience: A History from Colonial Times to the Present* (Garden City, NY: Image Books, 1985), 298.

18. Ibid., 409-10.

19. See Dolan, *The American Catholic Experiment*, 412; and Chinnici, "Dorothy Day: The Heroic Ideal," chap. 16 in *Living Stones*, 186-193.

20. Marilyn Miller, "Jessica Powers," *Mount Mary Quarterly*, 17 (March 1941), 11.

21. Dolan, *The American Catholic Experience*, 412-13.

22. *New Catholic Encyclopedia*, 1966 ed., s.v. "Literary Associations, Catholic," by Redmond Ambrose Burke.

23. Ibid., s.v. "American Literature: Poetry," by Joseph Schwartz.

24. See Margaret Mary Reher, *Catholic Intellectual Life in America*, The Bicentennial History of the Catholic Church in America Authorized by

the National Conference of Catholic Bishops, ed. Christopher Kauffman (NY: Macmillian, 1989), 123; and Paul R. Messbarger, "The
Failed Promise of American Catholic Literature," *U.S. Catholic Historian* 4 (1985): 155.

25. Mary Luke Baldwin, "Burns the Great Lantern," *Catholic World* 168
    (February 1949), 361.
26. Miriam of the Holy Spirit, Interview by Siegfried and Morneau, taken
    from transcript p. 3, tape 1: side 1.
27. Mary Luke Baldwin, "Wisconsin Poet Integrates Rural Upbringing,
    City Life, Monastery," in *(Milwaukee) Times Review,* 2 January 1986,
    9.
28. The Pegis children were Charles, Richard, Gerard, Sylvia, Marina, and
    Jessica. See "Services Set For Pegis, 72, Ex-Prof at MU," newspaper
    clipping taken from Jessica Powers Papers (Box 10: Folder 3), AMU.
29. See Robert Morneau, introduction to *Selected Poetry,* by Jessica Pow-
    ers (Kansas City, MO: Sheed & Ward, 1989), xvii; and Mary Luke
    Baldwin, "Burns the Great Lantern," *Catholic World* 168 (February
    1949): 358-59.
30. "The Story of Jessica Powers and Her Search for Happiness," *(Mil-
    waukee) Catholic Herald Citizen*, April 1942, 42.
31. See Miriam of the Holy Spirit, Interview by Siegfried and Morneau,
    taken from transcript p. 3-5, tape 1: side 1; and Powers, *Selected Po-
    etry*, 193.
32. Befor her entry into the Carmelite community in Milwaukee under the
    religious name of Sister Miriam of the Holy Spirit, Jessica Powers
    used several pen names including Justin Powers, Delia Trainer, Anne
    Dalling, Catherine Hyde, Helen OTroy, and Agnes de la Poer.
33. Melita Marie Garza, "Nuns Collected Poems Resurrected Since
    Death," *Milwaukee Journal,* 5 August 1989, 4 (A).
34. See Miriam of the Holy Spirit, Interview by Siegfried and Morneau,
    taken from transcript, p. 5, tape 1: side 1; Powers, *Selected Poetry*,
    193; and Morneau, introduction to *Selected Poetry,* xvii-xviii.
35. See Marilynn Miller, "Jessica Powers," *Mount Mary Quarterly,* 17
    (March 1941), 8; and Mary Luke Baldwin, "Burns the Great Lantern,"
    Catholic World 168 (February 1949): 358.
36. See Mary Luke Baldwin, "Burns the Great Lantern," *Catholic World*,
    357; for Laube's obituary, see *New York Times*, 22 August 1974, 36.
37. See Miriam of the Holy Spirit, Interview by Siegfried and Morneau,
    taken from transcript, p. 5, tape 1: Side 1; Powers, *Selected Poetry*,
    193; "So He Printed His Own Lines: Clifford Laube Then Found He
    Was a Publisher Too," *The New York Sun*, 9 March 1939, clipping
    taken from Jessica Powers Papers (Box 7: Scrapbook), AMU; and
    "Laube Lauds Woman Poet: Spare-Time Publisher Produces Second
    Volume," *The New York Times Book Review*, 8 October 1939, clipping
    taken from Jessica Powers Papers (Box 7: Scrapbook), AMU.

38. Leckey, "Notes On A Poets Life," *Spiritual Life,* 144.
39. "Laube Lauds Woman Poet: Spare-Time Publisher Produces Second Volume," *New York Times Review,* 8 October 1939.
40. Mary Luke Baldwin, "Burns the Great Lantern," *Catholic World,* 358.
41. Miriam of the Holy Spirit, Interview by Siegfried and Morneau, taken from transcript, p. 5-6, tape 1: side 1.
42. "An anthology of Wisconsins Leading Poets." *(Milwaukee) Journal,* 1937. Newspaper clipping taken from Jessica Powers Papers (Box 7: Scrapbook), AMU.
43. Raymond Larsson, "A Little New Years Poem for Jessica Powers: Staten Island: 1940-41," in Jessica Powers Papers (Box 9: Folder 5), AMU.
44. Raymond Larsson, "Letter from the House of Exile," in Jessica Powers Papers (Box 7: Scrapbook), AMU.
45. Miriam of the Holy Spirit, "Diary/Journal," entries from 1971 while on the West Coast, taken from Jessica Powers Papers (Box 3: Folder 8), AMU. On 11 February 1971, Jessica was reading *Saints at Prayer* by Raymond Larsson and sometime within this time period, she wrote her idea of the two best poets of her times. For a discussion of Jean Toomer (1894-1967), see p. 40 above.
46. Larsson wrote of his friendship with E. E. Cummings and Mrs. Cummings more than once in his letters to Jessica. He spoke of Jessica to them when they visited him. Letters from Jessica Powers Papers (Box 9: Folder 5), AMU.
47. See Raymond Larsson, Letter 13.IX.1962, p. 2, in Jessica Powers Papers (Box 9: Folder 5), AMU.
48. Miller, "Jessica Powers," *Mount Mary Quarterly,* 13.
49. Catherine OHearn, "Of Interest to Women," *Torch* (February 1940), clipping taken from Jessica Powers Papers (Box 7: Scrapbook), AMU.
50. For details of the retreat movement known as the Cenacle, see Chinnici, "The Cenacle, Soul of Catholic Action," chap. 14 in *Living Stones,* 157-72.
51. Miriam of the Holy Spirit, Interview by Siegfried and Morneau, taken from transcript, p. 6, tape 1: side 1.
52. Ibid.
53. Leckey, "Notes on a Poets Life," in *Jessica Powers Symposium,* 6.
54. Miriam of the Holy Spirit, Interview by Siegfried and Morneau, taken from transcript, p. 6, tape 1: side 1.
55. Boudreau, "A Meadow Moreover," in *Jessica Powers Symposium,* 12.
56. Jessica Powers, "The Master Beggar," in *Selected Poetry,* 23. Also translated into Italian under the title, "Il mendicante," in *Luogo di splendore,* 20-21.
57. Ibid. For a discussion of this poem, see Kieren Kavanaugh, "Jessica Powers in the Tradition of St. John of the Cross: Carmelite and Poet," in *Jessica Powers Symposium: Proceedings of the Symposium in Mil-*

waukee, Wisconsin, August 26, 1989, by Marquette University (Milwaukee, Wisconsin: Marquette University, 1989), 31,33; Robert Morneau, "An Experience of God: Reflections of a Poets Journey," *Emmanuel* 93 (November 1987): 491; Mary Luke Baldwin, "Burns the Great Lantern," *Catholic World* 168 (February 1949): 360; Miller, 11; Geigel, 33-34; and Berlingeri, 540.

58. Ibid.
59. See Mathew 10:37-38; 16:24; Mark 8:34; and Luke 9:23.
60. Powers, *Selected Poetry*, 23.
61. Jessica Powers, "The First Pentecost," in *Selected Poetry*, 25; published in 1937; and in *The Lantern Burns*, 15.
62. Acts 2:1-4.
63. Powers, "The First Pentecost," in *Selected Poetry*, 25.
64. See Jessica Powers, "The House of the Silver Spirit," in *Selected Poetry*, 125-26; *Forge* 4 (1929): 137-38; published in 1937; and in *Lantern Burns*, 4-5.
65. Ibid. For a discussion of this poem, see Regina Siegfried, "Jessica Powers: The Paradox of Light and Dark," *Studia Mystica* 7 (Spring 1984): 29-30; Baldwin, "Burns the Great Lantern," 355-56; Timothy, "The Silent Poet," 52; Mary Luke Baldwin, "Wisconsin Poet Integrates Rural Upbringing, City Life, Monastery," (*LaCrosse, WI*) *Times Review*, 2 January 1986, 8; Geigel, 27-28; and Berlingeri, 537.
66. Ibid.
67. See Reher, *Catholic Intellectual Life in America*, 122.
68. Jessica Powers, "The Mountains of the Lord," in *Selected Poetry*, 8; *Spirit* 5 (July 1938): 70; and in *The Lantern Burns*, 32-33.
69. See Mathew 5:14.
70. See John 4:10.
71. Psalm 3:2.
72. John of the Cross, "Song of the Soul That Rejoices in Knowing God Through Faith," in *Collected Works*, 723-24.
73. Psalm 3:5.
74. Powers, "The Mountains of the Lord," in *Selected Poetry*, 8.
75. John of the Cross, "The Ascent of Mount Carmel," in *Collected Works*, 68.
76. John of the Cross, "The Dark Night," in *Collected Works*, 71.
77. John of the Cross, "The Living Flame of Love," in *Collected Works*, 717.
78. John of the Cross, "The Dark Night," in *Collected Works*, 711.
79. Powers, "The Mountains of the Lord," in *Selected Poetry*, 8.
80. See Jessica Powers, "Manuscript of Heaven," in *Selected Poetry*, 54; and *The Franciscan* (January 1938): 15. For a discussion of this poem, see Siegfried, "Write Me Down As a Small Adjective Attending Light, the Archangelic Noun," in *Jessica Powers Symposium: Proceedings of the Symposium in Milwaukee*, 25.

81. Jessica Powers, "Bird at Daybreak," in *Selected Poetry*, 180; and *Commonweal* 28 (May 6, 1938):44.

82. See Jessica Powers, "Bird at Evening," in *Selected Poetry*, 181; and in *The Lantern Burns*, 9.

83. See John 1:26-27.

84. Luke 7:37-38.

85. See Luke 23:55-56; John 20:11ff; Matthew 27:61; 28:1,9; and Mark 15:47; 16:1, 9-11.

86. See Jessica Powers, "The Valley of the Cat-Tails," in *Selected Poetry*, 161; and in *The Lantern Burns*, 51. For a discussion of this poem, see Berlingeri, 536-57.

87. See Jessica Powers, "Old Bridge," in *Selected Poetry*, 104; *Forge* 2 (Summer 1926): 12; and in *The Lantern Burns*, 22. For a discussion of this poem, see Richard Boudreau, "A Meadow Moreover: The Wisconsin Poems of Jessica Powers," in *Jessica Powers Symposium: Proceedings of the Symposium in Milwaukee, Wisconsin, August 26, 1989*, by Marquette University (Milwaukee, Wisconsin: Marquette University, 1989), 11; and Siegfried, "Jessica Powers: The Paradox of Light and Dark," 29.

88. See Jessica Powers, "Place of Ruin," in *Selected Poetry*, 75; *Commonweal* 30 (August 11, 1939): 375; and in *Lantern Burns*, 41.

89. See Jessica Powers, "Morning of Fog," in *Selected Poetry*, 9; and in *The Lantern Burns*, 31. For a discussion of this poem, see Kiley, 76-77; and Geigel, 39, 41.

90. See Jessica Powers, "Belmont Harbor," in *Selected Poetry*, 156; and in *The Lantern Burns*, 49. Also published in Italian in *Luogo di splendore*, 18-19. For a discussion of this poem, see Baldwin, "Burns the Great Lantern," 358; Baldwin, "Wisconsin Poet Integrates Rural Upbringing, City Life, Monastery," 9; and Geigel, 2.

91. See Jessica Powers, "Human Winter," in *Selected Poetry*, 113; and *America* 68 (December 19, 1942): 299. For a discussion of this poem, see Siegfried, "Write Me Down As a Small Adjective Attending Light, the Archangelic Noun," in *Jessica Powers Symposium: Proceedings of the Symposium in Milwaukee*, 21.

92. See Jessica Powers, "No One Can Stay," in *Selected Poetry*, 98; published under the alternate title, "No Man Can Stay," in *The Lantern Burns*, 42; and in *The House at Rest*, 11.

93. See Jessica Powers, "The Terminal," in *Selected Poetry*, 134; and in *The Lantern Burns*, 21. For a brief discussion of this poem, see *Catholic Worker* 7 (May 1940); and Berlingeri, 538.

94. Jessica Powers, "Night of Storm," in *Selected Poetry*, 36; *Spirit* 6 (May 1939): 52; and in *Lantern Burns*, 3.

95. Ibid. For a discussion of this poem, see Kavanaugh, "Jessica Powers in the Tradition of St. John of the Cross," 30; Miller, 9; and Geigel, 35, 37, 57, 68.

96. See Jessica Powers, "The Kingdom of God," in *Selected Poetry*, 20; and in *The Lantern Burns*, 53. Also published in Italian under the title, "Il regno di Dio," in *Luogo di splendore*, 38-39. For a discussion of this poem, see Baldwin, "Burns the Great Lantern," 359; and Geigel, 56.

97. John of the Cross, "The Dark Night," in *Complete Works*, 711

98. See Jessica Powers, "Let There Be Light," in *Selected Poetry*, 28; and in *The Lantern Burns*, 18. Also translated into Italian under the title, "Fiat lux," in *Luogo di splendore*, 14-15.

99. Ibid. For a discussion of this poem, see Geigel, 67.

100. Ibid.

101. See Jessica Powers, "The Books of Saint John of the Cross," in *Selected Poetry*, 132; and in *Lantern Burns*, 13. For a discussion of this poem, see Kiley, 78; Baldwin, "Burns the Great Lantern," 359; Baldwin, "Wisconsin Poet Integrates Rural Upbringing, City Life, Monastery," 9; and Geigel, 39, 64.

102. See Jessica Powers, "If You Have Nothing," in *Selected Poetry*, 91; *Commonweal* 31 (March 8, 1940): 431; in *Place of Splendor*, 63; in *Mountain Sparrow*, 5; and in *The House at Rest*, 14. Also translated into Italian under the title, "Se non hai nulla," in *Luogo di splendore*, 70-71. For a discussion of this poem, see Siegfried, "Jessica Powers: The Paradox of Light and Dark," 36-37; Morneau, "The Spirituality of Jessica Powers," 16; and Geigel, 31.

103. See Jessica Powers, "The Heart Can Set Its Boundaries," in *Selected Poetry*, 151; *America* 65 (June 21, 1941): 300; and in *The House at Rest*, 12. Also published in Italian under the title, "Confini," in *Luogo di splendore*, 44-45. For a discussion of this poem, see Thomas P. McDonnell, "The Nun as Poet," *Spirit* 26 (March 1959): 24.

104. See Jessica Powers, "The Little Nation," in *Selected Poetry*, 39; published in *Washington Post*, February 1941; in *Place of Splendor*, 29; and in *Mountain Sparrow* (Reno, Nevada: Published by Carmel of Reno, 1972), 7.

105. See Jessica Powers, "Letter of Departure," in *Selected Poetry*, 43-44; *Spirit* 8 (July 1941): 78-79; in *Place of Splendor*, 25; *Spirit* 35 (January 1969): 60-61; and in *The House at Rest*, 21.

106. Genesis, 19:23-26.

107. Powers, "Letter of Departure," in *Selected Poetry*, 43-44.

108. See Mathew 22:37-40; Mark 13:28-33; and Luke 10:25-28.

109. Powers, "Letter of Departure," in *Selected Poetry*, 43-44. For a discussion of this poem, see Morneau, "The Spirituality of Jessica Powers, 17; Baldwin, "Burns the Great Lantern," 360; and Geigel, 33, 69.

110. See Mathew 10:9-10; Mark 6:7-13; and Luke 9:1-6.

111. John of the Cross, "The Ascent of Mount Carmel," in *Collected Works*, 68ff.

Chapter 5

1. "Wisconsin Poet Enters Carmel Here," *(Milwaukee) Catholic Herald Citizen*, 18 April 1942.

2. Leonard Feeney, review of *The Lantern Burns*, by Jessica Powers, in *America* 63 (May 1940): 192.

3. Miriam, Interview with Siegfried and Morneau, transcript p. 6, tape 1: side 1, AMU.

4. Miriam, Interview with Siegfried and Morneau, transcript p. 10, tape 1: side 1.

5. See Baldwin, "Burns the Great Lantern," *Catholic World*, 361; and Sally Fitzgerald, "Rooms With a View," in *Katallagate* 8 (Summer 1982): 10.

6. See "The Milwaukee Foundation," in *Carmel of the Mother of God*, edited by the Discalced Carmelite Nuns (Milwaukee, WI: Privately printed, 1942), 28-33; and Discalced Carmelite Nuns of the Association of Mary, *Carmel in the United States*, 137.

7. Discarded Carmelite Nuns, *Carmel in the United States*, 137.

8. Doris Trainer Scully, "Jottings/prose/poetry," from the Jessica Powers Papers (Box 3: Folder 5), donated on 26 August 1989, Department of Special Collections and University Archives, Main Library, Marquette University, Milwaukee, Wisconsin, 1.

9. "The Carmelite," chap. 8 in *Carmel of the Mother of God*, 56.

10. Ibid., 57.

11. Ibid.

12. Ibid., 58.

13. Ibid.

14. Ibid.

15. Ibid., 64.

16. Mary Jo Flanagan, "Jessica Powers: Contemplative, Carmelite, Poet," *Catholic Herald* 29 December 1983. Mary Bernadette of the Immaculate Conception worked as a lay person for Sears & Roebuck in the Chicago office. Miriam of the Holy Spirit and Mary Bernadette of the Immaculate Conception celebrated their fortieth anniversary of profession together in 1983. Mary Bernadette of the Immaculate Conception died 6 April 1989 and is not to be confused with Bernadette of the Immaculate Conception (Ranallo) from the Albuquerque, NM community who transferred to the Pewaukee community in 1969 and is still living as a member of the Pewaukee Carmel.

17. "Friends Crowd Small Chapel For Investiture At Carmel," (*Milwaukee Catholic Herald*, 2 May 1942, newspaper clipping in Jessica Powers Papers (Box 2: Folder 11), AMU.

18. Ibid.

19. The family members in attendance included: her brothers from Mauston, John Powers and Dan Powers; an aunt from Lyndon Station, Agnes Fuller; her cousin from Sparta, Mary Trainer; and her cousins

from Milwaukee, Mr. and Mrs. Edmund Powers. The group of friends included Sister Mary Lucille, OP, who had been her former elementary school teacher in Mauston, and Ruth Mary Fox, her mentor from her Milwaukee days. For further details, see "Friends Crowd Small Chapel For Investiture at Carmel," (*Milwaukee*) *Catholic Herald*, 2 May 1942.

20. "Miss Powers, Poet, To Take Orders Vows," *Milwaukee Journal*, 9 August 1946.

21. "A Day in Carmel," chapter 7 in *Carmel of the Mother of God*, 52-55.

22. "Carmel of the Mother of God [A Physical Description of the Cloister]," chapter 5 in *Carmel of the Mother of God*, 34-42.

23. Morneau, "The Spirituality of Jessica Powers," *Spiritual Life*, 159.

24. See Discalced Carmelite Nuns, *Carmel in the United States*, 197-98; and Scully, Papers on "Family History," 2.

25. See Powers, *Selected Poetry*, 193; and Mary Timothy, "The Silent Poet," in *Spirit*, 53.

26. See Discalced Carmelite Nuns, *Carmel in the United States*, 138.

27. "Lake Site Is Donated for Nuns Community: Discalced Carmelites to Erect Monastery on Seven cre Tract in Pewaukee Area," unidentified newspaper clipping dated 6 December 1956, [page] 10, in Jessica Powers Papers (Box 3: Folder 3), AMU.

28. Mary Timothy, "The Silent Poet," *Spirit*, 53.

29. Ibid.

30. Jessica Powers, "No Pity for Lovers," (alternate title) "The Parting of Lovers," in Jessica Powers Papers (Box 4: Folder 1), AMU.

31. Jessica Powers, "Souvenir, Wisconsin River," in *Selected Poetry*, 166. For a discussion of this poem, see Boudreau, 9.

32. Nuns of the Pewaukee Carmel, "Sister Miriam of the Holy Spirit, OCD," *Carmelite Digest* 4 (Summer 1989): 10.

33. Mary Timothy, "The Silent Poet," *Spirit*, 54.

34. Ibid.

35. Ibid.

36. Ibid.

37. Ibid.

38. For examples of Jessica's (Miriam's) references to the feminine or motherly attributes associated with the concept of God, see her "O Spirita Sancta," *Selected Poetry*, 29; "The Masses," *Selected Poetry*, 90 or pp. 82-83 below; "Ruah-Elohim," *Selected Poetry*, 133 or p. 94-95 below; and "Millet's Feeding Her Birds", *Selected Poetry*, 138 or p. 128 below.

39. See Jessica Powers, "I Hold My Heart As A Gourd," in *Selected Poetry*, 46; *Catholic Woman* 3 (August 1941): [no p.]; and in *Place of Splendor*, 35. Also translated into Italian under the title, "Reggo il cuore come unanfora," in *Luogo di splendore*, 56-57.

40. Ibid.

41. Ibid.
42. Ibid.
43. Ibid.
44. See Jessica Powers, "The Place of Splendor," in *Selected Poetry*, 123; *Commonweal* 43 (November 9, 1945): 92; in *Place of Splendor*, 13; and in *The House at Rest*, 46.
45. Ibid. For a discussion of this poem, see Siegfried, "Jessica Powers: The Paradox of Light and Dark," 35-36; Baldwin, "Burns the Great Lantern," 361; and Geigel, 40, 60, 63, 70.
46. See Tobit, chapters 5, 6, 9, and 11.
47. Powers, "The Place of Splendor," in *Selected Poetry*, 123.
48. Ibid.
49. See Jessica Powers, "The Garments of God," *Selected Poetry*, 21; *Spirit* 12 (September 1945): 111; in *The Place of Splendor*, 66; and in *The House at Rest*, 36. Also translated into Italian under the title, "La vesti di dio," in *Luogo di splendore*, 74-75.
50. Ibid. For a discussion of this poem, see Morneau, "The Spirituality of Jessica Powers," 14; Morneau, "The Garments of God," *Emmanuel* 92 (June 1986): 264-267/287; and Geigel, 38.
51. See Jessica Powers, "The Cedar Tree," in *Selected Poetry*, 176; *Commonweal* 43 (October 19, 1945): 10; in *Place of Splendor*, 65; in *Mountain Sparrow*, 10-11; and in *The House at Rest*, 62. Also translated into Italian under the title, "Il cedro," in *Luogo di splendore*, 72-73.
52. Ibid. For a discussion of this poem, see Boudreau, "A Meadow Moreover," 11-12.
53. See Jessica Powers, "The Legend of the Sparrow," in *Selected Poetry*, 4-5; and in *Place of Splendor*, 85.
54. Deuteronomy 33:11.
55. John of the Cross, "Poetry," in *Complete Works*, 721-22. John of the Cross described traits of birds in detail and used this language to speak of spiritual things. See John of the Cross, "Maxims and Counsels: Maxims on Love," no. 42, in *Complete Works*, 677.
56. Therese of Lisieux, *Story of a Soul: The Autobiography of St. Therese of Lisieux*, 197-200.
57. See Jessica Powers, "There s a Homelessness," in *Selected Poetry*, 86; *Sign* 26 (August 1946): 43; in *Place of Splendor*, 50; and in *The House at Rest*, 10. Also published in Italian under the title "Vè un esilio," in *Luogo di splendore*, 66-67.
58. Ibid. For a discussion of this poem, see Baldwin, "Burns the Great Lantern," 360; Baldwin, "Wisconsin Poet Integrates Rural Upbringing, City Life, Monastery," 9; and Geigel, 31-31, 38.
59. Ibid.
60. Ibid.
61. Ibid.

62. See Jessica Powers, "Doxology," in *Selected Poetry*, 191; in *Place of Splendor*, 98; and in *The House at Rest*, 72.
63. See Jessica Powers, "The Wind of Pentecost," in *Selected Poetry*, 26; and in *Place of Splendor*, 81. Also published in Italian under the title, "Vento di Pentecoste," in *Luogo di splendore*, 90-91. For a brief discussion of this poem, see Berlingeri, 541-42.
64. See Jessica Powers, "This Is a Beautiful Time," in *Selected Poetry*, 27; in *Place of Splendor*, 96; and in *The House at Rest*, 67. Also translated into Italian under the title, "E bello il nostro tempo," in *Luogo di splendore*, 92-93.
65. Ibid.
66. See Mathew 13:33; and Luke 13:20-21.
67. Isaiah 40:4.
68. See the discussion of "Winds of Pentecost," p. 81 above.
69. Powers, "This is a Beautiful Time," in *Selected Poetry*, 27. For a discussion of this poem, see Geigel, 63.
70. See Jessica Powers, "The Masses," in *Selected Poetry*, 90; and *Commonweal* 45 (April 11, 1947): 641.
71. Ibid.
72. See Jessica Powers, "Night Prayer: To The Prophet Elijah," in *Selected Poetry*, 61; *Commonweal* 47 (October 17, 1947):9; and in *The House at Rest*, 34.
73. Ibid. For a discussion of this poem, see Siegfried, "Jessica Powers: The Paradox of Light and Dark," 38-39.
74. Ibid. See 2 Kings 2:12.
75. Powers, "Night Prayer: To the Prophet Elijah," in *Selected Poetry*, 61. See 1 Kings 17:3-6.
76. See Jessica Powers, "God Is A Strange Lover," in *Selected Poetry*, 16; *Commonweal* 45 (January 24, 1947): 369; in *Mountain Sparrow*, 12-13; and in *The House at Rest*, 24.
77. Ibid. For a discussion of this poem, see Morneau, "An Experience of God: Reflections of a Poets Journey," 492-93; Baldwin, "Burns the Great Lantern," 360; 360; and Baldwin, "Wisconsin Poet Integrates Rural Upbringing, City Life, Monastery," 9.
78. Ibid. See Luke 7:36-50.
79. See Jessica Powers, "The Mercy of God," in *Selected Poetry*, 3; and *Spirit* 14 (January 1948): 157.
80. Ibid. For a discussion of this poem, see Morneau, "The Spirituality of Jessica Powers," 16; and Kavanaugh, "Jessica Powers in the Tradition of St. John of the Cross," 33.
81. Ibid.
82. See Jessica Powers, "The Flower of Love," in *Selected Poetry*, 41; and *Commonweal* 49 (November 5, 1948): 90.
83. See John of the Cross, "To Maria de la Encarnacion, Prioress of the Discalced Carmelites in Segovia, July 6, 1591," letter #24 taken from

Minor Works: Letters, in *Collected Works*, trans. by Kieran Kavanaugh and Otilio Rodriquez, 703.

84. See Jessica Powers, "The Book of Ruth," in *Selected Poetry*, 60; and *Commonweal* 49 (December 31, 1948): 302.

85. See Jessica Powers, "Renunciation," in *Selected Poetry*, 109; *Spirit* 15 (May 1948): 43.

86. See Note of Jessica Powers, *Selected Poetry*, 109. The quote attributed to St. Threse of Lisieux, *Autobiography*, 197: "To compose the most sublime poetry is of less worth than the least act of self-renunciation," is based on these actual words of hers: "the smallest act of PURE LOVE is of more value to her than all other works together"; or Therese of Lisieux, "Letter to Mother Agnes of Jesus, Marie of the Sacred Heart, and Genevieve (June 1897)," in *Letters of St. Therese of Lisieux*, trans. John Clarke, vol. 2, *General Correspondence (1890-1897)* (Washington, D.C.: Institute of Carmelite Studies, 1988), 1129. She draws her inspiration from St. John of the Cross, *Spiritual Canticle*, stanza 29, no. 2, *Collected Works*, 523: "For a little of this pure love is more precious to God and the soul and more beneficial to the Church, even though it seems one is doing nothing, than all these other works put together."

87. See Jessica Powers, "Enclosure," in *Selected Poetry*, 128: in *Catholic World* 166 (February 1948): 433. For a discussion of this poem, see Kavanaugh, "Jessica Powers in the Tradition of St. John of the Cross," 30.

88. See 1 Kings 18:42.

89. Powers, "Enclosure," in *Selected Poetry*, 128.

90. See Jessica Powers, "To Live With the Spirit," in *Selected Poetry*, 38; *Commonweal* 51 (December 30, 1949): 345; and in *The House at Rest*, 68.

91. Ibid. For a discussion of this poem, see Kavanaugh, "Jessica Powers in the Tradition of St. John of the Cross," 30.

92. Ibid.

93. Ibid.

94. See Jessica Powers, "Not Garden Any More," in *Selected Poetry*, 18; *Catholic World* 171 (September 1950): 451.

95. See Jessica Powers, "Israel Again," in *Selected Poetry*, 93; and *America* 83 (June 17, 1950): 316. For a discussion of this poem, see Kavanaugh, "Jessica Powers in the Tradition of St. John of the Cross," 31.

96. See Jessica Powers, "Counsel for Silence," in *Selected Poetry*, 85; *Spirit* 18 (September 1951): 112; in *Mountain Sparrow*, 15; and in *The House at Rest*, 22.

97. Ibid. For a discussion of this poem, see Siegfried, "Jessica Powers: The Paradox of Light and Dark," 39; and McDonnell, "The Nun As Poet," 25.

98. See Jessica Powers, "But Not With Wine," in *Selected Poetry,* 17; *Catholic World* 173 (April 1951): 58; and in *The House at Rest,* 55.
99. Ibid.
100. See Isaiah 51:21; and Acts 2:15-21.
101. See Jessica Powers, "Christ Is My Utmost Need," in *Selected Poetry,* 152; *America* 88 (October 25, 1952): 101; and in *The House at Rest,* 23.
102. For a discussion of "Garments of God," see p. 77 above.
103. Ibid.
104. Ibid.
105. Ibid.
106. Ibid.
107. See Jessica Powers, "And Wilderness Rejoices," in *Selected Poetry,* 7; *AD* 3 (Winter 1952): 42; and in *the House at Rest,* 22.
108. Powers, "And Wilderness Rejoices," in *Selected Poetry,* 7. For a discussion of this poem, see Kavanaugh, "Jessica Powers in the Tradition of St. John of the Cross," 32.
109. See Isaiah 35:1-6; 29:7; 41:18-19; 49:8; and 55:12-13.
110. Acts 1-4.
111. See Matthew 13:1-9; Mark 4:1-8; and Luke 8:4-8.
112. See Jessica Powers, "Repairer of Fences," in *Selected Poetry,* 14; *Sign* 31 (February 52): 15; and in *The House of Rest,* 42. For a discussion of this poem, see Rembert Weakland, "A Spiritual Journey," in *Wisconsin: Milwaukee Journal Magazine* (Milwaukee), 15 April, 1990.
113. Isaiah 58:12.
114. Robert Frost, *Poetry and Prose,* ed. by Edward Connery Lathem and Laurence Thompson (NY: Holt, Rinehart, and Winston, 1972): 6-17.
115. Powers, "Repairer of Fences," in *Selected Poetry,* 14.
116. See Jessica Powers, "Ruah-Elohim," in *Selected Poetry,* 33; and *Catholic World* 179 (June 1954): 199.
117. Ibid. See "The Masses," pp. 82-83 above.
118. John of the Cross, "The Spiritual Canticle," 26, in *Collected Works,* 715.
119. See note of Jessica Powers, *Selected Poetry,* 37.
120. See Jessica Powers, "Come, South Wind," in *Selected Poetry,* 37; *Spirit* 21 (September 1954): 102; and in *The House at Rest,* 13.
121. Ibid. For a discussion of this poem, see Morneau, "The Spirituality of Jessica Powers," 17.
122. See Jessica Powers, "A Meadow Moreover," in *Selected Poetry,* 174; and *America* 92 (January 8, 1955): 382.
123. Ibid. For a discussion of this poem, see Boudreau, "A Meadow Moreover," 10.
124. See Jessica Powers, "Take Your Only Son," in *Selected Poetry,* 153; *America* 95 (September 15, 1956): 560; and in *The House at Rest,* 16.
125. Genesis 22:1-18.

126. Powers, "Take Your Only Son," in *Selected Poetry*, 153.

Chapter 6

1. The Carmel of Pewaukee participated in the national gatherings of Discalced Carmelite Nuns in the United States. For example, see the photographs and article on "Meetings of Contemplative Nuns with Most Rev. Augustine Mayer: Representatives of Fifteen Carmels Interested in Forming an Association (April 26, 1976)" in *Encounter: An Inter-Monastery Quarterly of the Discalced Carmelite Nuns of the United States* 11 (Summer 1976): 48.

2. Carmelite Communities Associated, *Charter of Life* (Reno, Nevada: privately printed, 1979), 13. Other members of the Charter Task Force included Sister Claudette Blais, Sister Mary Paul Cutri, Sister Constance FitzGerald of the Baltimore Carmel, Sister Laureen Grady, Sister Carolyn OHara, Sister Mary Roman, Sister Mary Catharine Scanlan, Sister Vilma Seelaus, and Sister Carmen Womack of the Oklahoma City Carmel.

3. Ibid., ii.

4. Ibid., 1.

5. Ibid.

6. Ibid.

7. Ibid., 2-3.

8. See *Charter of Life*, 3; and "The Liturgy as the Source and Summit of Carmelite Life," in papers from Secretariatus Pro Monialibus (Rome: Curia Generalis, 1971), IX,3-15; X, 11-12. The U.S. Carmelites were familiar with these papers because they were part of the formation program in Carmelite spirituality which came from the generalate in Rome. In "The Liturgy as the Source and Summit of Carmelite Life," the rhythm of prayer in Carmelite spirituality is linked to certain times of the day, the month, and the season of the year in such a way that a cosmic significance is symbolized. Also the document summarizes this aspect of Carmelite prayer by stating that, if there is one grouping within the human community which is able to celebrate this "mystery of human time by affirming its redemptive character and stressing the primacy of God in the great and little things of the history of humanity, it is precisely the contemplative community" (IX,3).

9. See *Charter of Life*, 5-6.

10. Ibid., 1-12.

11. Ibid., 11.

12. Ibid.

13. Carmen Womack, member of the Carmelite Monastery of Saint Joseph in Piedmont, Oklahoma, interview by author, 10 January 1992, telephone conversation, Piedmont, Oklahoma. The Association of Mary Queen of Carmel draws its membership from the Carmelite communities of Discalced Nuns in Pewaukee (Milwaukee), WI; Piedmont (Oklahoma City), OK; Jackson, MS; Little Rock, AR; San Antonio,

TX; New Caney (Houston), TX; Santa Clara, CA; San Rafael, CA; Long Beach (Solvang), CA; Eugene, OR; Hawaii; and the Byzantine Carmel of Sugar Loaf, PA.

14. Scully, "Family History: Pewaukee," 2; Discalced Carmelite Nuns, *Carmel in the U.S.*, 138; and Sister Bernadette Ranallo and Sister Mary Joyce King, interview by author, 23 October 1991, Mother of God Carmelite Monastery, Pewaukee, WI.
15. Dolores Leckey, telephone interview by author, 1 November 1991.
16. Bernadette Ranallo and Mary Joyce King, interview by author, 23 October 1991.
17. Miriam of the Holy Spirit, *Diary/Journal (1971)*, in Jessica Powers Collection (Box 3: Folder 8), AMU.
18. Nuns of the Pewaukee Carmel, "Sister Miriam of the Holy Spirit, OCD," *Carmelite Digest* 4 (Summer 1989): 10.
19. Nuns of the Pewaukee Carmel, "Sister Miriam of the Holy Spirit, OCD," 9.
20. For details of her last illness, see Nuns of the Pewaukee Carmel, "Sister Miriam of the Holy Spirit, OCD," 8; and Morneau, introduction to *Selected Poetry*, xxii.
21. Nuns of the Pewaukee Carmel, "Sister Miriam of the Holy Spirit, OCD," 10.
22. Morneau, introduction to *Selected Poetry*, xv.
23. Bordreau, "A Meadow Moreover," 11.
24. Ibid., 12.
25. See Jessica Powers, "Pure Desert," in *Selected Poetry*, 154; *America* 105 (May 27, 1961): 375; and in *The House at Rest*, 25.
26. Ibid. For a discussion of this poem, see Kavanaugh, "Jessica Powers in the Tradition of St. John of the Cross," 31; and Siegfried, "Jessica Powers: The Paradox of Light and Dark," 40.
27. Ibid.
28. Ibid.
29. Jessica Powers, "The Hidden Christ," in *Selected Poetry*, 80; and *Commonweal* 79 (November 22, 1963): 259; *Journey to Bethlehem*, 9.
30. Ibid.
31. Ibid.
32. See Mathew 14:13-21; Mark 6:30-44; Luke 9:10-17; and John 6:1-13. Also see Matthew 15:32-39; and Mark 8:1-10.
33. Jessica Powers, "In Too Much Light," in *Selected Poetry*, 79; *Spirit* 30 (February 1964): 157; and under the alternate title of "Places of Light," in *Journey to Bethlehem*, 10.
34. Ibid.
35. Therese of Lisieux, *Story of a Soul: The Autobiography of St. Therese of Lisieux*, 266.
36. Jessica Powers, "Suffering," in *Selected Poetry*, 106; and *Spirit* 32 (March 1965): 15.

37. Ibid.
38. Jessica Powers, "One Answer," in *Selected Poetry*, 107; and *Spirit* 32 (March 1965): 15. This poem is also published under an alternate title, "Encounter of Love," in *Selected Poetry*, 51.
39. Ibid.
40. Jessica Powers, "Sign at Sexagesima," in *Selected Poetry*, 158; and *Spirit* 32 (March 1965): 7.
41. Ibid. See Genesis 6:8-22; 9:1-17.
42. Genesis 12:1-9; 15:1-19.
43. Jessica Powers, "Abraham," in *Selected Poetry*, 66; *Bible Today* 33 (December 1967): 23-24; and in *The House at Rest*, 15. Also published in Italian in *Luogo di splendore*, 40-41. For a discussion of this poem, see Kavanaugh, "Jessica Powers in the Tradition of St. John of the Cross," 30.
44. Acts 2:1-33.
45. Jessica Powers, "Only One Voice," in *Selected Poetry*, 148; *America* 116 (June 17, 1967): 853: in *Mountain Sparrow*, 16; and in *The House at Rest*, 52. Also published in Italian under the title, "Solo una voce," in *Luogo di splendore*, 98-99.
46. Ibid. See Matthew 9:20-22; Mark 5:25-34; and Luke 8:43-48.
47. Jessica Powers, "Everything Rushes, Rushes," in *Selected Poetry*, 163; *Sign* 49 (January 1970): 30; and in *The House at Rest*, 56. For a discussion of this poem, see Boudreau, "A Meadow Moreover," 12.
48. Siegfried, "Write Me Down the Archangelic Noun," Aquinas Institute of Theology Lecture Series, 27 September 1991, 1.
49. Robert Morneau, introduction to *Selected Poetry*, xxi.
50 Jessica Powers, "Siesta in Color," in *Selected Poetry*, 76; *Poetry: Magazine of* 115 (March 1970): 375; and in *The House at Rest*, 54. For a discussion of this poem, see Boudreau, "A Meadow Moreover," 10; and Siegfried, "Jessica Powers: The Paradox of Light and Dark," 31.
51. Jessica Powers, "For a Proud Friend, Humbled" in *Selected Poetry*, 111; *Sign* 49 (March 1970): 34; and in *The House at Rest*, 30.
52. Ibid.
53. Jessica Powers, "Los Angeles Earthquake," in *Selected Poetry*, 101.
54. See editor's note in *Selected Poetry*, 101.
55. Powers, "Los Angeles Earthquake," in *Selected Poetry*, 101.
56. Ibid.
57. Sister Bernadette Ranallo and Sister Mary Joyce King, members of the Carmelite Monastery of the Mother of God in Pewaukee, Wisconsin, interview by author, 23 October 1991, Pewaukee, Wisconsin.
58. Jessica Powers, "The Mystical Sparrow of St. John of the Cross," in *Selected Poetry*, 11; and in *Mountain Sparrow*, 2-3.
59. See John of the Cross, *The Spiritual Canticle*, no. 28-29 of the second redaction, translated by E. Allison Peers from the critical Spanish edi-

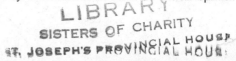

tion by P. Silverio de Santa Teresa (Garden City, NY: Image, 1961), 236 for the stanzas of the poem in context, and 418-22 for an exposition of the stanzas; and John of the Cross, *The Spiritual Canticle*, no. 28-29 of the second redaction, in *The Collected Works of St. John of the Cross*, trans. by Kieran Kavanaugh and Otilio Rodriguez, with Introductions by Kieran Kavanaugh (Washington, DC: Institute of Carmelite Studies, 1979), 413 for the stanzas of the poem in context, and 523-26 for an exposition of the stanzas.

60. Powers, "The Mystical Sparrow of St. John of the Cross," in *Selected Poetry*, 11.
61. Jessica Powers, "Wanderer," in *Selected Poetry*, 124; *Commonweal* 106 (March 16, 1979): 140; and in *The House at Rest*, 63. For a discussion of this poem, see Regina Siegfried, "Jessica Powers: The Paradox of Light and Dark," 40-41.
62. Hildegarde of Bingen, *Scivias*, trans. by Bruce Hozeski, with Forwords by Matthew Fox and Adelgundis Fuhrkotter (Santa Fe, NM: Bear, 1986).
63. Powers, "Wanderer," in *Selected Poetry*, 124.
64. Jessica Powers, "The Vision," in *Selected Poetry*, 1-2; *Desert Call* 10 (Spring 1975): 8; and in *The House at Rest*, 38-39.
65. Ibid. For a discussion of this poem, see Kavanaugh, "Jessica Powers in the Tradition of St. John of the Cross," 30.
66. Ibid.
67. James Weldon Johnson, "The Prodigal Son," in *Gods Trombones: Seven Negro Sermons in Verse* (New York: Viking, 1968), 21-26.
68. For a discussion of the poem, "Petenwell Rock," see p. 25-26 above.
69. Powers, "The Vision," in *Selected Poetry*, 1.
70. Exodus 2:15; 3:1-3.
71. Powers, "The Vision," in *Selected Poetry*, 2.
72. Jessica Powers, "This Trackless Solitude," in *Selected Poetry*, 6; and in *The House at Rest*, 64.
73. Ibid. For a discussion of this poem, see Morneau, "The Spirituality of Jessica Powers," 15; and Kavanaugh, "Jessica Powers in the Tradition of St. John of the Cross," 30, 32.
74. For a discussion of the poem, "Cabaret," see p. 26-27-28 above.
75. Jessica Powers, "This Paltry Love," in *Selected Poetry*, 48; and in *The House at Rest*, 26.
76. Ibid. For a discussion of this poem, see Kavanaugh, "Jessica Powers in the Tradition of St. John of the Cross," 33.
77. 1 Kings 19:14.
78. See John of the Cross, "Stanzas of the Soul," 1, in *The Complete Works of Saint John of the Cross*, trans. and edited by E. Allison Peers from the critical edition of P. Silverio de Santa Teresa, vol. 1, *Dark Night of the Soul* (Westminster, MD: Newman, 1959), 325, for translation used in "The House at Rest," in *Selected Poetry*, 12.

79. Jessica Powers, "The House at Rest," in *Selected Poetry*, 122; and in *The House at Rest*, 9.

80. Ibid. For a discussion of this poem, see Morneau, "The Spirituality of Jessica Powers," 17; and Kavanaugh, "Jessica Powers in the Tradition of St. John of the Cross," 29.

81. Ibid.

82. Jessica Powers, "Yes," in *Selected Poetry*, 137; and in *The House at Rest*, 37. For a discussion of this poem, see Morneau, "The Spirituality of Jessica Powers, 18.

83. Jessica Powers, "The Homecoming," in *Selected Poetry*, 53; and in *The House at Rest*, 70. This poem was read at her funeral and appeared on her funeral card. For a discussion of this poem, see Rembert Weakland, "Homily on Trinity Sunday delivered by Archbishop of Milwaukee" (Milwaukee, Wisconsin, 17 June 1984), 3-4, photocopied; and Morneau, "The Spirituality of Jessica Powers," 17.

84. Luke 15:11-32.

85. Jessica Powers, "The Great Mystery," in *Selected Poetry*, 100; and in *The House at Rest*, 33.

86. Ibid. For a discussion of this poem, see Boudreau, "A Meadow Moreover," 11.

87. Julian of Norwich, *Showings*, trans. and Introduction by Edmund Colledge, with a Preface by Jean Leclercq, The Classics of Western Spirituality (NY: Paulist, 1978), 279, 293, 295.

88. Jessica Powers, "Millets Feeding Her Birds," in *Selected Poetry*, 138; and in *The House at Rest*, 61.

89. Ibid.

90. Jessica Powers, "The Leftovers," in *Selected Poetry*, 112; and *Bible Today* 24 (September 1986): 309.

91. 2 Kings 5:42-44.

92. See Mathew 14:13-21; Mark 6:30-44; Luke 9:10-17; and John 6:1-13.

93. See Mathew 15:21-28; and Mark 7:24-30.

94. Jessica Powers, "The Rock Too High for Me," in *Selected Poetry*, 187; and *Bible Today* 25 (January 1987): 28.

95. Ibid.

96. Jessica Powers, "God Is Today," in *Selected Poetry*, 13.